THE BUSINESS OF SALES

Uncloaking The Mysteries!

First Edition: January 2014
Printed in the United States of America
ISBN-13: 9780615884295
ISBN: 0615884296
Library of Congress Control Number: 2013950042
CreateSpace Independent Publishing Platform
North Charleston, South Carolina

For the purposes of this writing, the following terms shall be utilized interchangeably:
- Company(s), business(s), organization(s), and entity(s).
- Prospect(s), customer(s), purchaser(s), and consumer(s).
- Offer(s) and offering(s).
- Solution(s) and service(s).
- Gender references: her, him, Ms., Mr.

The Business Of Sales: Uncloaking The Mysteries!
By Steven M. Monks
The Business Of Sales: Uncloaking The Mysteries!

To order additional copies of this book, contact:
www.CreateSpace.com
www.Amazon.com
www.TheBusinessOfSales.net
TheBusinessOfSales@gmail.com

DEDICATION

A special thanks goes out to my parents, Martha Kjosness (Monks) Torline and Edward (Ed) Monks, who have provided endless love, encouragement, caring, kindness, understanding, and friendship. I also thank each of my family members, who have provided such great and memorable life moments and lessons, while all the time continuing to show how special and instrumental a family's love should be. For without the involvement of my grandparents, parents, siblings, and extended family in my life, anything accomplished would not be nearly as meaningful, special, or rewarding. Thank You from the bottom of my heart for everything each of you have done and continue to do on a daily basis!

CONTENTS

Acknowledgments

This writing is an accumulation of education, professional training, observations, trial and error, and experiences acquired over twenty plus years of sales, marketing, observations, and interactions. There are far too many individuals to list and thank individually who have assisted me along the way, but they include colleagues, friends, customers, mentors, and family members. I would like to let each of these individuals know how much I appreciate each and all of the sales, personal, and life lessons and experiences they provided. These interactions and experiences have provided motivation, direction, and guidance throughout my life and helped shape and mold a rewarding professional career and wonderful life.

This writing is an opportunity to give back to a profession that has been very exciting and provides me an opportunity to assist others along their journey throughout a successful professional sales career.

FOREWORD

The author has been marketing, presenting, and selling solutions (software, hardware, products, services, etc.) that assist thousands of users across multiple industries for more than twenty years.

During his award winning professional sales career, he has held various titles (VP of sales, national sales representative, sales executive, sales consultant, national account manager, etc.) focusing on the goal of dedicating his efforts and abilities to perform, present, and provide, solution offerings to multiple markets and industries and a wide range of organizations across the United States and internationally.

Throughout his career, much effort has been devoted to learning, practicing and utilizing numerous sales methodologies and techniques. This dedicated mindset and motivation was instilled early-on as a student of the sales process, and inspired his interest in exploring the psychology (the mental or behavioral characteristics of an individual or group) and physiology (the functions and activities of life or of living matter) of the selling and sales process.

In preparation for writing this book, much research and time was dedicated to focus on sharing experiences (events and actions) that have been learned and tried over his career. The knowledge was gained from a myriad of experiences and exposures of years of day-to-day sales activities, mentor lessons, books, publications, articles, and multiple sales trainings and seminars delivered by sales industry experts focusing on various aspects of the selling and sales process.

Throughout his many years spent in the sales arena, as well as, applying educational sales instruction there seemed to be some areas of the sales process less clearly outlined and defined making it more challenging to complete the entire sales process. It is customary, for sales seminars and trainings to be designed and focused on a certain element(s) of the sales process, which can be beneficial, as long as the person possesses an understanding of *each* of the elements involved in the *entire* sales process.

Therefore, locating a resource that provides a guide for administering, performing and managing *each* element throughout the *entire* sales process assisting in a higher level of success, seems more difficult to find.

What would have been helpful throughout his career would have been a guiding methodology revealing and outlining the sales elements, process, and procedures, and therefore removing the mysteries of "How-to-Sale"...*The Business Of Sales* is *that* guide!

This book is to be utilized by a salesperson to walk through the various steps of the selling process explaining the *why* and *how* individuals and companies purchase while *"Uncloaking The Mysteries!"*

BIOGRAPHY

Born in Colorado Springs, Colorado, Steven (Steve) Monks grew up in a small rural town on the eastern plains of Colorado, where agriculture and ranching were and continue to be the area's staples. He attended the local elementary, middle, and high schools, where he participated in a variety of sports, including football, basketball, wrestling, track, and rodeo, and other extracurricular activities, such as band, choir, theater, and student government.

He graduated from Colorado State University with a Bachelor of Science (BSBA) degree in Business Administration/Management. While attending college, he received recognition of scholastic performance, as well as athletic awards. Steve received multiple awards and honors as a member of the National Intercollegiate Rodeo Association (NIRA) and went on to participate and represent his college teams at the College National Finals Rodeo (CNFR).

During his high school and college days, he also competed in multiple amateur rodeo associations within the United States, leading to competing at the highest level of the rodeo sport...the Professional Rodeo Cowboys Association (PRCA).

After graduation from college, he continued competing at both the amateur and professional levels of rodeo for a number of years, learning the importance of delivering one's best performance *every day* as the sport of rodeo rewards and competitors are compensated by their performance.

Another of his long-time interests has been in the realm of personal fitness and nutrition, where he has been an active enthusiast for over thirty years. Many of the relatable analogies, scenarios, and stories depicted in this writing stem from experiences in the sales, athletics, personal training, and rodeo arenas and venues.

Preface

There are a number of sales and marketing publications and audio recording available today, so why should anyone be interested in spending their hard-earned money on this particular book?

This book was written for a wide variety of audiences, ranging from individuals who are interested in or just entering the sales profession to those who have been in the profession for a number of years. It was also written for anyone who feels or has been told, "You can never do that!"

When I first entered the sales arena and the sales profession, I was told the possibility of me completing a sale was equal to the same chance an ice cube has of surviving in a very hot place. I was told that not only would it be improbable, it would be almost impossible for me to succeed in sales!

Well, in the face of what seemed to be almost insurmountable odds and with individuals telling me I had very little chance of being successful, this writer went on to a successful sales career.

My message to the reader is that you should not allow someone else's opinion and words to define "you"—your capabilities and levels of success you can achieve. If you are willing to work hard and focus on *performance, processes,* and *perseverance, "you"* can define your level of success in whatever field and career *"you"* select.

The intent of this author is to assist those individuals who are currently or potentially looking at a sales role as a career and to remove the cloak of mysteries behind the selling processes while identifying essential elements, methodologies, and techniques involved in improving success in the sales profession.

I will be up front by telling you that I have made every conceivable mistake, of which only a small number are mentioned in this book, in regard to the selling process. Initially, the sales process may seem to merely require a short time to *learn,* but then it is quickly realized that it may take a lifetime to *master.* One of the biggest challenges to sales is there does not seem to be a "magic" or "single" approach that works "every time," and therefore, each sales opportunity provides ample opportunity for mistakes to be made, which can negatively affect the completion of a successful sale.

It is these enigmatic elements in the sale process that make a sales career so exciting and unique, as rarely will any two sales opportunities, or even two sales days, be exactly the same. It is also the many elements involved in the sales process that need and require focus in order to avoid making errors and impeding moving forward toward the completion of a successful sales opportunity.

The sales cycle can be an interesting and enjoyable experience for both the salesperson and the potential purchaser(s) if the process is handled appropriately and correctly. However, this process can also quickly and easily become an experience and act of futility if not addressed with the appropriate knowledge and training.

Because the possibilities of any two sales opportunities being exactly the same are remote, it is imperative to gain and utilize the knowledge of how to move through a sales cycle. It is possible to become complacent and make mistakes or skip over important elements by attempting to rush through the sales process. Believe it or not, even with years of experience, if appropriate focus is not given to each sales opportunity and process, this writer can catch himself making mistakes—even today!

My intent with this writing is to assist those individuals with an interest in the sales and selling process with a guide that identifies and illuminates the essential sales elements necessary to successfully complete sales opportunities.

This book is designed to be read in its entirety and then for you to utilize the lessons, contents, steps, elements, and provided diagrams on a daily basis. The material is designed in a format that allows for referring back to lessons prior to an interaction (meeting, phone call, etc.) with a potential purchaser(s). It is my intent to have this book be read and then referred back to often. I would recommend highlighting or utilizing page marking techniques, noting particular sections of interest, allowing the reader to quickly refer back to the lessons.

The diagrams (lists, etc.) are provided to be utilized to assist in moving sales processes and opportunities forward toward the successful completion of a sales opportunity.

My intent is to help every reader by exposing the sales process in a logical order and flow, like a blueprint guide to building a structure, it will assist the reader to follow steps to complete the structure, or in our case...the successful sale!

It is not my intent to describe how to close hundreds of sales at once but rather to provide a methodology (elements and structure) allowing for closing *one* sale successfully and then repeat the process...*hundreds of times!*

INTRODUCTION

It's Monday morning, 7:00 A.M. on a beautiful Colorado day. I am driving into my company's Colorado Springs office with a magnificent view of the Rocky Mountains directly in front of me—specifically, a spectacular view of Colorado's most popular and majestic mountain, Pikes Peak.

As I drive, I am feeling extremely nervous about today's events. It had been an exceedingly busy and nerve-racking weekend, involving early mornings and late nights of researching, studying, and memorizing computer hardware system components and attributes of a recently released family of computer hardware servers from a prominent computer hardware vendor that my company represents.

The reason I had dedicated the weekend to learning about the new line of hardware servers was that they had just been released the previous week, and I was preparing for an important meeting with individuals (potential purchasers) from a large distribution company on the East Coast of the United States. Today, the individuals would be traveling to the company's office in Colorado Springs for an important meeting involving a presentation for evaluating and investigating a potential investment in one of the newly announced computer hardware servers, along with my company's software solution offering(s).

The individuals attending the meeting from the prospect's company would include the CEO, President, and VP of operations, and as if this was not enough pressure, representatives from my own company, including the President, VP of sales, and the sales manager, would also be present.

If this meeting went as planned, it would result in a significant purchase for the prospect's business and would be the computer hardware server and software applications utilized to run their entire organization for the next several years.

This also meant a significant revenue opportunity for my company as it not only involved the purchase of a new computer hardware server but also software applications and service fees associated with the installation and implementation, along with ongoing annual licensing fees.

As I drove to the office, I kept repeating the many server models and statistical attributes that I had learned over the past few days to ensure I wouldn't mix up or confuse any of the individual computer hardware models' information during the meeting. Also, I wanted to appear as knowledgeable as possible to all the meeting attendees, both the prospects and my company, by accurately referencing all of the specifications of the hardware and software systems being presented.

The meeting was scheduled to start at 10:00 A.M. and last for approximately two hours. This was going to be my first opportunity to present as a sales representative for the company since being promoted from a customer service position. Since several of my company's management team would also be attending the presentation, I wanted to show and prove to them that they had made the correct decision by promoting me to a sales position.

Having only been with the organization for a little over a year, I had recently approached the company president with a request for a salary increase for continuing to perform the duties of my current customer service position. The president of the company stated, "If you want a salary increase or to make more money, you should consider moving into sales, where you will be compensated on the ability to complete sales opportunities and therefore be eligible to receive sales commissions based on your sales performance."

Well, whether the president knew it or not, he had me convinced the minute he said, "Make more money!"

At that point, I began watching the company's job opening list, and as soon as a sales position became available, I applied and was fortunate enough to be selected; I was promoted from a customer service role to the new position of...SALES REPRESENTATIVE!

But now, only a few hours away from the first chance to show some of the most influential people in my company my sales abilities, I began thinking, *What have I done?* How could I have been so foolish to ask for the sales representative position? I had no sales experience or formal sales training, had never sold anything before, and only knew a couple people who were in the sales profession. I had never discussed with them anything about *how to sell* anything, let alone the steps and elements involved in a sales cycle, along with its many processes and procedures... *what* to do...or *how* to do it!

Upon arriving at the office at approximately 7:30 A.M., I could feel my anxiety level beginning to rise as reality set in. This would be my first official sales meeting, performance, and presentation since becoming a salesperson just a few weeks ago. I quickly went to my desk to check phone messages and e-mail for any communication from the prospect stating the meeting would need to be cancelled due to some unforeseen travel issue(s). If so, I would be off the hook for today's meeting. Rescheduling would allow additional time to reschedule and learn more about the information needed to prepare for the meeting. Since there were no messages regarding the meeting cancellation, I began checking and double-checking the equipment in the meeting room.

Around 8:00 A.M., my coworkers were beginning to file into the office, indulging in the normal "Monday morning" conversation: what they had done over the weekend, how their sports teams had performed during the weekend's games, what they had planned for the coming week, etc.

The company's office policy was to send out a message informing employees when prospects and customers were going to be visiting the company's home office. Therefore, my coworkers were aware of the day's meeting, the company, names of the individuals who would be attending, and why they were visiting.

So, there I was, dressed in the only suit I had at the time, straight off the discount rack. Since suits were required of salespeople when a prospect or customer visited the home office, it was quite evident that I was involved in the day's meeting. As coworkers approached me, they politely said, "Good luck with your meeting today!"

Immediately, the thought in my mind was, *Good Luck?* Why would I need good luck?

Did these people know something about the customer or my sales management team that I did not? Suddenly, the weight of the success of this presentation and potential sales opportunity grew exponentially. Now I felt my position, job, and length of employment with the organization could possibly be on the line, depending on how the presentation went today.

The morning hours seemed to fly by, and with only forty-five minutes until the visitors were scheduled to arrive, I was a nervous wreck and unable to hold a complete thought in my head. What was the processor speed; what was the memory capacity; what components could be added to each system? I began thinking, *What have I done?* Why would I have put myself into this position? I should have just stayed at my prior position within the company and kept my mouth shut about wanting an increase in compensation.

Then, I began thinking through possible meeting exit strategies. Maybe it was time to suddenly become ill, requiring me to leave the office right away? How and how badly would I have to injure myself before I could leave the office immediately, and therefore not have to put myself through this agonizing and potentially career-ending meeting?

As I continued to think about potential exit strategies to avoid the day's meeting, the president of my company saw me pacing down the hall and said, "You ready to sell something today?" With much anxiety and nervousness, I swallowed hard and responded with very little confidence, "Ah, well, sure...I think?"

In retrospect, my response to the president probably was not the best response to instill confidence in regard to my preparedness and the prospect of the meeting's success.

I returned to my desk, trying to avoid wearing out the carpet as I paced up and down the hallways. I tried to avoid other coworkers who, unbeknownst to them, were making me even more nervous by offering "good lucks" or, worse yet, "let me tell you what went wrong during my meeting" stories.

Every time someone said something to me about the meeting, how important the prospect would be as a customer, the revenue implications to the company, etc., the weight of the presentation increased.

Some coworkers began asking me questions about the prospect. Who was attending? What were their roles? What did the company do? What were their revenues? How many employees? How many locations? What hardware and software are they utilizing? What is their purchasing time frame? Why are they interested in purchasing from our company?

I began asking myself, why didn't I ask more questions about the issues and needs of the prospect prior to scheduling this meeting? What did I really know about what the new hardware and software system would and could provide for them and their company? How would it address their needs and requirements, not only today but also in the future? Now, even more panic set in as I began to realize the information and knowledge I did *NOT* possess about the prospect and their purchasing and business requirements.

Then, came the moment I had been dreading all morning...the phone at my desk rang. Upon picking up the receiver, the receptionist voice stated, "Your ten o'clock appointment is here."

I responded in a trembling voice, "Thank You. I'll be right there." I remember just staring at the phone for several seconds, thinking, *I am in deep trouble. If I can somehow get out of this situation, I will do all I can in the future to avoid this type of feeling again when it comes to a prospect or customer meeting.*

Unfortunately, however, the time had arrived. The receptionist knew I was in the office, the boss knew I was in the office, and the prospect now knew I was in the office. There's no turning back...as unprepared as I was...the meeting must now go on.

Suddenly, a coworker walked by my desk and stated, "Your prospect is waiting up front," causing me to break from the trance of staring at the phone. I slowly stood up, checking how my suit and tie looked in the office window reflection, and then slowly turned and walked down the hall toward the reception area. Just before turning the hallway corner and reaching the reception area, I put a big smile on my face and eagerly greeted each of the individuals with an enthusiastic "Nice to meet you, and Thank You for coming to visit us today!"

I quickly escorted them into the company meeting room, where they took their seats around a large wooden conference table surrounded by leather captain chairs while making casual conversation regarding their travels to Colorado.

Within a few minutes, individuals from my company's management team began to walk into the room. To my surprise, a few more individuals from my company also attended. After some brief introductions, everyone politely took their seats in the room and began staring directly at me.

At that point, if there had been any way for me to evaporate into the ceiling or melt into the floor, I would have done it. Unfortunately, neither of these were an option. It was now show time...and it was my show!

Up to that point, I had not thought about how I would begin the meeting. I was so inundated, focused, and concerned about all the many hardware server systems and their characteristics and capabilities that I had not thought about how to begin the meeting, set the stage, or prepare for the presentation, let alone consider how to potentially engage the prospects.

As all eyes looked at me, I did not know what to do. I began stumbling through and repeating introductions, including names and titles, which included bungling my own management team's names and positions, along with about two dozen...*ahs* and *ums*. As if my verbal nervousness was not enough, I began unconsciously moving around and fidgeting in front of the room, trying to determine a way to smoothly move into the prepared presentation.

After completing introductions and not having any prepared opening or planned way to set the stage for the presentation, I simply went to the computer in front of the room to begin the presentation. As I touched the computer key to begin, it was then I realized I had overlooked actually opening up the presentation to the first slide. The presentation was loaded on the computer but needed to be accessed, opened, and put into presentation mode. As I stood looking at the computer screen in horror, I quickly apologized and began the steps to get the presentation onto the screen. In reality, this process only took a few seconds, but it seemed to be a lifetime as no one said anything. They all just sat there, staring at me, making uneasy sounds, clicking their pins, and turning notebook pages while I continued to apologize, trying to pass time and make some form of conversation with the audience.

Finally, I found the folder, found the file, opened it, and selected presentation mode. I brought up the first slide and quickly turned to the audience, who seemed to have been waiting forever. I then looked at the first slide on the screen...and then my mind went completely blank!

This particular presentation had been developed and created by my company's marketing department, and although I had reviewed it previously and felt comfortable with the information, it was not my presentation. For whatever reason, most likely due to the anxiety and stress of the situation, I had forgotten everything I wanted to say about this first slide. It was literally like I had never seen this slide.

At that point, I panicked and thought, *You have got to say something!* Having nothing come to mind quickly, I started thinking, *What is the backup plan?* I quickly realized, *Backup plan?* I did not even have an initial plan for the meeting, let alone a backup plan!

In my panicked state, I quickly clicked the computer to the next slide just to have something happen and draw the attendee's eyes to the screen instead of everyone just looking at me, wondering if I was okay or if some-thing had happened to my audible abilities.

Having seemingly forgotten what I had learned over the past few days and not knowing what else to do, I simply began reading the infor-mation on the screen to the audience as if they could not read it for them-selves. At least I was speaking rather than just having an uneasy silence in the room.

Luckily, the presentation slides reflected most of the model's at-tributes, figures, statistics, and capabilities. However, the font size of the information listed about each system was so small that it was difficult to see, let alone for the audience to read. It looked like the bottom row on an eye examination chart. To add to the difficulty the audience had in seeing and reading the information presented on the screen, my nervousness had me speeding through the statistical information, sounding like an auction-eer throwing out all kinds of performance figures, capabilities, and num-bers of each model and then moving to the next slide as quickly as possible.

During this entire time, I never even looked at my audience as I was just focusing on reading the information that appeared on the screen in front of me.

I now realized I had not provided any background or set the stage for why any (or all) of this was important or what all the specifications meant, the value and benefits, and how this information might address any of their problems, issues, or goals.

Looking back, it would have been nearly impossible for anyone in the audience to understand or make sense of what I was trying to communi-cate...let alone what it meant to "them."

However, the meetings' attendees sat very politely, even though they had no idea where we had started or where we were headed. They were probably afraid to stop or interrupt, fearing I might start over again from the beginning and they would have to endure this whole experience again!

I am sure the prospects felt it would be better to let me get it all out while trying to grasp some of the information from the presentation in hopes someone else from my company could sort it out and articulate what I was talking about.

While continuing to speed-read out loud the figures displayed on the screen of each of the server models, which seemed to go on forever, my mouth became so dry, I could not speak anymore. I had to stop to take a drink of water from the glass positioned next to me on the podium. After lifting the glass to my mouth to take a drink and nearly splashing half of the water over the sides of the glass caused by my nervous shaking, I finally looked at my audience, who I had not looked at since beginning of my monologue almost a half hour before. I reluctantly asked, "Are there any questions?"

I was hoping it would be a rhetorical question and no one from the audience would have anything to say. If they did, I hoped they would politely say something like, "We need to think about what we have seen and heard and discuss it and get back with you regarding questions and our decision."

However, to my sheer horror, the prospect's company president's hand shot into the air.

I was terrified of what the question might be as I had completely forgotten all the information I rehearsed while driving to work that morning, but I politely looked directly at him and with a nervous and somewhat quivering voice said..."Yes, sir?"

The next few and simple words out of his mouth would change the direction and help shape my sales career... *FOREVER!*

Those fateful words were, *"So what? What does any of this information mean to me and my company?"*

Like being hit in the forehead with an open hand, it was then I suddenly realized I had not made any of the facts relevant or important to him and his company.

I had not asked enough questions prior to the presentation to understand their current environment and situation...I did not know and understand their current issues and challenges...I did not know and understand their future needs...I did not know and understand their personal or company goals.

I had not set the stage for the presentation, had not made the presentation engaging, or connected with the audience, let alone addressed their individual and company's needs/challenges/issues. I had not showed or explained what the new systems could do for their company, how it would make them more effective and efficient, save money, improve customer service, proof sources, Return on Investment (ROI), testimonials... nothing was provided to the prospect showing and describing the value and benefits they would receive from investing in a new hardware sever and software solution.

The presentation simply included throwing out a plethora of "facts and figures" on the different available hardware servers to the audience and then expecting them to somehow connect the dots and make sense of all the information. They would then have to determine what the information might mean to them and somehow come to a logical conclusion that purchasing a new system would benefit their company, although they might not really understand why.

This book focuses on activities and actions that should have been performed for this and other sales opportunities to ensure a successful sales cycle and process resulting in a W-3...*Win* for the customer, *Win* for your company, and *Win* for your sales career!

LESSON 1

WHAT IS THIS BOOK DESIGNED TO ACCOMPLISH?

It has been said, *"If a person ever sees a turtle sitting on top of a fence post, you can be assured it had some help getting there!"*

The intent of this book is to share knowledge and experiences learned and tried over time and to provide examples of both "failures

1

and successes"...and what has worked and what has not...along with *"how"* and *"why"* some were successful and some fell short of the desired goal(s) and outcome(s). It also contains recommended daily/weekly/monthly actions, activities, and illustrations to be utilized in assisting in the sales cycle and process(es), culminating and ultimately improving the reader's ability and probability of being more successful in their sales career.

This book is meant to assist every level of sales professional from a novice just getting started in a sales career to a seasoned salesperson.

This book is designed to allow readers to follow a structured sales guide, allowing for moving through the sales cycle and processes more effectively and efficiently while decreasing potential risk(s) from pitfalls and setbacks, which reduce the possibility of completing a successful sales experience. It also provides ideas and concepts designed for shortening the learning curve, and sales cycle, by providing specific examples preventing the reader from reinventing the process for each sales opportunity.

During my sales career, it would have been extremely beneficial to have a guide to assist with managing the individual and separate steps involved in completing successful sales opportunities. This writing and included illustrations provide a guide along with instructional reasoning involved with each step. The material is supplemented with lists of items and recommendations aimed at improving the chances of more sales successes.

Looking back over my career and evaluating the lost sales opportunities that were not successfully closed, I realized each one presented signs during the sales process that indicated the opportunity was not moving forward and progressing in the appropriate manner.

There can be a myriad of reasons why any particular sales opportunity can become at risk (or greater risk), and many times, the risk indicators can develop due to various circumstances. The indicator(s) can also appear in clear or subtle manners, such as slowing responses and/or communication stoppage.

There were many times I chose, voluntarily or involuntarily, to ignore signals and indicators from the potential purchaser(s) indicating the opportunity was not progressing and moving forward in an appropriate and productive manner. I continued ignoring the red flags in hopes of completing the opportunity in spite of them.

In reality, each time the warning signs were ignored, it introduced risk(s) with the opportunity, causing it to become stalled, delayed, or lost. The lesson learned over time is that it does not pay off to ignore sales warning signs in hopes they will simply disappear without being addressed and the opportunity will progress forward and close anyway. This rarely ever happens!

This is why it is so important and beneficial for a salesperson to have a structured process for following, acknowledging, and completing each step of the sales cycle and process before moving to the next step(s). This guide allows the process and cycle to progress toward a successful completion in a logical manner, making sure each step is presented, clarified, and acknowledged with the potential purchaser(s). If a salesperson utilizes a logical sales cycle flow combined with structured procedural steps, then the probability and chances of a successful sales campaign are increased dramatically, allowing for the entire sales cycle and process to flow and culminate to a successful result for all the parties involved (purchasing company, solutions company, and the salesperson).

It has been my experience that it is never too late to learn and/or evaluate one's sales strategies, methodologies, processes, and procedures. This writing attempts to assist in educating, as well as serving as a reminder of the elements that are crucial and critical to completing a successful sales campaign.

Having attended many professional sales training programs provided by many different companies and industries; reading many sales philosophy books, articles, and blogs; and participating and attending Internet-based programs such as webinars, simulcasts, and podcasts focusing on sales elements, the number of sales techniques to which this writer has been exposed are numerous. However, I have found if some of these techniques are not adopted, utilized, or implemented on a regular basis into one's sales strategy and methodology, they can become simply stored away or forgotten, no matter what level an individual is in their career.

It is my goal for the reader to gain many ideas and concepts, as well as generate additional thoughts from reading this book. The value of this book will be worth the price paid if the reader learns to *focus on selling "value" to potential purchasers...rather than selling solution(s), product(s), and service(s)!*

By just comparing definitions alone, which would you prefer to purchase and invest your money in as a consumer, product(s) or value?

> **Product**: Something produced by human or mechanical effort or by a natural process.
>
> **Value**: Worth in usefulness or importance to the possessor; utility or merit. A principle, standard, or quality considered worthwhile or desirable.

If salespeople will focus and concentrate on finding out what is important to potential purchaser(s) and then provide value, benefits, and supporting proof for addressing what is important to the potential purchaser(s), they will find greatly improved potential for completing successful sales opportunities, which equates to achieving their sales goals along the way to a successful sales career.

SUMMARY

It has been said that there are "some" people who have fifteen plus years of sales experience. However, the majority of salespeople have less than five years sales experience.

This may speak to the fact that a sales career is not the easiest career. Therefore, it is important to try to gain any advantage possible. Hopefully, reading this writing is one of those advantages.

If this book helps one person improve or increase their sales opportunities, assists in increasing the monthly sales forecast, increases quarterly sales numbers, increases annual sales performance, and, as a result, increases commission(s)/bonus(s), and/or learns some new ideas, concepts, and methodologies...the book will have been worth the time taken to write it.

Keep in mind, the intent of this writing is to not try to cover "every" conceivable and possible sales and marketing technique and methodology. Especially, given the current speed of and changes to technological advances, as technology will continue to play an important part in the sales environment. The intent is to provide ideas, concepts, techniques, methodologies, and scenarios of this salesperson's experiences to assist others in their sales endeavors.

Focus on selling "value" to potential purchasers, rather than solution(s), product(s), or service(s)!

Focus on selling *"what"* solution offering(s) provide (value and benefits) to the potential purchaser(s) as opposed to *"how"* they do it (features and functionality).

To rework the quote at the beginning of this lesson: "Should a salesperson be successful in achieving their personal sales goals and quota(s), you can be assured they had some help getting there!"

LESSON 2

VALUE OF INVESTING IN YOURSELF!

A young kid once asked me, "What do you do for work?"

I responded, "I am a salesperson for a company that assists people and companies to improve their business processes and procedures."

He looked at me with the proverbial "deer in the headlights look," and after thinking about what he had heard for a second or two, he said, "What does that mean?"

The young kid's question and associated follow-up question started me thinking of a couple things.

In many professions, family members and friends have an opportunity to observe what other family members do each day in their occupation and *"how"* and *"what"* they spend their time doing while at work. As an example, family members can visit the workplace and see the area where their family member works or maybe even have an opportunity to visit the office and observe their family member doing their job.

On the other hand, it is probably rare for a family member to observe a sales process, let alone to participate in a prospect or customer meeting.

The average person will spend approximately forty years—83,200 hours—working, which equates to roughly 40 percent of one's adult life. Therefore, if people are going to dedicate almost half their life to an occupation, it would seem to make sense for them to find enjoyment in doing so. Also, it would make sense for people to allow time, energy, and effort to maximize the effectiveness of their time and want to improve their craft and performance on an ongoing basis.

Due to the amount of time most people will spend at their occupation, I recommend seeking out an occupation that you find interesting, as well as enjoy and feel fulfilled doing a good job for your customers. A sales career provides an opportunity for the level of success to only be limited by the willingness to dedicate time and energy to learning as much as possible about the craft, just like any other professional performer or athlete. It has been said that time, effort, and resources individuals invest to learn and improve their career and profession will pay off exponentially in improved performance results.

I was watching a television documentary of a popular musical group that had released albums/CD's over the past three decades and still continue to sell out large venues. As the documentary highlighted and presented the achievements of the group, along with details of its individual members' lives, I found it interesting to learn one of the musicians had sought out an iconic figure in the percussion world from who to take lessons—even after being the group's drummer for over a decade and releasing multiple albums/CD's.

This information confirms we should be taking actions to continually improve to stay at the top of our profession.

SUMMARY

There is a saying..."The more someone practices, the luckier they get."
My belief is this saying is accurate. The more a person practices and is prepared for situations, the more likely that person will be successful. Therefore, what appears to be simply "luck" to the outside world in regard to someone's career is more than likely linked to that person's ongoing practice and preparation routine. This will allow the individual to succeed in opportunities more than others, and therefore, their success is viewed as luck. In reality...they are better prepared to be successful.

LESSON 3

THE SALES PROCESS BASICS

Taking a high-level view of the steps and elements involved in a standard sales process and then distilling them down to the rudimentary steps involves the following elements. Each will be covered in further detail as the reader proceeds through this lesson and through the book.

1. *Marketing*: activities focused on generating curiosity, value, benefits, features, functions, etc.
2. *Prospecting*: researching, investigating, contacting, and communicating with potential purchaser(s) regarding their current environment, situation(s), and potential opportunity(s), utilizing criteria, such as customer demographics, geography, industries, and strategic targets.
3. *Relationship Building*: providing information and credibility to decision makers, building trust, becoming a resource and obtaining willingness to continuing communication and interaction.
4. *Analysis/analytics*: techniques and methodology for identifying opportunities, such as the prospect(s) current solution, what is working, what is not, why, motivation to look at alternatives, etc.

5. *Value Proposition:* how a salesperson's solution offering(s) addresses the issue(s), challenge(s), need(s), goal(s), etc., along with decision maker(s) willingness to look and consider alternative solution(s). Then, supporting with proof sources, such as: case studies, references, Return on Investment (ROI) models, etc.

6. *Performance and Presentation:* opportunity to present/demonstrate the proposed solution offering(s), including themes, visual and audio enhancement(s), audience involvement and interaction, creating relevant and memorable value(s), and benefit(s).

7. *Negotiation:* pricing, payment options, contract items, implementation, training, etc.

8. *Closing:* items associated with signing and completing contract agreement(s).

9. *Implementation:* installation, project management, and initial and ongoing training and professional development, along with applicable and associated time frames.

10. *Follow up:* addressing open items, ongoing communications, and feedback on the customer status.

11. *Reference:* activities focused on continuing to build and strengthen ongoing relationship(s).

In considering a salesperson's responsibilities at a high level, a salesperson should be able to understand and effectively communicate the value(s) of the company and its solution offering(s) to potential purchaser(s), including:

1. Identify and target industries, market(s), and market segments (niches) for opportunities.

2. Identify and target individual purchasers (contacts) within each of the industries, market(s), and market segment(s).

3. Provide activities directed at promoting and increasing curiosity and interest in their company and solution offering(s).

4. Generate and ask appropriate questions to ascertain the potential purchaser's current environment and situation.

5. Be a good listener with the ability to understand and discern challenges/needs/goals facing potential purchaser(s).
6. Understand and clarify the "consequences" of any current and future challenges/needs/goals the potential purchaser(s) is facing and the results of those consequences on the company and its stakeholders.
7. Explain potential resolution(s) and the value(s) and benefit(s) of implementing the proposed solution offering(s), including approximate time frame(s) and financial considerations.
8. Perform and present the solution offering(s) as they pertain to addressing and resolving potential purchaser's criteria, challenges, and goals.
9. Negotiate contract agreement items, such as pricing and terms.
10. Follow up on implementation and ongoing reference communication.
11. Continue performing relationship-building activities.

SUMMARY

These essential sales elements/steps should be addressed with a potential purchaser(s) to discover and clarify any questions and opportunities. Receiving approval and agreement to continue with the sales process/steps will assist in avoiding situations in which the salesperson feels the purchaser(s) is ready to complete and close the contract agreement and then experiences delays due to the decision maker(s) not being ready to move forward because an element(s) was not completed satisfactorily in the purchaser's mind.

If there are issues or unanswered questions, the earlier the salesperson is aware of them and can address them, the quicker it is to continue to move the sales process forward toward a successful and agreeable completion of the sales opportunity.

LESSON 4

UNDERSTANDING THE SALES PROCESS!

CLASSIC SALES INTERVIEW QUESTION

Interviewing for a sales position can be rather unique in that a potential employer rarely has an opportunity to observe the individual going through a complete sales cycle, which consists of prospecting, performing, negotiating, etc., prior to hiring. Therefore, there seems to be a common and classic sales interview question. At some point in the interview, the interviewer will look around the area, pick an item (e.g., pencil, stapler, etc.), and say something like..."Sell this to me." This question is an attempt to provide an opportunity for the interviewee to demonstrate knowledge of the sales process.

It was early in my sales career when an interviewer asked me this question, and I was caught off guard. I was not sure what to do or what to say. It felt similar to a situation where you walk up to a comedian and say, "Make me laugh!"

So, I quickly started thinking and trying to discern "features" of the item, such as color, size, shape, potential uses, etc. After struggling to come up with any real significant reasons why the interviewer would be interested in the object, the interviewer said, "I think I have a feel for your sales knowledge." The interviewer quickly moved through a few more obligatory questions, and then the interview concluded. Oddly enough, I was not selected for the sales position with that organization.

However, this somewhat embarrassing situation was a real eye-opening experience and made me become aware of the importance of knowing, understanding, and being able to articulate the selling process, procedure, elements, and steps.

ELEMENTS OF A PROCESS

When thinking about the importance and benefits of knowing and understanding the elements of a process, I am reminded of a story where a college student had been attending a psychology class in which the students learned the cognitive processes of the mind.

As with most college courses, the professor administered a final examination to provide an opportunity for the students to demonstrate and exercise their knowledge gained during the course. This particular final was held on the last day of the regular semester class. The students came into the classroom knowing the final examination was scheduled for a two-hour period.

The professor handed out four blank sheets of standard 8.5 x 11-inch paper to each student in the class. He stated that there would be additional paper available on his desk should it be needed.

After handing out the designated number of blank pages to each student, he returned to his desk and instructed the students that they would have two hours to complete the final examination. He asked if there were any questions before he provided the test and the examination commenced.

Since there were no questions from the students, the professor requested each student put their name and the page number at the top of each of the four pages.

When the students completed the professor's request, the professor then walked to his desk, reached into his jacket pocket, and produced an apple. He said in a clear voice, "The final examination question is, how can you convince me that this apple, which I am currently holding in my hand, does not exist?" Then he took a seat at his desk in front of the class and set the apple at the edge of the desk in view of all the students.

Almost immediately, the students began writing feverishly, knowing they only had two hours to complete the final examination, which would be a significant portion of their semester and final grade.

However, one student just sat at his desk, staring at the apple in deep thought for several moments before picking up his writing utensil. He then picked up one of the pieces of blank paper and began to write.

Within a few seconds, the student put down his writing utensil and sat there, staring at what he had written. He then collected the sheets of paper in his hands, stood up, and walked toward the professor's desk. By this time, the professor had taken a book out of his other jacket pocket and had begun to read as experience had taught him most of the students would need the entire time to complete the examination question.

As the student approached the desk, the professor looked up and asked, "Would you like additional pieces of paper?"

The student responded, "No, thank you!"

The professor then asked, "Is there something you require of me?"

The student responded, "No, thank you. I've completed the examination," and handed the sheets of paper to the professor.

The other students in the class quickly looked up, amazed to overhear the student say he had completed the examination as most of them were just getting started.

With a doubtful look on his face, the professor reluctantly reached out his hand to take the pieces of paper from the student's hand and adjusted his glasses prior to glancing down at the paper.

Upon reading what the student had written on just one of the pieces of paper, the professor's face quickly produced a smile. The piece of paper only had two words written on it: *WHAT APPLE?*

The professor set down the student's paper on his desk. Reaching into his jacket pocket, he produced a felt tip marker and quickly wrote an A+ at the top of the page.

The moral of the story is that it is not the number of features or functionality that is important to potential purchasers. It is the value and benefit(s) sought out and received and how a provided solution addresses the needs and issues of the intended user. It is understanding the potential purchaser's current environment, the needs and/or issues, and the decision-making process(es).

Whether considering the example of college psychology class or in the sales arena, it is extremely important to have a clear understanding of the steps and processes involved in a situation. Like the examination question, a prepared salesperson can save precious time, energy, and resources by having a better understanding of the complete sales cycle and decision-making process within each sales opportunity.

So, now let's refer back to the situation in which the interviewer requested that I attempt to sell him an object from the top of his desk. Rather than stumbling through and stating obvious features about the object, color, size, function, etc., what should I have done?

The answers are revealed in this book!

The response to the question posed by the interviewer should have included asking a few questions. In essence, the questions asked would have allowed for a brief but important analysis, such as:

- What is the need for the item?
- What task(s) does the item currently complete?
- How is the item utilized today?
- Who utilizes this item?
- Where is this item utilized?
- What is liked about the item and how it performs?
- What should be changed about the item?
- Who or how is this item currently procured?
- How would the user's daily activity(s) change with and without the item?
- How would the item impact individuals in the company and the company overall?
- What is the approximate *"value"* of the item to the user and company?

- Would the user like to continue to invest in using the item?
- How many would be needed?
- When would the item be needed?
- How would the user like to purchase the item?

Gaining a level of knowledge about the current environment and situation, interest level, needs and issues, likes and dislikes, and perceived value to the user and company, allows for an opportunity to move to the next step(s) toward completing the sales process.

Without acquiring some level of knowledge and interest level of the interviewer, my earlier attempt was simply pointing out features and functions without knowing if any of them mattered or addressed the needs, challenges, and issues of the interviewer.

SUMMARY

A salesperson should always be prepared for the classic sales question, "Sell this to me," whether it comes from an interviewer or prospect.

Should this happen, be prepared to ask questions, allowing you to gain information that can be utilized to move effectively through the next step(s) of the sales cycle.

A good method of accomplishing this is to be able to walk through a sales analysis, gaining additional information regarding the purchaser's needs, challenges, issues, and goals. Realize it is not the quantities of features and functionality but rather the value and benefit(s) the user will receive and the impact the solution offering(s) have on the user(s) and overall organization that matters.

The responsibility of a salesperson is to conduct activities that move the opportunity forward and to ensure completion of a successful sale.

LESSON 5

WHAT IS A SALES PROFESSIONAL?

It has been said, "People like to *purchase* items, but do not like to be *sold* items."

You may be saying to yourself...*What's the difference?*

Let's begin by taking a look at the two definitions:

Purchase/Purchasing: Acquisition through the payment of money or its equivalent value.

Sold (Sell): To give up or surrender in exchange for a price.

Just by the definitions alone, which one would you think most people would be more willing to do...acquire or surrender?

You might be saying, "Isn't it really the same result?"

One difference is how individuals "perceive" the interaction, transaction, and overall experience.

When individuals "purchase," they feel they exercise some element of control and are participating in an interaction and interchange of information. They perceive the salesperson to be providing answers to their questions, pointing out value and benefits. They understand how the individual(s) are going to utilize the solution and how it fits into their specific environment and situation. How can it provide additional uses the purchaser may not have considered previously regarding their purchasing decision criteria.

When people are sold, they "perceive" they have little control in the process and therefore must "give in" or surrender in order to complete the transaction, which leaves them feeling pushed into a decision that might not meet their purchasing criteria. This could be for a variety of reasons, such as the item not having the particular desired characteristics (color, size, shape, look, etc.). When a situation of being "sold" occurs, the individual being "sold" often leaves the interaction feeling it was a less-than-positive experience.

Example:

A potential buyer has interest in a certain item and asks the salesperson, "In what colors does this item come?"

The salesperson responds, "Absolutely any color you would like...as long as you only want green."

Upon receiving this information, the purchaser moves forward with the transaction, knowing they need the item but wishing it would have been available in the color preferred, which was blue.

In this example, the purchaser is partially satisfied knowing they wanted or needed the functionality of the item but feeling the value and, to some degree, the benefit of the item is reduced as it did not meet the purchasing criteria and they had to settle for what was available.

It should be the responsibility and goal of a salesperson to have each customer (purchaser) walk away from the experience feeling positive and good about the purchase. This goes back to the adage that a satisfied customer shares their story and experience with a few people and an unsatisfied customer shares their story and experience with many people.

SALESPEOPLE'S HISTORICAL IMAGE

There are individuals who have an impression and image of a salesperson that resembles, and is often presented in, historical Western movies. The image is that of a nicely dressed salesperson who travels from town to town. Upon arriving at the newest location, he stands atop an elevated platform (flatbed wagon, steps, etc.) and begins speaking in a loud voice, requesting anyone within the sound of his voice to gather around. He begins pontificating the varied sort of remedies and cures, resulting in the use of some miracle elixir(s) or salve(s).

During this old Western scene, the salesperson makes many bold claims, many of which may be outrageous and potentially unproven, of assorted uses and miracle cures. He attempts to sell as much of the potion as possible and then quickly moves to the next town before any of the individuals who are "sold" the product have time to use it or to witness the promised miraculous results.

There is another stigma of salespeople represented by a movie scene in which a salesperson locates a person with purchasing authority, sets the individual down, and produces a gold pocket watch or some other sparkly, shiny object from their pocket. While holding it by a chain, the salesperson slowly swings it in front of an individual's face, requesting that the person focus on the moving object with their eyes. The salesperson speaks calmly to them ultimately putting them in a mystical trance.

While the person is in this trance, the salesperson quickly produces a writing utensil and puts it in the individual's hand. The salesperson slides the document (contract, purchase order, etc.) under the individual's hand. Holding the writing utensil, the individual unknowingly signs the document.

Then, the salesperson snaps their fingers, and the person is brought out of the trance, not remembering what happened. However, for some unknown reason, the unsuspecting victim is willing to just accept the consequences of their signature and fulfill the obligation of the document that was signed while in the trance.

Hopefully, the reader finds these two simple and unrealistic examples of the historical image of salespeople and the sales process humorous, but let us be realistic about the image some salespeople have with society. It may be true that some in today's society have a distorted view of salespeople and the sales profession and still view them as individuals with questionable morals and/or ethics.

Another misnomer of salespeople is that they are pushy and try to utilize strong persuasion tactics until they gets what they want, which is the completion of a sale.

How many times have you or someone you know purchased an item requiring a significant investment from someone who they did not like or did not trust?

I learned early in my career that if a solution was sold that did not meet the purchaser's expectations and did not address their needs and goals, then the customer would either request a return of the solution and return of the investment or be unwilling to make a purchase again.

SALES PROFESSION RELEVANCE

Salespeople provide a vital service to individuals, companies, businesses, entities, communities, nations, and the world. They provide service(s) to private, public, government, and profit or nonprofit entities, including small, medium, and large organizations.

It is a company's sales force that is largely responsible for communicating the company's current solution offering(s), newly developed solutions, technology, and services to potential purchasers.

EVERYONE IS A SALESPERSON...WHETHER THEY KNOW IT OR NOT!

The reader may have heard someone say, "I could never be a salesperson!"...or..."I would never be a salesperson!"

The response to someone making this statement should be, "Sure you could!" or, more appropriately, "Sure you are!"

Think about a time when you had a particularly good experience purchasing an item. Think about the salesperson's actions and what they offered/provided to make the experience unique and special. What was your opinion of the salesperson, as well as of the company and the solution offerings at the time of the purchasing experience? How did you feel about the interaction and experience over the next few weeks while utilizing the solution?

Is it not true that everyone would like to experience a positive feeling and enjoy a good experience making purchase(s)... *EVERYTIME?*

Believe it or not, it is still possible to have a good and enjoyable experience purchasing an item, and the salesperson is a big piece of how the experience is perceived.

SALES ELEMENTS ARE EVERYWHERE

Not only do sales professionals provide an important service, role, and function in our society, but if we stop and think about it, the reality is that we all "sell" in one form or another, whether it is to our children, spouse, parents, friends, associates, coworkers, boss, etc.

The art and finesse of selling an individual or group of individuals (organization) on an idea that we think would improve another's life or situation has probably been around since the beginning of humankind. Possibly, one of the first persons to try to sell an idea was Eve in the Garden of Eden when she so eloquently presented Adam with the "benefits" of taking a simple bite of an apple.

When thinking about the sales process in its simplest and basic form, it is providing another person(s), company, organization, entity, etc., with the "value, benefit(s), and outcome(s)" of performing some action and/or the potential consequences of not taking some action and how the outcome(s) of the decision is going to impact the situation.

CONSULTATIVE SALES

Sales professionals are focused on performing "consultative" and "advisory" based experience(s) and service(s) to the potential purchaser(s). Therefore, it is imperative to commit time, effort, and energy to building and nurturing a personal and ongoing relationship with potential purchasers.

Typically, the sales opportunities involving a consultative sales professional require such elements as higher monetary investment, longer term commitment, and larger impact on the individual's and company's overall success. The salesperson should focus on building relationships, allowing not only an initial selling opportunity, but also potential recurring sales opportunities and a reference account.

SALES ELEMENTS

Here are some of the elements involved in the sales process:
1. Having knowledge and understanding of a potential purchaser's current environment and situation, along with needs, issues, challenges, future needs, and goals.
2. Listening, understanding, and processing how the current situation is affecting and impacting the situation (whether it is an individual, organization, company, entity, etc.).
3. Skill and technique for asking appropriate discovery analysis and clarifying questions, ensuring a solid understanding of the purchaser's goal(s).
4. Delivering and explaining a value proposition, such as value(s), benefit(s), result(s), etc., that can be provided and expected.
5. Ability to communicate, demonstrate, explain, and expand the value and benefits of solution(s).
6. Techniques for having conversation(s), performing, and presenting solution offering(s) as they pertain to attaining the purchaser's goals.

7. Attaining approval from the potential purchaser(s) that the solution offering(s) being proposed addresses their needs/goals.
8. Negotiating an acceptable purchase price for exchange of the value and benefits provided by the solution offering(s).
9. Agreement on contract terms (payment, etc.), implementation, and project completion time frame(s).
10. If needed, an implementation model/timeline with projected benchmarks (with associated time frames for completion).
11. If applicable, any support and maintenance items.
12. References. What other prospects does the customer know who could also benefit from the solution offering(s)?
13. Ongoing relationship-building communication and activities.

SOME OF THE BEST SALESPEOPLE ARE NOT SALES PROFESSIONALS

Some of the best salespeople I have witnessed were not sales professionals and did not have a sales profession title or role.

Some individuals seem to have the natural ability, personality, and characteristics to sell others on an idea or concept that also happens to benefit them. It is truly an art form and magical to observe, as these individual go through a process consisting of setting the stage while explaining the scope of a situation. Then, continuing to describe the "relatively" inconsequential involvement of other person(s) that would allow them to complete the task, and...oh, by the way, allowing those involved to gain the benefit of feeling good about assisting in the process.

Sales professionals, including myself, should be glad when these individuals don't choose to work for any competitors. They are truly masters of getting individuals to realize, understand, and assess the situation. Resulting in achieving their goal, while providing you an opportunity to feel good about helping them. If these individuals would have chosen the sales profession, they would have had an extremely successful and rewarding sales career.

So, how do these individuals (each of us probably all know one or two) with no professional sales training understand, exercise, and accomplish the processes and elements of a sales process successfully?

They do this armed with basic knowledge of simple but important elements, which are also desirable in achieving success in the selling arena:

1. They maintain a personable, friendly, and outgoing personality. This allows others to easily and quickly engage with, interact with, and enjoy being around them.

2. They represent a willingness to "want" to help others ("would help if they could" attitude).

3. They exude a genuine kindness and sincerity when making a request for the action desired.

4. *Prospecting*: They locate an individual or individuals who have the wherewithal to assist them in achieving their goal.

5. *Marketing*: They make the initial request for some action that is or would be a relatively trivial commitment (requiring little effort, small investment, etc.). The commitment may lead to an increased commitment or larger decision as the process continues.

6. *Analysis*: They ask questions about how they may be able to address the item(s) needed to achieve the goal. This allows the other person(s) to become involved since they are providing advice/direction.

7. *Performance and Presentation*: They provide value(s) and benefit(s) for the person(s) they are assisting, and how helping will allow them to gain something, even if just the satisfaction of helping out another individual.

8. *Negotiating*: They continue to further expand the benefit(s) of assisting them.

9. *Close*: They explain and establish the "Win-Win!" A Win for those who help and a Win for the person accomplishing their goal.

10. *Reference(s)*: They share with others about the act(s) of kindness and the willingness to assist them...and who doesn't like to hear others

say nice things about them, especially in front of supervisors, sales management team, coworkers, peers, family, friends, etc.?

WILL EVERYONE (OR ANYONE) BUY?

When I was first starting my sales career, I was told by other sales individuals it would be beneficial to have thick skin if I wanted to have a chance at a lengthy sales career. This information and advice was helpful and true.

If a survey was taken of sales professionals, it would reflect that they have experienced and heard..."No, thank you"..."Not at this time"..."Maybe later"...many times during their career.

Individuals get into the sales profession for many different reasons: the challenge, the adventure, the rewards. However, I feel the occupation will be much more enjoyable and allow for a longer career if the experience and journey of the sales process is embraced.

To make the most out of a sales career, my advice is to truly enjoy the sales process and genuinely want to assist individuals and companies. The daily activities required of a sales position (prospecting, cold-calling, marketing, customer satisfaction issues, travel, reporting, etc.), will be more satisfying and rewarding if the journey and experiences are appreciated, enjoyed, and celebrated along the way.

It is likely that almost every salesperson during their career will hear or receive some rejections—maybe even on a regular (daily/weekly/monthly) basis.

Therefore, I feel it is essential for a salesperson to find some level of enjoyment and satisfaction in their role of assisting others (prospects and customers) while making an impact (improving individuals and/or companies, etc.), as well as acknowledging successes along the way. Without the enjoyment and satisfaction of the selling process and assisting others, the number of potential rejections could impact the level of dedication needed to achieve sales goals.

HIRING SALESPEOPLE PHILOSOPHY

Many companies tend to have a sales hiring philosophy that falls into one of two categories:

1. Hiring or transferring an individual with technical experience and background (typically someone who has been with the company/industry for an extended time) who has possibly has been in the development and/or installation/implementation department and may have been involved in installing solution(s)/applications for customers. If the individual comes from within the company (but different department) they usually have a good knowledge of the company's history, solution offering(s), and potentially familiar with the industry and customer base. In this scenario, the sales management team then provides necessary sales training allowing the candidate to gain the company's sales philosophy and methodologies (process, procedures, etc.).

2. Hiring a professional salesperson that possesses appropriate experience, training, and skill set, including sales methodologies, strategies, techniques, etc., and provide them with appropriate information regarding the company's solution offering(s), including any required technical aspects, etc. Both philosophies may incorporate assistance from other individual(s), or department(s) during the sales cycle and/or presentation(s).

The sales personnel hiring strategy that is exercised by a company is dependent on each specific company's philosophy and may consist of a mixture of the individuals described. The level of success realized by the utilized strategy seems to be determined by each individual's ability to grasp whatever knowledge or skill set is lacking from the equation of:

- Knowledge of the sales process.
- Company's solution offering(s): specific solution/application or suite (group) of solutions, with associated service(s), etc.
- Unique and specific value proposition(s).
- Market/Industry knowledge.
- Company's market positioning.

- Prospecting/Marketing (territory/region, accounts, geography, etc.).
- Understanding and expressing value(s) and benefit(s).
- Technology utilization and benefits.
- Implementation and installation elements.
- Services (training, ongoing support, etc.).

Then, evaluate what knowledge area, skill set, or expertise is needed and what resources are available to shore up and strengthen any weak area(s), allowing the salesperson to appropriately represent the company's solution offering(s) to purchasers.

My experience has been that it involves a shorter time frame to inform a sales professional about the value and benefits of the solution offering(s), than to teach an individual who has the solution offering(s) knowledge the entire sales processes.

This is not a statement or reflection on any individual's skill set, but as an example, it is rare to see mechanic(s) of a national racing team actually operating as the driver of the vehicle during the actual competition. Similarly, it is rare to see a commercial airline mechanic also being the pilot of the plane. Both have extremely important responsibilities and skill sets; however, they are very different responsibilities and skill sets.

SELLING IS A WORK IN PROCESS (WIP)

Keep in mind that the selling process and ongoing professional development process is a "Work in Process," and as such, there are elements to learn and continue to perfect along the way: learning what works for you, when it works, why it works, and what does not work.

I recommend making sure to not only enjoy the process and the journey of sales but also continue to be open to learning throughout the process as *each* sales opportunity is likely to provide learning and educational moments, as well as personal growth opportunities.

Activities associated with selling, such as prospecting, conversations and interactions, analysis, performances, presentations, and demonstrations are likely to present challenges and, as such, may not always go perfectly or even as planned. However, as long as the salesperson is willing to be open to continuing to learn from each opportunity and continues to move forward, allowing themselves the freedom to be curious, adventuresome, and willing to think out of the box, many new things will be learned, making them more improved and experienced salesperson as their career progresses.

One of the realities of a lengthy sales career is that it is likely that a salesperson will not win every opportunity they encounter (for any number of reasons), so it is important to enjoy and appreciate the opportunities won (secured contract), as well as to challenge themselves to learn equally (if not more) from those opportunities that are "not won."

Another reality is that there is a likelihood that some mistakes may be made along the way. Acknowledge this reality, and do not be afraid to make a mistake. Depending on the type of mistake it is and how it may impact the potential purchaser's decision, and/or the sales opportunity, it may provide an opportunity to demonstrate a level of professionalism and integrity to the potential purchaser by admitting the error and providing the correct information and appropriate corrective action(s).

I have also discovered it is easier to admit the mistake when recognized rather than trying to move forward with the hope(s) the potential purchaser(s) will not find out about it. If this is a long-term customer, the likelihood of the truth being discovered is high. I have realized it is better and more appropriate to address and rectify the issue as quickly as possible.

Another reason for a salesperson admitting and rectifying any error(s) quickly is that if the salesperson is going to be selling in an industry over a long period of time, they may encounter a number of the same people and/or companies along their career path and may continue to see and/or communicate with these individuals. It is not uncommon for individuals to stay with the same company, or the same industry with a different company, over an extended period of time. Whether a salesperson successfully completes a sales opportunity or not, there may be an opportunity to work with this person again, or they may even know someone who you are (or will) work with on a future sales opportunity(s). Should this opportunity happen, you will be better served to have left a positive impression as a person with integrity.

The president of a successful company for which I worked once told me, "Make mistakes quickly, learn from them, and do not repeat them!"

This is good advice to pass on to you. Remember, a high-level US official once stated, "Trees cause pollution"...and went on to have a successful political career, so it's possible to make a mistake and still go on to become successful.

PRIORITIZING SALES TIME

It has been said in real estate that it is all about...Location, Location, Location! If this is accurate, then in sales it's all about...Time, Time, Time!

Time is one of the most precious commodities any salesperson (or any person, for that matter) has, and therefore, this commodity should be managed with much care and focus.

Salespeople seem to prioritize their *time* based on two variables and potential outcomes:

1. Prioritizing activities that focus on "gaining" achievements. Focusing on those activities that will move them toward their goals and therefore appearing in a motivated (offensive) stance.

2. Prioritizing activities that focus on "reducing" anxiety and concern. Focusing on those activities that are going to keep them out of a predicament with their sales management team and company administration and therefore appearing as a defensive stance.

The reality seems to be that salespeople and sales managers focus on item #1 when the salespeople (and/or company) are ahead of their sales projections, and focus on item #2 when the salespeople (and/or company) are behind their sales projections.

Another method is to prioritize time for sales-focused activities, allowing a salesperson the best possible chance to achieve sales goals (set by the salesperson or by sales management). The following example is based on an 8-hour day and 40-hour week:

- 45 percent of time (3.5 hours/day, 18 hours/week) focusing on prospecting and marketing activities (new opportunities in the sales process).
- 25 percent (2 hours/day, 10 hours/week) focused on moving identified sales opportunities forward to the next step(s) in the process.
- 15 percent (1.2 hours/day, 6 hours/week) focused on existing and reference customers.
- 15 percent (1.2 hours/day, 6 hours/week) on e-mail and internal company activities (scheduled weekly and monthly calls, administrative activities, expenses, travel, etc.).

Salespeople should prioritize their time based on individual sales goals, sales management goals, or a combination of both goals.

My recommendation is to have open and clear communication with your sales management team, allowing both the salesperson and sales management to know and understand the goals. These additional and supplementary internal company activities, such as e-mail, conference calls, expenses, travel, etc., are important and necessary activities for a sales position. However, if not prioritized and monitored appropriately by a salesperson, ancillary activities have a way of taking away from valuable selling time and those activities that are required to meet sales goals.

A sales manager once said to me, *"Inspect what you expect."* This means that Sales management should focus on and communicate about those activities and results that they *expect* from their salespeople (sales team) and then *inspect* information provided to achieve these results.

SALES ACTIONS

Sales roles have various titles, including Sales Executive, Sales Representative, Sales Associate, Account Manager, among others. Regardless of the title and job description, it is customary for a sales position to be associated with a geographic territory (city, state, multiple states, international, etc.), sales accounts, or a combination of both, allowing opportunities to communicate and interact with prospects and customers.

The responsibilities of a salesperson may require the "sales office" to fluctuate between a desk/cubicle at the corporate office, the home office, airports, airplanes, hotels, rental cars, and prospects' and customers' office(s).

As modern technology continues to expand and evolve, it provides opportunities for the majority of us to be more and more connected and therefore have additional and better access to voice mail, e-mail, Internet, etc., via electronic devices that salespeople carry with them.

The portability of today's information and technology assists with communicating with potential purchasers more quickly. Also, the continued advances in technology will make it easier to communicate and interact with others. However, it also means individuals with whom salespeople are trying to communicate are also busier and more inundated with activities because they also have access to similar advances in communication where individuals both inside and outside of their work environment are vying for their time. The increasing number of potential distractions exacerbates the importance of providing concise and relevant information during communications with potential purchaser(s).

PROFESSIONAL SALES CHARACTERISTICS

Throughout the years of being involved in sales, there appears to be a pattern of characteristics of those individuals who have been recognized as being successful in the sales arena. The following are some of the characteristics that have been observed:

- Passion for providing solution(s) to improve entities (companies, divisions, departments, groups, etc.) and lives of individuals.
- Commitment to doing the right thing(s) for the right reason(s).
- Perseverance (not adverse to hearing rejection and does not take rejection personally or internalize objections).
- Drive (performing and communicating the company's message every day)!
- Character and personality (the type of person others want to associate with and are willing to interact with regularly).
- Motivation (the ability to continue to progress and achieve while facing adversity).
- Good communicator (able to provide information others can clearly understand, along with the ability to think on their feet, overcome objections, etc.).
- Performer (ability to command the attention of an audience and be memorable).
- Dedication (to achieving their own personal goals, as well as company's defined goals).

It will also be beneficial to a salesperson's career if they can determine a way to cope with and understand why they may receive rejections. One way to keep from becoming discouraged when hearing rejection(s) is to understand that what the potential purchaser is really saying is that they do not clearly understand the value, benefits, option(s), etc., being offered and how they would improve their company. So, the rejection may be simply a notification that they require additional information in order to better understand how the value and benefits being offered impact the purchaser(s).

SUMMARY

Remember, individuals like to *purchase* things, but do not like to be *sold* things.

Salespeople provide a vital service to individuals, companies, businesses, entities, communities, nations, and the world by providing service(s) to private, public, government, and profit or nonprofit entities, including small, medium, and large organizations.

Not only do sales professionals provide an important service, role, and function in society, but the reality is that we all "sell" in one form or another, whether it is to our children, spouse, parents, friends, associates, coworkers, boss, etc.

The selling process(es) involves some of the very basic and innate processes of human nature in each of us. Whenever individuals want something, they tend to focus energy and effort on showing and/or convincing other(s), or even themselves, the value and benefits of obtaining or achieving the thing being sought.

Some of the challenges of being a salesperson have been mentioned; however, understand that it is not necessary to apologize for being a sales professional. This career has been chosen by a large number of individuals, and few entities can continue to be successful without some type of sales activity and the associated revenue it generates for the company.

Any rejection may be simply a notification that the purchaser(s) require additional information in order to better understand how the value and benefits being offered impact them.

Time is one of the most precious commodities to a salesperson (and to any person). I recommend utilizing this commodity carefully and working with your sales management team to prioritize and manage time effectively to achieve your personal sales and company goals.

The selling process and ongoing personal development is a "Work in Process," and as such, there are various elements to learn and continue to perfect along the way...learning what works for you...what does not... when it works...and why it works.

The portability of today's information and technology assists with making communications with potential purchasers happen more quickly. However, it also means individuals with whom salespeople are trying to communicate are also busier exacerbating the importance of salespeople providing clear, concise and relevant information to prospect(s)/customer(s).

Keep in mind, successful completions of sales opportunities are designed to be beneficial for the customer and the company you represent... just keep in mind a Win-Win mentality, and it will assist you in being able to present the appropriate solution offering(s).

To make the most out of a sales career, it would be my recommendation to enjoy the sales process and genuinely want to assist individuals and companies.

A world champion rodeo cowboy once told me, "It's not who I face as competition that defines my ability to be successful, but rather how I perform against competition that determines if I will be successful."

LESSON 6

UNDERSTANDING WHY PEOPLE PURCHASE!

The goal of the sales process is to allow individual(s) and entities (companies, organizations, etc.) to make an informed decision based on values, benefits, features, and functionalities best suited and fitted to accomplish the intended result to achieve current and future goals.

To help achieve a successful sales career, it is important to understand why people purchase.

1. What makes them curious about purchasing a solution?
2. What helps them make the decision(s) to purchase?
3. What are the entity's need(s) and goal(s)?
4. What are the purchaser(s) need(s) and goal(s)?
5. Why they "may" and "may not" purchase from a particular company.
6. Why they "may" and "may not" purchase a specific solution offering.
7. How can a salesperson assist in the decision-making processes?

An element often overlooked when it comes to understanding why people purchase is the reality that individuals involved in the decision-making process may have varied levels of knowledge and experience of "decision making." Each individual's own personal decision-making processes and procedures may influence their decision making for not only themselves but also for any company or organization with which they are involved.

Individuals may not have a formalized or structured purchasing process, but most have been purchasing items for themselves and potentially others for a period of time. Therefore, they have developed some type of decision-making process and procedure, whether it is formal or informal.

By the time most individuals reach young adulthood, they have more than likely made hundreds of personal purchases and purchasing decisions (albeit many of these purchases may be trivial, requiring a small investment). Regardless of the number of decisions or the purchase price point, each individual usually has what can be referred to as an "informal" purchasing process or structure. Individuals will make decisions based on their "informal" process for the majority of their lives, utilizing a more "formalized" decision-making process when involving work- or job-based decision(s). A salesperson needs to be aware and try to ascertain the purchaser's individual "informal" decision-making process(es) and how this will affect the formalized decision process that is utilized by a committee or group for an organizational decision.

Most individuals begin making simple and small purchasing decisions at a relatively early age. Even if these purchases and purchasing decisions did not involve money, the purchases may have involved the "barter" system involving negotiation(s).

As an example, kids learn to trade items (toys, candy, etc.), stating, "I'll trade this item I have for that item you have."

Utilizing this rudimentary process and system is how most of us learned to obtain and/or exchange items and therefore began honing our decision-making skills early on in relation to school, food, and daily chores, among other things. It is also at this young age that we begin to learn negotiation skills (covered in a later lesson).

MOTIVATION TO PURCHASE

One of the most important elements of the sales process that needs to be identified and understood in order to be successful is knowing what the curiosity and motivation is for someone being initially interested in wanting something and ultimately completing a purchase.

These individual purchasing curiosities and motivations can be as varied as one can imagine...including making an individual and/or entity more effective, efficient, or profitable; saving money; increasing customer service, loyalty, etc. Because almost every purchase involves some form of curiosity and/or motivation, it is the salesperson's responsibility to determine what this curiosity and motivation is for each potential purchaser.

To accomplish the task of identifying the curiosity and motivation behind a potential purchase, the salesperson needs to obtain as much appropriate information as possible, such as the current environment situation and status of the challenge(s) and issue(s), to be addressed with this purchase. What is the result for the business if not addressed, what is the urgency and timing, what is the budget, is there an impending event (deadline for expiration of existing contract, change in business practices, regulations, etc.) that requires or makes sense for the issue(s) to be addressed now or in the near future?

Most individuals will complete a purchase to make their lives and/or their company's business "better" in some manner (e.g., more effective, more efficient, increase margins, reduce costs, doing more with less, improve customer satisfaction, etc.).

DOES EVERY PROBLEM NEED TO BE SOLVED?

A salesperson should be cognizant and not assume that even though they have identified or are aware of a particular company/industry issue that each company in that industry *"wants"* to address (resolve) *"that particular issue."*

There have been times when I was made aware of a company's particular operational issue and tried to explain to individuals within that company how they could address this situation by simply purchasing my company's solution offering. Only to have it explained to me that the prospective company did not want to explore addressing the issue (for whatever reason) or they did not view it as a major area of impact to the company. Therefore, the company was not interested in investing time or resources in investigating potential resolution options.

I met with individuals from a large organization who were interested in exploring a *"specific"* module's functionality of the solution I was representing, which focused on Enterprise Resource Management (ERP) including inventory control.

Through my experience with similar companies, it struck me that if they were struggling in *one* particular inventory control area, they were also probably experiencing issues in *other operational areas* associated and affected by the inventory control operation(s).

Being a salesperson interested in expanding any sales opportunities within a company, I suggested that the company could also utilize another of my company's solution modules to gain additional operational control, which in turn would allow for overall improvement in the organization.

The president of the company looked at me and asked, "Why do you think we have problems in other areas of our company?"

The look on his face was one of disgust, and I quickly realized I had unintentionally touched on a sensitive area of the company. To make it worse, the topic was brought up in front of the entire management team and departmental leaders.

The president went on to say in a stern voice, "We do not have any problems with operational control in the area you just mentioned, and we are here to *specifically* explore our options in the inventory control area for which this meeting was scheduled!"

I quickly began backpedaling and trying to recover and move forward, focusing on what they had requested be presented, but the damage had been done. As they say, "It's a lot easier letting the cat out of the bag than it is getting the cat back in the bag."

My assumption that since they had an issue in *one* area of the company, *another* area of the company might be affected, and therefore, they would also be interested in hearing or exploring additional options was obviously incorrect.

It was later explained that the person responsible for the inventory control area that the president was not interested in addressing was managed by his son. Therefore there was no need for any improvement in that particular area!

It was a tough lesson to learn, but moving forward taught me to ask more discovery analysis and clarification questions before assuming that just because an organization was interested in one area of a solution, or addressing one area of concern the organization also *wanted and needed* to address additional areas for improvement.

The lesson is to point out the importance of identifying not only what the company's issue(s) and challenge(s) might be, but more important, determining if the company is interested in investigating and pursuing potential resolutions in addressing the area(s) of concern(s).

A COMMON MISTAKE

One of the common mistakes made when selling is that when someone expresses an interest or curiosity to salespeople, they assume:

- The individual wants to address the issue(s).
- They have the budget to purchase.
- They have authority to purchase.
- They want to purchase...from us!

Let us assume that an individual who expresses curiosity and motivation wants to do something about the current challenge(s)/issue(s), has the budget to address them, and has the authority to purchase. How do they decide from whom to purchase when the time comes to make the purchasing decision?

Think about how you and people you know decide where and from whom to purchase.

One big influence on the decision of where to purchase is referrals. Individuals who have an issue/challenge they are unsure how to address ask friend(s), family, neighbors, and coworkers for advice on where to purchase based on their experience(s).

Well, believe it or not, many companies go through this same type of decision-making process. They query others in the industry or ask other companies with which they conduct business that may share similar types of issue(s)/challenge(s).

The reasons include:

- Approximately 80 percent of people believe referrals from friends, family, colleagues, etc., to be highly credible.
- Approximately 50 percent of people believe written or online information to be highly credible.

So, even in today's digital age, referrals still have an impact on individual and business purchasing decisions.

One reason for referral(s) still being prominent and powerful is that both individuals and companies are trying to mitigate risk. This reduces the chances of making an incorrect decision and the solution offering(s) not meeting the need(s) or addressing the specific issue(s), challenge(s) and goal(s). As a result, if a potential purchaser knows an individual (friend, family, coworker, etc.) who had a good purchasing experience from a specific provider, most potential purchasers will accept this recommendation versus taking a chance of doing business with some random and unknown provider.

SUMMARY

To assist in achieving a successful sales career, it is important to understand *why* people purchase.

Each individual's own personal decision-making processes and procedures influence their decision making for not only themselves, but also for entities with which they are involved.

A salesperson should confirm the potential purchaser(s) willingness to explore and address potential issue(s)/challenge(s) prior to offering potential resolution(s).

One important element is to identify and understand the curiosity and motivation for someone being interested and wanting to complete a purchase.

Keep in mind, referrals are a large influence on an individual's purchasing decisions.

LESSON 7

THE ROLE OF A SALES PROFESSIONAL

To assist in positioning and illustrating the overall goal(s) of a sales professional, think about the following.

How would someone explain the concept, ideas, and/or goals of a particular sporting activity to another person who had never seen the actual sporting activity/event before? Since they have never seen or heard about the sport, they are not familiar with any of the objectives, rules, or outcomes.

I understand it might be a rare instance where an individual does not know the basic concept(s) of most professional sports, but for illustrative purposes, just imagine how someone (salesperson) would explain the sport from a conceptual and descriptive perspective, containing items, such as the layout of the field/court, the rules, the players' responsibilities, scoring, etc.

This is similar to the situation of how a potential purchaser(s) may feel regarding the salesperson's solution offering(s), as the potential purchaser(s) may have little to no knowledge of the solution offering(s), the company the salesperson represents, or the salesperson, let alone the value(s), benefit(s), features, functionality, usage, and usability. It is also possible the individual(s) has never heard or seen whatever the salesperson is providing as a solution offering(s).

Therefore, it is the responsibility of the salesperson to set the stage early in the conversation and/or meeting to provide information that builds curiosity and interest while providing a basis of value. If this is the first time the salesperson is communicating on the phone or in a meeting, it is imperative that the salesperson set the stage and provide some form of high-level structure and outline for the reason(s) for the interaction and topics to be discussed.

This is especially important whenever a group of people gets together for a meeting, as most audiences would like to have some idea as to the purpose of the gathering: what the agenda is, what topics will be covered, issues and challenges to be addressed, value(s) and benefit(s), next step(s) and action(s), and what goal(s) will be accomplished. By providing and establishing this information early, individual(s) attending the meeting have a chance to understand why there is an interaction taking place.

This also provides the salesperson an opportunity to deliver a high-level value proposition and a quick commercial on value and benefits, as well as positioning the salesperson's company's solution offering(s), allowing the potential purchaser(s) an understanding of what type of information will be presented and offered during the call/meeting.

So, let's now return to the illustration mentioned earlier and how someone (salesperson) might explain a professional sporting activity that a potential purchaser is unfamiliar with.

For the sake of this illustration, image pulling into the parking lot of an empty football stadium along with a person (potential purchaser) who has never before seen a professional football game.

I would imagine their first question may be, "Why are we here, and what happens or takes place here?"

This is similar to what prospects want to know when first contacted by a salesperson. "Why are you contacting me, and what is the topic of interaction?"

Upon parking the vehicle, the salesperson and potential purchaser both walk into the stadium and walk up to the point where both are standing on the stairs of the first level of seating.

So, in the sales process, the salesperson has gotten a foot in the door, and the prospect has enough curiosity to allow the salesperson the privilege of continuing to share more information.

Now that the salesperson has created interest and received permission to continue, the task is to quickly explain the reason for contacting the prospect.

In our scenario, it is time to explain the game of football to the other person in a manner that will make sense using reference points, such as shared or common experiences, allowing the prospect to more easily understand.

The salesperson leads the prospect to the seats, which are located on the 50-yard line, allowing them to see the entire field, and produces a football symbolizing one of the main topics.

The salesperson begins explaining, "This is a football, and the objective of the sport of football is to take this oblong, leather ball and move it down the field and ultimately over the goal line." The salesperson references by pointing toward the final line across the field indicated by two orange end zone markers.

Since the prospect has never seen the game (or, in our case...the solution offering), the potential purchaser asks with a puzzled look on their face, "How difficult could it be to take the football and move it down a perfectly manicured, seemingly level grass/turf field and across the goal line?"

The salesperson responds, "What a great question! Let me share a little bit more about the details" (solution offering). As is often the case, the devil is in the detail(s).

Now it is time for the salesperson to begin explaining the details, providing a clearer picture of the game (solution offering).

Now that the potential purchaser has a general idea of what the concept of football (or the salesperson's offering) is, the salesperson can begin to explain high-level items (values and benefits) of the game (solution offering), such as:

- There will be two teams on the field competing against each other.
- Each team consists of several players but can only utilize eleven at a time during official play.
- The ball is made of leather and filled with air. Its oblong formation allows it to thrown more easily, but it also bounces unpredictably if dropped on the ground.
- The team with possession of the ball is known as the offense, and the team defending their goal line is known as the defense.
- Scoring. If the ball is passed or ran across the goal line, it is worth six points, and then the scoring team has an opportunity to either kick it through the uprights for an additional point or run/pass it for two points.
- General rules. Penalties are assessed against either team for rule infractions.

After stopping to address any questions at this point, the salesperson can proceed, providing more information based on the prospect's questions, curiosity level, and needs for additional information. The salesperson can continue to provide additional details, such as:

- Specific team members' positions/roles and substitutions.

- Possession rules and downs.
- Additional scoring methods and strategies.
- Time limit for the game.
- How to win the game.

Hopefully, the reader understands the concept of this illustration, which is to point out the number of complexities that can be involved in what was "initially" described as explaining a simple concept...the game of football.

These same complexities are also involved in the selling process. Many times, the salesperson *assumes* the potential purchaser(s) understands what the solution offering(s) provides and what it means to the purchaser(s).

This scenario is similar to the sales process as some people have the perception that selling is simply showing up and telling people about a solution (features and functionality) and receiving a signed order (contract). But as described in the football illustration, it can be much more complicated than originally thought...and so is the sales process!

WALKING WITH THE POTENTIAL PURCHASER(S)

Without setting the stage, the potential purchaser can quickly become confused as the salesperson begins to explain the value(s) and benefit(s) that the offering provides. Remember, the salesperson is familiar with the offering, so they have a tendency to want to move through all of the offering(s) in its entirety. This process can become overwhelming to the potential purchaser(s), especially if they are trying to determine how all the possible features and functionality being presented will benefit them and their company.

This is why it is so critical for salespeople to not just throw out "all" the features and functionality (show up and throw up mentality) and then leave it to the potential purchaser(s) to figure out what all the features and functionality mean to them and try to connect the dots as to how they could utilize the solution offering(s) to improve their lives and business processes.

Here's a little secret...most potential purchaser(s) are usually too busy to take time to go through the mental exercise of trying to connect all the pieces of information, saying, "If the solution offering(s) has the ability to do *this*, then that means we can do *that*, and the benefit will be *this*." Therefore, it is imperative that the salesperson finds out what is important to the potential purchaser(s) and provide information on those areas, assisting the purchaser(s) in making sense of each of the values and benefits and what they mean to them, along with features and functionality in regard to the purchaser(s) needs before proceeding forward to the next need and benefit(s).

Along with being able to explain values, benefits, features, and functionality of your company's offering, it is also very important for the salesperson to clearly understand and comprehend the potential purchaser(s) current environment (situation, issues, challenges, goals, etc.) and be able to address (explain, show, and demonstrate) how the solution offering(s) is going to address each of these areas without overwhelming the audience with numerous features, functionality, and options the solution offering(s) can provide.

If this step is not completed carefully and strategically, the salesperson risks the prospect(s) becoming confused or overwhelmed, which in turn can make the solution offering(s) look and feel as if it is convoluted and difficult to utilize.

Therefore, it is instrumental when explaining and presenting the value(s) and benefit(s) of the solution offering(s) that the salesperson confirms the audience members' understanding often by asking validating questions.

In many cases, if audience members get confused about what is being stated and presented, the salesperson risks the audience members not asking them to clarify the information being communicated and instead allowing the salesperson to continue to move forward in the hopes of figuring out any misunderstanding later in the meeting.

When this situation happens, the salesperson risks the audience members missing key concepts and ideas presented, along with how the solution offering(s) could assist them and their organization.

Remember, it is the salesperson's responsibility to ensure that the audience understands the value and benefit of what is being discussed and proposed as a resolution(s) to the prospect's issues/needs/goals and how the organization benefits from utilizing the solution offering(s).

If the salesperson feels the audience members may be confused or do not clearly understand what is being said or presented, which may be indicated by confused looks or disengaging in the meeting, it is a good idea to stop and ask simple questions about the information previously presented. If there are no answers or inaccurate answers, then quickly go back to the last section where the audience was comfortable with what was being presented and provide a quick overview of the information. Many times, audience members have just missed a small section or point of what was being presented and can quickly understand what was said, allowing everyone to be caught up and the meeting to move forward.

If the potential purchaser(s) does not clearly understand and follow along with the salesperson as the solution offering is being discussed and presented, it will make the solution seem complicated and difficult to utilize, resulting in the audience deciding to do the following:

1. Request the salesperson to come back and present again to additional people, or provide additional proof sources (white papers, references, case studies, ROI, etc.) to try to substantiate the company and its solution offering(s). These actions typically extend the sales cycle, which can potentially affect contract closing and any associated implementation/installation dates.

2. Do nothing, deciding to continue with the status quo. The potential purchaser(s) makes no changes and decides to keep the solution they are currently utilizing. When this occurs, the salesperson forfeits time and resources spent on the opportunity.

3. Internal alternative(s). Prospect(s) figure out a different way to address the task(s), causing them challenges/issues, potentially utilizing different internal processes, or existing company resources.

4. Outside alternatives. Explore additional vendors (competitors) offering similar options and alternatives. Although it is preferred to avoid having potential purchaser(s) bring in competition, some companies' policies may deem it necessary to receive multiple vendor proposals (usually two or three). If this is company policy, the salesperson should have uncovered this during the analysis questioning prior to the meeting. If, however, additional vendors are invited due to the prospect's opinion of your solution offering(s) being inadequate (confusing, difficult to utilize, etc.), then this certainly reduces the chances of successfully completing the sales opportunity.

Therefore, it is important for the salesperson to understand the potential purchaser's environment (situation) and for the potential purchaser(s) to understand the value(s), benefit(s), and applicability of the solution offering(s) as it addresses and relates to the potential purchaser(s) need(s)/goal(s).

Think about this situation from your own experience. Have you purchased an item where the salesperson speaks at a level that does not allow you to completely feel comfortable that you understand how this item is going to address your specific needs? If this happens, do you purchase the item, not understanding how the item works or what/how it is going to address your particular needs, especially if the item requires a sizable monetary investment to acquire?

If this happened to you, did you go ahead and make the purchase, or were alternative measures explored, such as trying to speak with a different salesperson, looking for an alternative store location, or speaking with friends, family, or coworkers who could provide a reference or improve your understanding in a manner that ultimately allowed you to make a decision?

USING VISUAL INFORMATION

Think back to the football scenario and how much easier it would be to explain the game and objectives if some visual assistance could be utilized. What if the salesperson could have utilized some television footage of a football game, a whiteboard for diagramming, or even taking the potential purchaser to watch an actual football game?

Visual assistance (diagrams, charts, prototypes, etc.) can make explaining an idea, concept, and solution offering(s) easier to understand not only during an initial meeting(s), but also during the presentation/demonstration phase of the sales process.

Visual assistance adds another dimension to an explanation, which allows the potential purchaser(s) to gain an enhanced picture in their mind of how the solution offering works and how it will address their issue(s)/need(s), as well as encouraging questions during the sharing of information.

The number of visual assistance elements to be utilized during a meeting may be adjusted depending on the length of time allotted. The meeting time frame may affect how detailed the salesperson is with the solution offering(s), as well as the diversity of visual aids that may be utilized during the performance presentation.

COMMUNICATION SKILLS

One of the wealthiest individuals in the world once said, "If someone wants to increase their annual income by twenty percent, they should learn to communicate better and spend time learning to write and speak well."

There is little doubt that being able to communicate clearly, both verbally and in writing, can assist in presenting ideas and concepts to prospects, customers, coworkers, friends, etc., and is a critical part of an individual's success level. Being a good communicator allows an improved opportunity to be more thoroughly understood when providing and explaining ideas and concepts.

In today's modern world, the use of technology provides an opportunity for us to interact more easily and frequently than ever before. However, just because there are mechanisms and technology available to communicate faster and more easily does not necessarily mean the *quality* of communication is improving at the same level and speed as the technological advances.

If one would like to believe and trust in the words of one of the most financially successful people in the world, then it might be good advice to spend some time and invest in resources (classes, books, etc.) on improving the effectiveness of a salesperson's communication skills.

The communication skill set is especially important due to the fact most initial sales communications and interactions can be very brief (thirty seconds to a couple of minutes). During this time, it is imperative for the salesperson to make a compelling and positive impression, as well as to be able to express the value and benefits of continuing communication regarding their company's solution offering(s).

WHAT COMPANIES PROVIDE

When looking more closely at the overall and high-level purpose of what an entity provides for prospects, customers, and society as a whole, it could probably be condensed to a handful of very important elements and actions involving:

1. Providing communication to individuals, such as prospects, customers, vendors, employees, etc.
2. Providing information/education about new or improved ideas, concepts, solutions, products, and services.
3. Providing solution offering(s) addressing and solving individuals' and entities' issues/challenges/needs.
4. Providing some form of customer and/or client service(s), whether it is new or ongoing support services for a new or improved offering(s).

5. Contributing to society by providing solution offering(s) designed to improve and benefit society.

There might be other areas and elements companies provide, but it would be difficult to locate an entity providing solution(s), product(s), concept(s), idea(s), and/or service(s) that do not strive to provide most (if not all) of the items listed.

SALESPEOPLE = REFLECTION OF THE COMPANY

Most individuals have experience interacting with some level of salesperson and from those interactions are aware salespeople have many different characteristics, some strengths and some weaknesses. Many sales professionals have similar characteristics, such as a desire to assist individuals and entities, a drive to succeed, self-motivation, and an outgoing personality.

So, why does an individual and/or company purchase from one salesperson over another?

It could be for a myriad of reasons, such as the company and offering(s) reputation, the solution offering(s) applicability and fit, needed requirements, the company and offering(s) longevity, local support and service(s), references, and monetary investment amount. However, it is my belief that individuals and companies purchase and do business with people (salespeople) they trust as a resource, with whom they enjoy working, and with whom they feel are an advocate for the purchaser(s), entity, and their personnel. Therefore, in many cases, prospects and customers view the salesperson as the "company" or at a minimum a reflection of the company.

In some "commodity-based" industries, it is common for similar entities to offer similar types of services, making such things as purchase price (investment) and service(s) with little difference between available options. So, what is the possible variable(s) making a difference when it comes to consumers making their choice? One possible option is the person (people) they interact with on a periodic or regular basis while conducting business with these entities.

Again, do you or people you know continue to purchase from individuals (entities) who you or they do not like, where you or they do not receive favorable customer service, or where services are not provided on a timely manner at an acceptable level? Would you or they prefer to purchase from people (entities) with whom they prefer to work when things are acceptable, and more important, when there is a problem or issue?

As an example, if a consumer contacted three different vehicle dealerships in the same city and requested a price quote for the same vehicle, and each price quote response was similar, what would one possible differentiator and decision maker be? Might it be how the consumer felt they were treated during contact with the salesperson and company?

Remember, most individuals and companies making any type of significant purchase (large investment) do not feel like they are just purchasing from a company. They feel like they are purchasing from a person...a salesperson.

Most individuals and companies are fond of the idea of "one head to pat and one tail to kick" should things go as expected or not as expected! This is another reason why it is so important to have potential purchasers view a salesperson as someone they can trust and view as a resource, an industry expert, the face of the company providing the solution offering(s), an expert on their own company, and an advocate who can get things done should something go differently than expected.

EVERYONE IN A COMPANY IS A SALESPERSON

It has been said that few things happen in regard to a company's revenue-generating stream and capability...until a sale is completed.

Trying to ascertain a business entity that does not provide a solution, product, service, or idea is more difficult than finding a needle in a haystack.

During my years spent working with a number of companies, it was interesting to observe individuals within each of these companies who were outside of the sales department, stating, "I'm not concerned about sales. It is the sales department's responsibility, not mine or my department."

If looking only at a company organizational chart, the statement made is probably accurate as others in the company (outside the sales department) have specific responsibilities (accounting, development, marketing, warehousing, etc.). However, without some type of revenue (sales, services, etc.), a company can experience difficulty continuing to provide "all" individuals within the company with employment. Therefore, it would seem reasonable for "everyone" participating and involved in the company to present themselves in a manner that would contribute to promoting the company.

It would seem beneficial and advantageous for everyone in an organization to think and act as if they were a company representative, regardless of their role or title, when interacting with prospective clients, customers, and vendors. These are the group of entities largely responsible for the continued success of their organization.

Thus, individuals within organizations should be treating communications and interactions with prospects and customers as if their paycheck and continued employment depended on it...because in reality...it does!

It is true. Sales are the lifeblood of profit-based organizations, which is why it is so important to have reliable, knowledgeable, and dedicated individuals handling what is arguably one of the most important parts and functions of any company's revenue-generating stream.

Simple examples of "everyone is a company representative" can be seen and experienced in our daily routines. These company representatives may have various titles (sales associate, guest advocate, etc.), but no matter their title, they are offering each patron the opportunity to purchase something extra or in addition, such as:

- Coffeehouse in the morning: "Would you like a pastry with your beverage?"
- Restaurant at noon: "Would you like to add a side salad or apple slices with your order?"
- Restaurant in the evening: "Would you be interested in dessert? We have fresh pie that is amazing."

UNDERCOVER BOSS

I have a friend who owns and is the chairman of the board of a medium-size company (approximately three hundred employees) consisting of multiple locations around the United States. Since he allows his management team to run the day-to-day operations, he is not widely known by the employees at each of the company locations.

He periodically meets with the management team and employees at each site. He makes it a practice to arrive early (an hour before the office opens for business) and sit in the parking lot, dressed in casual clothes (ball cap, blue jeans, casual shoes, etc.) or a simple disguise (facial hair, sunglasses, coveralls, etc.) and observes the employees arriving for work (noting early and late arrivals, etc.).

He also likes to approach employees as they are about to enter the building and ask them a few quick questions, such as:

- I am looking for work and wondering if you feel this is a good company?
- If you were me, would you apply for employment with this company?
- How do you like working here?
- Do you feel the company is run efficiently and effectively?
- What is your impression of the company and the leadership team?
- What do you not like about the company and the leadership?

Then, after spending time observing, asking brief questions, and conducting brief interviews, he goes back to a location and changes into more suitable clothing expected of the owner and returns to his company's office, where a meeting is held with the entire location's employees and management team. He provides feedback and observations regarding what was witnessed and heard from individuals he encountered earlier in the day.

He also provides "on the spot" monetary bonuses for those individuals who conducted themselves in the manner the company strives to portray and deliver to its prospects and customers.

His philosophy and actions promote the belief...that everyone "in" the company "represents" the company, and therefore, it is critical everyone conduct themselves in a manner that promotes the company.

IT PAYS TO BE NICE...EVEN TO PEOPLE YOU DO NOT KNOW

Years ago, I was running a little late to a sales appointment and had the misfortune of being pulled over to speak with a state patrolman regarding the possibility of my vehicle speedometer being inaccurate and/or my foot being a little too heavy on the throttle pedal.

After giving my best plea for leniency, I was served with a speeding citation, which was accompanied by an opportunity to provide the state with additional revenue.

Since the traffic citation was issued in a rural area with few vehicles occupying the road and the conditions were almost perfect (75 degrees, clear skies, dry roads), I decided to take the chance to plead the case at the local courthouse for a possible reduction in the fine and/or associated driving license points.

The court hearing was scheduled to be held in a small community of about fifteen hundred people. On the day of the court hearing, I arrived early in hopes of getting my hearing completed quickly, allowing me to get back to work as soon as possible.

So, arriving at the courthouse building about 7:30 A.M. on the day of the scheduled hearing, I walked up to the courthouse building, where it was discovered the doors were still locked and the courthouse was not yet open for the day's business. I returned to the vehicle in front of the courthouse building to await the doors being unlocked.

After sitting in the vehicle for approximately ten to fifteen minutes, I noticed a suburban vehicle pulling up and backing in toward the main courthouse doors. A gentleman who appeared to be a just a few years older than I was got out of the vehicle and walked over, unlocking the courthouse doors and then headed back to his vehicle. I observed him opening the two back doors of the suburban and begin stacking boxes and transporting them toward the courthouse.

Wanting to be first in line, I hurriedly got out of the vehicle and walked toward the doors. I arrived about the same time the gentleman arrived back at the doors with three or four boxes stacked in his arms. He reached the doors just before I did, and when he tried to open the door to go into the building, he dropped the boxes. They fell open, spilling the contents (lots of files) all over the ground.

I said, "Let me help you," and began to pick up the files and put them back into the boxes. The gentleman thanked me for helping, and we finished picking up the contents on the ground and set the boxes inside the courthouse on a countertop just inside the doors. I then observed the gentleman again return to his vehicle, where there were still several more boxes.

I followed him out of the courthouse, asking if I could offer a hand. He agreed, and we made a couple more trips, carrying three or four boxes each trip, until all the boxes were unloaded. During this time, we made light conversation about how nice the weather had been over the weekend, the results of the local sporting teams, etc.

As we set down the boxes from the last trip, the gentleman said, "I certainly did not intend for you to assist and have to carry boxes this morning," but stated that he really appreciated the help.

About this time, several other courthouse employees had arrived, and since the doors were already open, I took a seat inside and waited for a counter person so I could check in.

After just a few minutes, the same gentleman who I had helped with the boxes came up to the counter and said, "How can we help you today?"

I started to explain my reason for being there was to address a traffic citation.

The gentleman said, "Someone will be here to help you in just a few minutes. Please take a seat."

After thanking him for his help, I sat down in a chair, and within a few minutes, a lady arrived at the counter and asked how she could help me.

I explained the reason for being there, and she asked for my name and looked up the information on her computer.

She then stated, "Please go through the double doors just to the left of the counter and take a seat in the courtroom. The court personnel will be arriving within a few minutes."

As instructed, I entered the courtroom area and found I was the only person present in the courtroom at that time. So, I took a seat in the middle of the large courtroom, anticipating other cited individuals to join soon.

After I had been sitting in the courtroom for about five minutes with no others joining, the gentleman whom I had assisted with the boxes walked into the courtroom through the same doors I had entered and stated, "Someone will be with you shortly." I thanked him and continued to sit rather nervously alone in this fairly large courtroom.

Within a few more minutes, the door in front of the courtroom behind the judge's bench opened. A lady came into the courtroom and took her place just to the right of the judge's bench.

A little nervous, I politely said, "Good morning!"

She looked up and said, "We will get started soon." My anxiety level was increasing as it appeared things were about to get started.

About two minutes later, the door in front of the courtroom opened again, and the lady said, "All rise," to which I stood up, being the only person in the courtroom who didn't work there. In walked the gentleman I had assisted with the boxes...donning a black judge's robe.

He sat down in the chair and started scooting a few papers around on his desk as the lady announced, "All be seated." The judge then asked the clerk to announce the first case.

Since I was the only other person present in the courtroom, I figured the chances were good it would be my case.

The lady said my name and asked me to approach the podium in front of the courtroom and state my name for the record.

After stating my name, the judge looked at me and said, "Since you are present today in the courtroom, I am assuming you are not here to plead guilty to the citation you received."

I responded, "Your Honor, I am here to explore options as to how we might be able to arrive at a resolution that would be fair and beneficial to both the court and myself."

The judge looked at me and then looked down at some papers in front of him for a few seconds. Then he looked up and said, "My decision is to drop the traffic citation charge in exchange for public service, which has already been served this morning!" and then he banged the gavel and said, "Have a good day!"

The point of this story is...often in sales, as in life, it never hurts to be kind to people (paying it forward), as you never know who and when you will encounter someone who can later have an impact on your life, personal or professional!

ASSISTANCE FOR REMEMBERING PEOPLE'S NAMES

One of the most important possessions of each and every person is their name. Most people will have and keep their names for most of their lives (they may change a portion of their name when getting married). But, for the most part, individuals will keep their given first and/or last name or at least use a derivative of it. So, it is important to each of us that people know and use our name(s).

The problem is it is difficult to remember people's names when meeting them briefly, in passing, or when seeing them on an occasional basis.

So, how can the chances of remembering people's names be improved? When meeting someone for the first time:

1. Focus and look at the person's face, mentally trying to memorize his or her face so you can recognize them again at a later date.

2. Once someone says their name, immediately repeat it, asking them if you said it correctly, and then ask them something about the name, such as are they named after someone (grandparent, Junior, etc.).

3. Say something associated with the person's name, and cross-reference it with something you know (e.g., my dad has that name also, my best friend has the same name, etc.). This will assist you in remembering their name next time you see them.

4. By this time, you have said their name three times in a very short period of time, repeated it after they were introduced, stated their name back to confirm your understanding, and stated something to cross-reference his or her name.

5. As you continue to speak with him or her, make sure you utilize his or her name during the conversation, such as, "Steve, are you planning to attend the trade show next week?"

6. Make sure when you have completed your conversation or when one of you is leaving the conversation, to use their name, such as, "It was nice meeting you, Steve, and I'm looking forward to seeing you next week at the trade show."

At the end of a conversation, it is likely you have had the opportunity to say his or her name three to six times, and this will allow for recalling his or her name more easily the next time you meet. Just remember, individuals like and appreciate when people remember and utilize their name.

SILENT SIGNAL

Members of my family know if they are accompanying me or walk up while I am speaking with someone and do not introduce them to the person(s), it means I am experiencing difficulty remembering the person's name, so that is a signal they should introduce themselves. When this happens, it provides an opportunity for me and others who may be around to simply say something like, "Oh, I apologize, I thought you probably already knew each other or had met before."

This silent signal and introduction accomplishes a couple things:

1. Provides an opportunity to hear each individual say their name as they introduces themselves to the new person, and
2. Avoids embarrassment because the persons involved did not know or could not recall the names of those present.

When attending social events, trade shows, large group meetings, etc., I have made it a habit when approaching an individual or group of individuals whom I have met previously but have not seen with in a while to introduce myself. This avoids putting someone in the position of trying to remember my name and potentially feeling uneasy or embarrassed because they do not remember my name.

I have found it is much easier to allow individuals to say, "Oh, yeah, I/we remember who you are" rather than having them look at me nervously, thinking, *I know this person but cannot remember his name,* and then after briefly speaking wanting to conclude the conversation before anyone else walks up and they are put in a position of having to introduce me.

I have found it much more comfortable to approach an individual or group of people, stating, "Hello, Bob. Steve Monks with S-M Enterprises. It is great to see you again." It allows people to be at ease and reinforces your name should they need to introduce you to someone else.

UNDERPROMISING AND OVERPERFORMING

It is often perceived (sometimes factually) that salespeople have "overpromised and underdelivered" when it comes to specific capabilities or a specific functionality of a solution offering(s). Regardless of what causes or leads up to the misunderstanding or mismatch, it is recommended to avoid this situation as it can lead to mistrust or weakening of the relationship.

It is my experience that should a misunderstanding or mismatching occur, it usually stems from a misinterpretation or confusion of perceived information and/or issue(s). The mismatched information and issue(s) is usually caused by an innocent mistake rather than a deliberate deception by either of the parties.

This may come about when a salesperson says (means) one thing, and it is interpreted by the audience as having a different meaning.

I have witnessed this type of situation happen in the computer software solution offering(s) arena. The salesperson is presenting current functionality and then mentions potential future functionality, and someone in the audience doesn't hear or confuses what is said and accepts what is being said as current functionality. If presenting/demonstrating or speaking about "future" capabilities, it is beneficial to reiterate what was stated, ensuring the audience is able to separate existing or current functionality from "future" planned features and functionality.

When it comes to mismatching or misunderstanding of information, one example is of the childhood game, in which a teacher or parent selects several children and puts them in a straight line, standing shoulder-to-shoulder next to each other. The adult (parent/teacher) will whisper a short phrase into the ear of the first child, who in turn must whisper whatever they heard to the child next to them (saying it only one time). This continues down the line going from child to child until the last child in the line says the phrase aloud. It is usually at this point that everyone has a laugh or chuckle because it is usually something completely different from the original phrase.

As an example, the phrase whispered to the first child in line is, "The sky is blue." By the time the phrase is whispered through all the children, the last child in line announces the phrase as "Is your shirt new?" or some wording rarely close to the original phrase.

Well, this type of situation can also happen with adult audiences. There is a myriad of reasons why this may happens. Maybe they did not correctly hear what was said, maybe they were briefly distracted, or maybe they were multitasking while listening to the speaker, etc. The issue for the salesperson is the audience member who misunderstood or mismatched what was said may not stop the salesperson to obtain clarification and therefore lets the salesperson continue speaking, even though there has been a misunderstanding or confusion of the feature/functionality being described.

Another example of the salesperson's message being misunderstood or confused can be the result of different company or industry terms and terminology utilized by companies and how each party utilizes and interprets the definitions of such. The result being...what was stated by the salesperson could have been interpreted as something different by the audience.

The salesperson may be referring and utilizing the word *system* as all-encompassing, including field laptops, corporate mainframe computers, handheld devices, and software applications, and the audience interprets the term "system" as just their corporate server.

Therefore, when the audience is asking questions referring to the "system," they are referring to their corporate server system, and the salesperson is answering utilizing a more global and all-encompassing description. Therefore, the audience is interpreting the answer based on their definition of what the "system" is and can do, and the salesperson is answering the questions based on the global company capacity and capabilities.

So, it is easy to see how even though the question and answers were provided and responded to in good faith, the different terminology or definitions utilized by the parties may have a person(s) misunderstanding what was asked and what was provided as an answer.

Most people have been exposed to the saying *"underpromise and overperform,"* which is a good motto to live by and one that I would recommend be strived to achieve every day. Doing so is important and can avoid potential issues moving forward for the salesperson to make sure they clarify and confirm the terminology utilized by the audience when addressing questions. The salesperson should not assume because one company or entity interprets terminology a specific way that other companies have also adopted and utilize the same terminology.

Therefore, whether talking about value, benefits, features, functionality, pricing, etc., make sure to clarify the question and then follow up to make sure the audience understands and is clear about the answer.

In most cases, purchasers would rather be pleasantly surprised by knowing something can happen that exceeds their expectations rather than receiving news that something that they were expecting to happen is not going to due to some unexpected reason.

Besides risking their credibility with the purchaser(s), the salesperson also risks alienating their interior adviser (individual within the purchasing company assisting with aspects of the opportunity, such as scheduling meetings, purchasing criteria, etc.). The risk is that by telling the purchaser(s) something is not going to be able to meet their expectation(s), individuals within the purchaser's company may also view the interior adviser with incertitude. If the salesperson's company is unable to perform and complete items prior to concluding the implementation/installation, what else did the salesperson communicate that is not going to happen and may have an impact on the purchasing company?

The result is that this not only negatively impacts the salesperson's credibility and relationship with the prospect but also could potentially effect the interior adviser's reputation with their management and coworkers.

AND EVERYTHING ELSE

Several years ago, I worked for a terrific sales manager who masterfully utilized the phrase…"and everything else" when talking to potential purchasers. This phrase is similar to utilizing the term *et cetera* (abbreviation "etc.") in written language. Et cetera means, a number of unspecified additional things, odds and ends. He would utilize the phrase "and everything else" in situations to infer there may be additional items and elements associated with the topic. The phrase would most likely be utilized in discussions where there was a mutual understanding of the overall picture of a sales opportunity involving multiple areas and where the potential purchaser(s) understood the solution offering(s) would incorporate additional elements, such as software applications, hardware, support, down payment, overall investment, and everything else, but the details and specifics of each of these had not yet been determined or completed.

As an example, if he was presenting to a prospect, he would say something like, "Our solution offering will not only address all your current purchasing criteria and goals, but also allows your organization to continue to address and meet future goals...and everything else" or "All that remains in order to move forward and complete the contract agreement is to receive the signed paperwork...and everything else."

This simple phrase "and everything else" seemed to address concerns from potential purchasers. If there was a situation where a purchaser would later have a question in what they were told or heard, this sales manager would say, "That was included in 'and everything else.'"

Keep in mind, the sales manager was not trying to be deceptive or deceitful. This phrase allowed him to cover large areas of the potential purchaser's concern(s) during communication without going into time-consuming details and also allowed him to diffuse potential mismatch or misunderstanding by stating..."That item/topic was what I meant and included in...and everything else."

SUMMARY

When performing the role of a sales professional, it is critical to be able to communicate and convey value(s), benefit(s), feature(s), functionality, ideas, and concepts to individuals/entities who may not have ever heard of you, your company, and/or its solution offering(s).

Then, be able to follow up and continue to discuss, perform, and present a more complete and thorough description of the solution offering(s) to the potential purchaser(s) during ongoing conversation(s) and/or meeting(s).

Visual assistance adds another dimension to an explanation, which allows the potential purchaser(s) to gain a clear picture of how the solution offering works and how it will address their issue(s)/need(s).

Remember, companies provide one or more of the following for individuals and/or entities: Communication, information/education, solution offering(s), and customer/client service.

It never hurts to be nice to people as you never know when you will encounter someone who can have an impact on your life.

To assist with remembering people's names, say their name *three* times in a very short period of time, repeat it after they are introduced, say their name back to them to confirm, and say something to cross-reference their name.

LESSON 8

EVALUATING SALES SKILLS

One of the most important elements for both the individual just getting started in sales and a seasoned salesperson is to identify their strengths. Equally important is to identify any weaknesses in their overall sales abilities and skills.

Communication skills, both written and verbal, are important elements for being successful in a sales profession. It is not only imperative for a salesperson to be able to communicate value, benefits, ideas, and concepts, but they must also be able to communicate these ideas to varied and diverse audiences and to multiple levels within a specific organization (management, departmental, end users, etc.).

As mentioned earlier, one of the wealthiest people in the world stated that being able to write and speak appropriately and professionally will add 20 percent to a person's lifetime earnings.

When you stop to think about this statement, it makes a lot of sense. If a salesperson cannot communicate appropriately and effectively to potential purchasers, then the audience may not be able to clearly understand how the proposed solution offering(s) is going to provide the desired and required goal(s). Therefore, they may not see any reason for continued and ongoing communication (calls, meetings, etc.) and have difficulty seeing any reason to invest any monetary and/or resources (time, energy, etc.). Therefore, the sales opportunity dissolves.

The reason self-evaluation of one's skill set is so important is to ensure the person is cognizant of where and how to utilize specific skill strengths. This knowledge will assist in identifying where to focus energy on areas in need of improvement(s) in order to continue to compete in the sales arena and to strive to raise their skill set to the next level.

It is my words of encouragement to each and every person to strive to become better not only in their professional lives but also in their personal lives by instilling a commitment to lifelong learning and continued improvement.

CHAMPIONS WORK AT IT EVERY DAY

During my time competing in both amateur and professional sporting activities, it was astonishing to see how those individuals performing at the top of their chosen competitive event(s) continued to train and practice on a regular basis in attempts to continually improve their technique, abilities, and improving their craft...*every day!*

While progressing through the competitive ranks of the sport of rodeo, occasionally there were days when I really did not feel like practicing for whatever reason. One of my best friends, who was also a roping professional, would say..."Do you think the world champions are practicing today?"

If the world champions are practicing every day while at the top of their game, and we expected to be able to compete at their level, how would this happen if we did not practice as much as they did?

These words were all that were needed to motivate us to practice because we understood that if the world champions practiced and were improving their skills set and abilities *"every day,"* we needed to also! In reality, we should practice more than the champions do to be able to perform competitively.

In an attempt to even stay equal or gain ground on the competition, it was obvious early in my rodeo and sales careers that it was imperative to do some daily activity focusing on improving an area of my skill set and abilities.

Now, you might be saying to yourself, there is not a "World Champion of Sales" title awarded each year. Although you might be correct, most companies have some form of acknowledging the top performing salespeople within their company. Even if the company for which you are currently working does not provide this type of award or acknowledgment... your competitor's company probably does!

Therefore, each salesperson should be working toward being the "number one" salesperson in their company by continuing to work on their skill set and abilities, realizing that the way to do so is to win deals and close opportunities. This also includes understanding that each sales opportunity and deal the competition closes is a sales opportunity you and your company did not close.

I would recommend picturing your competition and competitors as the current "World Champion of Sales" and pursue activities, time, and resources to improve your skill set and abilities to better position you to compete in the arena of sales...on a daily basis!

WAYS TO IMPROVE SKILLS

If you find yourself lagging behind in any specific area(s) of sales (e.g., communication, prospecting, marketing, performing and presenting skills, negotiations, etc.), I recommend acquiring assistance from any/ all of the following:

- Query the sales management team as to whom might be a good candidate to be a mentor. This individual could be a more seasoned salesperson with longer tenure with the company or more knowledge about the company's solution offering(s), customer base, prospects, etc. Most experienced salespeople would consider being asked to be a mentor as a privilege as it shows the person asking sees the person as a successful role model and would like to emulate them and their sales techniques and methodologies. As they say, imitation is the sincerest form of flattery!

- Approach a seasoned sales professional in your area who has been successful or has been recommended, and ask that person to be your mentor. Even though they may not work for the same organization as you, or even in the same industry, they can provide valuable assistance and feedback regarding potential sales techniques and methods.
- Search and research potential sales and marketing seminars and trainings being held in the local area. Oftentimes, employers may assist with offsetting cost(s) or even pay for attending as it is beneficial for their salespeople to be as effective as possible.
- Investigate local groups, classes, clubs, etc., which meet on a regular basis and focus on sales and marketing or elements such as speaking, presenting, performing, etc., to gain knowledge, techniques, and experience.
- Conduct an Internet search for possible local or distance learning opportunities (webinars/WebEx, classes, etc.).
- Read books/e-books, magazines/e-magazines, journals, blogs, periodicals, etc., focused on the area(s) of desired improvement.

There is an old adage: if someone wants to learn to do something, find a person who has done that exact thing and ask that person how they accomplished it. Then be open to their advice and see if it will also work for you.

If you want to be a great salesperson, I recommend locating a great salesperson and replicating what that person is doing. Chances are, you will also become a great salesperson.

MENTAL BARRIERS

Oftentimes when individuals first enter the sales profession, they may have a skill deficiency in one area(s) or another. Rarely do individuals begin their sales careers with all of their skills operating at the highest capacity.

There are individuals selling today who continue to work on their specific skill set(s) to improve any skill that might be lagging or just need some continued fine-tuning to stay at the top of their game.

Knowing it is rare for each salesperson to have every skill operating at its highest level, do not let a deficiency in one area impact the other areas that might be stronger and more effective. If a salesperson knows they are not as strong as they would like to be in a particular area, they should not let that area become a mental barrier and diminish other areas of strength. Simply focus time, energy, and resources on developing those skills that need to be advanced to the level of your stronger skills.

During my early weight training days, even though I had been training for some time, I was not able to bench-press 225 pounds, which is equivalent to two 45 pound plates on each side of a standard 45 pound Olympic weightlifting bar.

I continued to train regularly but was unable to lift the 225 pounds. It became a training obsession because many of the other guys in the gym could bench-press 225 pounds, and this weight level is sort of a benchmark leading to the next level of fitness.

So, on days I would go to the gym to train my upper body, I would begin the training session with the bench-press exercise as I wanted to try to perform the lift while at full strength and maximum energy.

After completing a few warm-up sets of the bench-press exercise, I would begin the training session in earnest.

During the warm-up sets on one particular day, I began speaking with a guy who had been weight training for many years and had competed at professional level in bodybuilding and had a physique which reflected his many years of hard work and dedication.

As we briefly discussed training concepts and techniques in between warm up sets, I reluctantly shared my bench-pressing situation and asked him if he would be willing to watch my technique and provide suggestions to be able to break the 225 pound barrier.

He agreed and begin observing my bench-pressing technique, asking me to begin with a weight I felt comfortable and then move up by adding incremental weight plates.

The beginning weight was 135 for ten repetitions, then 185 for ten repetitions, then 200 for ten repetitions, then 215 for a couple repetitions. Now it was time to try the elusive 225 pound weight mark.

Not sure how this was going to go, and thinking...*Why did I ask anyone to watch in the event I am not successful?* I hesitantly loaded the weight bar with the two 45 pound plates on each side of the bar and then began mentally preparing myself for what could potentially become a new Personal Record (PR).

Knowing this person who I respected was watching provided additional motivation and incentive to complete the lift. He came up to me just prior to the 225 pound lift attempt, offering words of encouragement and reinforced the earlier weights had presented little to no problem. At this moment, I felt like I was as ready as I had ever been to complete this lift.

Lying back down on the bench and completing my simple and quick "prelift" ritual, I thought to myself, *You are ready!*

With one deep breath, the bar was lifted off the bench-press standards (device which suspends the bar above the bench). Slowly lowering the bar in a controlled fashion to be positioned just above my chest, I was ready to begin the upward motion toward completing the lift. Providing maximum effort, the bar began slowly moving upward from my chest, and then quickly stalled when the arms approached a 45 degree angle, as had happened every time prior when attempting to lift this weight.

At that point, I began extruding maximum effort to push and move the weight, but the weight bar began to slowly move downward toward my chest, at which point a spotter (helper) quickly assisted with moving the weight bar back to rest again on the bench-press standards. In relative disgust and defeat, I slowly stood up from the bench and looked at the individual who I had asked to observe.

He stated, "I know the problem!"

I responded quickly, "You do? Great! What is it?"

He asked, "How long have you been working out regularly?"

Response: "For several months now."

He went on to ask, "And how long have you been trying to bench-press this particular weight?"

Response: "For several weeks 225 pounds is my current bench-pressing record and goal!"

He thought for only a second and then walked over to one of the weight trees (stand where extra weights are stored) and quickly removed two 5-pound weights. He walked over and placed one on each side of the weight bar...now making the overall weight 235 pounds!

He then looked at me with a stern face and in a rather loud voice said, "Do it!"

At that point, I looked at him and thought to myself, *Are you crazy? This may staple me to the bench! You just witnessed me failing at lifting 225 pounds, and you are going to add weight?*

But remember, this guy is a large individual and much bigger and stronger than I at the time, so I did not particularly want to irritate him.

I hesitantly replied, "Ah," and he quickly cut me off and again in a loud, stern voice said, "Do it!" and pointed at the bench-press bar.

Knowing at this point that my choices were very limited, I lay back down on the bench and again prepared myself with the quick "prelift" routine.

Just prior to lifting the weight bar from the weight standards, he said in a very calm and confident voice, "Don't worry about the weight. Just *focus on the technique* needed to complete the lift."

The bar was slowly lifted off the weight standards and then positioned to the proper starting position. This time, the focus was not on the weight of the bar as it really did not feel that much heavier, but rather on the *technique* required to successfully complete the lift.

The weight bar was once again slowly lowered to the bottom position just above the chest. I began extruding controllable but maximum effort, and again the bar began to rise...slowly...then the bar was a quarter of the way back up, then halfway (which had always been the sticking point), then past halfway, then three-quarters, and then, to my amazement, with one last exertion of effort, the bar was back at the beginning position.

The lift was completed, and I had set a new personal record.

From that day, I did not experience any problems with getting past the 225 pound bench-press barrier.

The moral of the story is that we all have "mental" barriers that have been either self-imposed or imposed by some outside force that might cause us to introduce limits on ourselves, and as life goes on, we seem to reinforce these barriers, whether we intend to or not, on a somewhat regular basis, making them even larger and more difficult to overcome.

Most of these barriers are self-imposed through some mental process, and we do not even know or recognize it.

My recommendation is to evaluate your own skill set and potentially self-imposed barriers. Then ask for assistance from a mentor, trusted friend, or colleague to evaluate your skill set and have them assist you in moving past your sticking point(s), utilizing and focusing on *technique(s)*.

The improvement(s) that will be realized from going through a self-evaluation process should provide some insight to your skill set and abilities and provide feedback for seeking assistance for strengthening any area(s) of potential weakness. But more than that, this process will identify areas that, if addressed, developed, and improved, will provide amazing results for improving techniques, methods, and confidence.

What is your new Personal Record (PR) goal?

BE A SALESPERSON *YOU* WOULD LIKE

Think about representing the type of salesperson you and your company would like and enjoy working with every day.

Consider the times you enjoyed working with a salesperson and the reasons that made the experience enjoyable. Next, think about what type of salesperson you want to be and are going to be.

Think about what type of image, reputation, and legacy you would like for your own career, and take actions to become that type of individual.

Think about what your prospects and customers are currently saying about you as a person—specifically, what type of salesperson you are and if they would recommend you to other prospects (individuals, entities, friends, family, and coworkers).

SUMMARY

Salespeople need to keep in mind that purchasers do not read a salesperson's resume. They may not care what a salesperson's performance has been, as they are more interested in what the salesperson can provide for them...*today!*

Therefore, it is essential for a salesperson to show up, perform, and demonstrate expertise, knowledge, and superior skills each and every day!

Like any other professional career, it is important to stay apprised of current issues and regulations and to try to be involved in the industry as much as possible. This will allow you to be viewed not just as a salesperson but as a knowledgeable and valuable resource to prospects and customers.

View yourself as a professional: a professional salesperson competing in the sales arena, just like any other professional person competes in their chosen field. Continue and constantly work to improve and hone your skill set in an attempt to be better prepared for the next sales opportunity and competition.

I have heard, "I was not sure what to do or how to do it, but knew I needed to do something to make a difference."

There have been entrepreneurs and business owners who have told me when they were first starting in their businesses, they were not sure what to do or if what they were doing and the decisions they were making were the correct ones, but they knew they had to do something, as doing nothing was not an option. They risked potentially making a mistake rather than sitting back and waiting until they knew exactly what to do, potentially missing an opportunity.

As a salesperson, you may also find times when you are not exactly sure what to do with prospecting, marketing, etc. If this should happen, I would offer the same advice that I once received. "When in doubt do 'something,' as it is likely no one is going to do it for you; while you are waiting, someone else will do it."

If need be, as the saying goes..."Fake it until you make it!"

LESSON 9

STARTING WITH A COMPANY OR SOLUTION OFFERING

When a salesperson is starting with a new company and/or a new solution offering(s), it often presents its own set of obstacles and challenges.

It can be difficult when first starting with a new company as the salesperson may be trying to learn multiple facets, such as how the company operates, the expectation of the role/position, identifying departments and personnel, and your company's internal operations and procedures.

In addition, it can also be equally challenging to learn a new solution offering(s), which may include such elements as an overall system application, along with assorted modules and/or suite of offering(s).

Learning the processes of a new company, along with a new solution offering(s), can seem to be an overwhelming and monumental task, especially when the sales management wants the salesperson to become effective immediately or within the shortest time possible.

So, here are recommendations that are applicable whether the person is a new employee learning a new company and solution offering(s) or a current employee tasked with learning a new solution offering(s).

LEARNING THE MOST IMPORTANT ELEMENTS FIRST

It has been said that the easiest way to walk up a mountain is one step at a time.

One step at a time is a sound approach when learning a new company and/or new solution offering(s).

It is difficult to learn everything about a new company or solution offering(s), so it is easier to learn if the facets and components can be compartmentalized, and potentially departmentalized, into learning the high level and overall features and functions of the components into smaller step/bite-size components, allowing a specific and specified amount of time to be spent on each.

As an example, if asked to learn *four* major components of a new company (human resource policies, travel and expenses, customers/prospects and territory, and solution offerings), I recommend trying to commit a specific amount of time each day to each component (*two* hours to each of the *four* components). Continue until gaining an acceptable knowledge of one of the components, and then continue with the remaining three components, committing approximately two and a half hours per day to each. Then, spend approximately four hours a day on each of the two remaining components until a significant amount of knowledge has been gained to cover all the specified components (it is also advisable to ask sales or company management personnel what component(s) or areas of the solution offering(s) are the most imperative to learn and focus on initially).

This process allows learning multiple facets of the organization at the same time, as well as having a more rounded knowledge of the company as the salesperson begins contacting prospects/customers.

TIME IS EVERYTHING

In the sales profession, *time* and *timing* are two very important elements—and possibly the two most precious commodities a salesperson possesses.

Time = A suitable or opportune moment and arguably the most important commodity for a salesperson—and actually anyone—is time, for nothing is possible or can be accomplished without it. Therefore, it should be considered by salespeople as the most important and critical element in their repertoire.

There are only so many working hours each day in which potential purchasers are available to be contacted for calls and meetings. Historically, potential purchasers were predominantly available to be contacted during their office or company hours. More recently, this has changed for some individuals and companies, and therefore, some individuals are available to be contacted during off hours or after hours. For the purposes of this lesson, a traditional 8:00 A.M. to 5:00 P.M. working day is utilized.

How a salesperson plans and utilizes time is extremely important. The sooner a salesperson can learn information about the company, internal processes, and solution offering(s), the quicker a salesperson can get into the sales role and begin contacting customers and/or prospects.

Timing = The art or operation of regulating occurrence or coordination to achieve the most desirable effects. This involves planning, designing, and delivering strategic approaches to getting the appropriate information to the appropriate person(s) at the appropriate time.

Depending on the complexity of the company and its solutions offering(s), it may not be possible to know everything about the company's solution offering(s) prior to beginning to contact customers or potential purchasers. If this happens, it is acceptable as long as the salesperson is armed with a good understanding of the high-level value and benefits along with at least the most popular of the company's solution offering(s). There have been several times when I have been asked to begin working a sales territory and contacting potential purchaser(s) without having complete knowledge of both the company and its solution offering(s), and I have survived to tell the story.

If the solution offering provides multiple application modules or a suite of solutions, make sure to be able to explain the top four or five main values and benefits for each application/module.

In the case of being new to a company, the initial calls and meetings may be with existing customers. Therefore, the salesperson should be focusing on learning about the customers' business and why they purchased the solution offering(s).

In a perfect world, a company would allow as much time as needed for each new salesperson to learn about the company history, internal and external processes, industries they serve, contacts, etc., as well as all of their solution offering(s). However, in reality and in this fast-paced world, companies hire new sales personnel as needed, and therefore expect them to be selling as soon as possible. Due to this urgency, most companies' training for sales personnel becomes a work in process (WIP). The companies allow the salesperson the opportunity to learn as they go, or, stated differently, learn as the salesperson needs to know or when prospects/customers ask them questions.

EVERYONE WAS NEW TO A COMPANY AT SOME POINT!

When salespeople join a new company or when someone within the company moves into a sales role, they should not be apprehensive acknowledging to prospects/customers that they are new to the company, role, or industry.

The reason is twofold:

1. Most individuals working at a prospect's/customer's business have started a new role or position at some point in their career and therefore are usually understanding and willing to provide information and recommendations if asked.

2. Individuals with whom the salespeople will be communicating can usually figure out the salesperson is new to the company, position, or territory. If they are an existing customer and have never spoken with a particular salesperson, they will know there is something new about the situation/person contacting them.

Letting existing customers know a salesperson is new can provide a good opportunity for the salesperson to ask questions and learn more about the market, industry, and the customer's company. The salesperson should utilize this opportunity to gain knowledge about the customer's company, as well as the individual contact, as this information will be important and needed for future sales opportunities with these organizations.

If the salesperson has been in a particular market/industry for a number of years but is new to a particular company, then they should acknowledge this is a new role but also share with prospects/customers that they have experience in the industry/market. This will inform the prospects/customers that the salesperson has knowledge of the industry and will assist in instilling confidence and credibility with prospects/customers and let them know the salesperson is familiar with their industry, such as terms/terminology, challenges, issues, etc.

LEARNING THE HISTORY OF YOUR COMPANY

One of the ways to build credibility with potential purchasers is to learn the history of your company. Even if the company and solution offering(s) have not been around for an extended period of time, learn the most significant events that have allowed the company to expand and achieve success.

Some examples of items the salesperson should know and be able to communicate to potential purchasers:

- When the company was founded and the founder's name(s).

- Why the company was started (what problems or challenges did they address, what was the company's niche, and how it has grown and expanded over time).
- Any major business acquisitions, mergers, and milestones, and why they are meaningful to the prospect.
- Significant/Strategic customers, as well as particularly large sales (franchises, recognized industry leaders, etc.).
- If someone within your company is well-known and what contribution(s) they have made to the industry.
- Is the company a recognized leader in the industry? If so, explain how such status was achieved.
- If not the leader in the industry, then mention why the company is well-known (fastest growing, geographical focused, etc.) and their strategy for becoming the leader in the industry.
- What is the success history and what do they provide that differentiates them from their competition?
- If the company has been in the industry for several years, explain the company's market position, market share, status, and effectiveness in the industry.
- Strategies for expanding the existing solution and/or any new solution offering(s).

BUILDING RELATIONSHIPS WITHIN YOUR ORGANIZATION

Just like it is important to build relationships quickly with prospects and customers, it is also important to build relationships quickly with individuals that the salesperson will be working with inside their own company.

These individuals (coworkers) will play an instrumental role in the success level of the salesperson as they assist with addressing prospects'/customers' questions and/or issues, such as those that arise as a result of an RFP (request for proposal), presentation(s), demonstration(s), installation(s), implementation(s), and ongoing customer support. All these areas can affect what customers are sharing with their peer group and the industry, as well as what they will be willing to share as a reference for additional sales opportunities.

Many individuals within your company are experts in the company (history, formal and informal organization chart, influencers and alliances), as well as the company's solution offering(s), services, and customers. Salespeople should make it a point to spend time with coworkers (either during working hours or off hours) to get to know the coworkers, on both a professional and personal level. This is especially important if the salesperson is working as a remote/virtual position. Exposure to coworkers may be limited and infrequent, and what limited exposure there is may revolve around prospects'/customers' request(s) or question(s)/issue(s) that may be time sensitive. Therefore, there may be limited time for casual conversation and/or an opportunity to gain additional information about the individual while they are assisting in resolving the issue(s).

Many coworkers can be a tremendous resource in regard to the results the company's solution offering(s) has produced and what the results have been for existing customers. Many also have existing relationships with the customer base through having assisted them with implementation(s), installation(s), training(s), etc., and can be a valuable resource as to which customers may be of assistance in your territory (e.g., references, hosting customer and site visits, etc.).

NEW COMPANY AND/OR NEW OFFERING COMPONENTS

It is important when a salesperson either joins a new organization and/or introduces a new product (suite of products) that the following elements are learned and can be clearly conveyed to potential purchasers.

The intention of the provided list is to assist in focusing energy, resources, and limited time to learning the elements of a new company and/or new offering and to gain the required knowledge to begin communicating value and benefits to potential purchasers as quickly as possible.

This list is equally applicable for learning a new solution/product as it is when joining a new company:

1. Learn and be able to communicate the company's high-level overview summary, including who the company is, what they do, and why customers do business with them. Also, be able to provide the overall value proposition.

2. What are the high-level value and benefit points provided by the solution offering(s) and to whom they provide, such as industries, market, companies, individuals, etc.?

3. What are the top 5-10 *main* reasons (value and benefits) other companies or individuals purchase this offering? Such as:
   a. Allows clients to be more efficient...and how.
   b. Allows clients to be more effective...and how.
   c. Saves money by reducing expenditures...and how.
   d. Increases revenues and margins...and how.
   e. Saves clients time, allowing time to focus on other activities...and how.
   f. Improve customer service...and how, such as meeting expectations and retaining existing customers, therefore discouraging competitors from gaining momentum in existing accounts.

4. Understand how new solution offerings (modules, applications) integrate and interface with existing solution offerings.
   a. How does it complement existing solution(s) currently being offered and/or utilized?
   b. How would the offering be utilized by new and existing customers?

5. Understand how the company is planning to advertise, market, and position the solution offering(s).

6. Understand how the company is planning to condition the market and how they plan to utilize the marketing department to create awareness about and advertise the solution offering(s).

    a. Is the solution offering(s) going to be targeted toward existing customers and/or prospects, as well as new markets? How does it complement, integrate with, and interface with the existing offering provided by the company or even complements other vendors' solutions that may be utilized by shared clients?

    b. What marketing campaign strategies are going to be utilized to provide exposure for the offering?

        1. Company website (video clips, customer testimonials, solution description(s), case studies, etc.).

        2. E-mail campaign(s).

        3. Social media.

        4. Mail/delivery service(s).

        5. Letter(s).

        6. Postcard(s).

        7. Brochures (printed materials).

        8. Trade shows.

        9. Seminars.

        10. Groups (user, geography, etc.).

    c. What is the time frame for release(s) of marketing campaigns?

    d. What are the follow-up strategies to the marketing campaigns? Who or what department is going to follow up, and through what method(s), such as calls, e-mails, meetings, etc.)?

7. Learn product requirements (hardware, software, networking, etc.) the new solution offering(s) requires, as well as an understanding of the associated pricing.

8. Learn implementation, installation, and training requirements, as well as approximate time frame(s) to complete.

9. Partners: Who else may also be selling the solution offering(s) in the marketplace, such as partnerships, resellers, and channel partners, etc.?

10. Competition: Who are the competitors, and how does your company differentiate themselves and their solution offering?

QUICK ADVERTISEMENT

One important element is for the salesperson to be able to explain to individuals what they and their company's solution offering(s) provides to potential purchasers in a brief and concise manner.

One way for providing this pertinent information is to develop a quick advertisement for your company and its solution offering(s) and commit it to memory. Having a quick advertisement prepared provides the salesperson with the ability to introduce themselves, their company, and solution offering(s) to individuals quickly.

This can be accomplished by writing down the quick advertisement and practicing delivering it until the salesperson is able to deliver the information utilizing their natural speaking voice (pace and flow) and with confidence. An added benefit of committing it to memory is that is allows for customizing it on the fly for specific individuals and/or situations.

A quick advertisement is a thirty-second to two-minute high-level overview providing information including an introduction of yourself and your company, your company's solution offering(s) and purpose(s), and any particular application and/or results that are applicable to their industry, company, etc.

The overall goal of the quick advertisement is the ability to deliver a *brief and consistent* message and introductory information as the salesperson meets potential purchasers. The more you do this, the more comfortable and relaxed you will be, and the more natural the information will flow.

The majority of the quick advertisement should be fairly consistent information. However, provide flexibility to revise portions to be varied and interchangeable when directing and focusing on a particular section of the message, such as particular solution offering, company, or role or position within the potential purchaser's organization.

The purpose of a quick advertisement is to provide information to individuals and decision makers, letting them know who you are, what organization you represent, and what value(s) and benefit(s) the solution offering(s) provide(s), along with any results that have been recognized by individuals/entities. It also allows for an opportunity for building curiosity and interest points with the potential purchaser(s) by encouraging an ongoing dialogue in which individuals have a chance to ask questions and make comments. This in turn allows for even further and continued dialogue, such as follow-up communication, as well as being referred or asked to speak with other individuals within the potential purchasing company.

Should this happen, it provides an opportunity for the salesperson to follow up with the referred individual with a lead-in: "Mr. /Ms. (Name) from your company recommended I contact you about my company and its solution offering(s)."

When designing and developing a quick advertisement, think about it as if you were walking down a sidewalk and happened to pass by a friend you had not seen in a while. After exchanging initial greetings, your friend asks, "What are you doing for work these days?"

During the conversation, you might mention some of the following details that could be incorporated into a quick advertisement utilizing the W-6's technique, such as:

1. **Who**...are you working with (name of company, etc.), who are the clients?
2. **What**...job are you performing (sales, customer service, etc.), company's offering(s)?
3. **Where**...where is the office (city, state, etc.), or the territory you are covering (geographic)?
4. **When**...do you perform the work (weekdays, weekends, nights, etc.)?
5. **Why**...why the company provides their offering, why you selected the company and work?
6. **hoW**...long have you been with the organization?

Just one of the benefits of the quick advertisement is that once it has been developed and committed to memory, it can be altered to fit particular situation(s) as necessary given the circumstances and the length of time available to deliver. The quick advertisement can be tailored to a specific person and/or position the person holds within the organization, along with the message you want to deliver, making sure main points, value, and benefits are delivered in a brief, concise, and interesting way, promoting curiosity and continuation of the dialogue.

THE VALUE OF QUICK ADVERTISING

Advertising is described as the activity of attracting public attention to a company's business or product offering and is essential for notifying the public (potential purchasers) about what a company is providing.

Ever wonder why television and radio advertisements are predominately scheduled for thirty-, sixty-, or ninety-second intervals, or why television advertisements provide clips of newly released movies containing thirty-, sixty-, or ninety-second clips and/or sound bites?

The reason is they *WORK!*

They grab people's attention and generate curiosity while providing enough information for the public to engage and to act on the information.

Turn on a television almost any time of the day, especially early morning and late night, and you will discover a plethora of infomercials being delivered—everything from the latest cookware to workout(s) and diet(s), houseware and healthcare items and remedies.

In the event that you might not be quite sold on the solution(s) being provided, they assist by instilling urgency, providing a limited time to act. By doing so, you receive something in addition (e.g., special pricing, additional items, etc.).

I would recommend thinking about how infomercials are designed and structured not only when developing a quick advertisement but also when preparing to perform a presentation/demonstration. The elements include:

1. Grabbing attention quickly and generating curiosity and interest.
2. Being relevant and relatable to potential purchasers.

3. Showing or describing issue(s), conflict(s), challenge(s), and how the solution offering(s) resolves these.
4. Showing value(s) and benefit(s), described in item 3.
5. Testimonials from industry experts or current users.
6. Call to action—where to obtain, where to see, where to call.
7. How to find out more information (website, phone number, location, etc.).
8. Creating a sense of urgency (e.g., special pricing, limited offer, limited quantity, etc.).
9. Summarize and review important/key information.
10. Be memorable. As a sales professional, you want to be remembered in a positive way by potential purchasers.

Most of these same elements are utilized no matter if the advertisement is a thirty second commercial spot or a thirty-minute program.

Companies providing these advertising commercials/programs spend hundreds of thousands of dollars designing and developing their message and having industry experts create, craft, and deliver it.

It just seems to make sense if companies are investing lots of money into designing and developing their advertising, salespeople should also design and develop their quick advertisement in the same structure, incorporating some of the same elements.

QUICK ADVERTISEMENT FORMULA

A quick advertisement may be designed utilizing the following formula:

1. The first section (first few sentences) should be an introduction of who the person is, what company they represent, and their specific role (e.g., "Hello, (prospect name). My name is Steve Monks, and I am a (salesperson's title/role) for (company name). I work with companies in your area and around the state (indicate territory), assisting with (company's high-level or overall value)."

2. The next section should be about the salesperson's company, what offering(s), purposes, and outcomes they provide to the industry, and successes customers have achieved utilizing the company's solution offering(s). (Company name) is the industry and/or market leader in the distribution industry, assisting over 50,000 companies, which is approximately 35 percent of the industry, helping companies like yours with inventory management and saving 15-20 percent of their inventory costs while increasing overall profit margins.

QUICK ADVERTISEMENT EXAMPLE

Hello, Mr./Ms. (*Prospect's Name*),

My name is Steve Monks, and I am a sales executive for S-M Enterprises. I work with distributors in your area and across the state, helping them to improve their inventory resource management.

S-M Enterprises is the industry leader in the distribution market, providing centralized and integrated solutions that are 100 percent web-based, allowing for extending a distributor's reach and capabilities beyond their buildings and locations, saving time, money, and resources for your organization.

Our company has been providing distribution solutions for over 25 years, and our solutions are currently utilized by one out of every three distributors. Our implementation process is managed by a dedicated resource, which is designed to be quick and easy, allowing for a smooth transition from your existing system to your new solution with no data loss or negative impact to your business.

Just some of the benefits companies realize from our solutions are:
1. Improving customer service, satisfaction, and delivery.
2. Increasing inventory control and management.
3. Decreasing costs and maximizing profits.
4. Allowing them to know *what* inventory resources they have, *where* each resource is located, and *what cost* structure is represented by each item.

Our solution(s) provide organizations instant business information regarding inventory resources, while allowing customers 24-7 access to your company's solutions, resources, and services. We can very easily show your employees how to take advantage of the features and benefits in the new system, leveraging existing resources and the environment already in place and therefore minimizing implementation time and cost.

Our partnership with our existing customers means the solution(s) we develop address distribution and distributor issues today and into the future, which is why our entire organization is built around the philosophy..."patron for life."

Rather than trying to cover all the solution offerings and services we can provide to your organization over the next couple minutes, I would like to understand what challenge(s) you and your organization are currently facing.

If you agree it is at least worth exploring the possibilities and hearing more about what we have been able to accomplish with other distributors, when would be a good time for me to contact you within the next few days to schedule a time to discuss what S-M Enterprises can provide for your organization?

QUICK ADVERTISEMENT BENEFIT(S)

The quick advertisement can be developed and learned in a short time frame. Once completed, it can be easily committed to memory. It can also be quickly adapted to different situations when speaking with prospects on the phone or in person.

Salespeople may also be surprised just how this scripted message of very precise and condensed information will engage individuals and further spur conversation while generating questions that can be either addressed during the conversation and/or covered in more detail during a subsequent discussion.

Because the quick advertisement takes such a short time to deliver, it is rarely interrupted prior to finishing, which provides an opportunity to deliver the message in its entirety before the individual responds with questions and/or comments. However, if interrupted for any reason because it is committed to memory, it is easily restarted from the point of interruption and completed without leaving out any information.

The individual(s) the salesperson is speaking with appreciates receiving significant information in a short, condensed message. Let them know relevant information about you, your company, the solution offering(s), benefits, and the overall value proposition without taking too much of their time or completely interrupting whatever it was they may have been doing.

QUICK ADVERTISEMENT VERSUS TRADE SHOW CONVERSATION

The quick advertisement allows for a different type of conversation from a standard initial conversation. It allows the salesperson the opportunity for more control of the direction of the conversation with fewer opportunities for the prospect/customer to break off from the conversation without learning important information about you, your company, your solution offering(s), and the value proposition.

Example:

Here is a familiar "initial" conversation when meeting an individual in passing while they are walking through a trade show booth area *without* utilizing the elements of a quick advertisement.

Salesperson: "Hello. How are you?"

Prospect: "Well, and you?"

Salesperson: "Am well also, Thank You. What company are you with and what do you do?"

Prospect: "President of ABC Company. We distribute pipe, valves, and fittings. Who are you, and what is it that you do?"

Salesperson: "Am a sales representative with S-M Enterprises, and we are here at the show providing company's information about our solutions. Has the show been beneficial for you? What activities are you planning on doing while at the show this week?"

Prospect (interrupting): "Excuse me, there is someone I've been looking for and just saw them over there. I will be back later."

Salesperson: "Before you leave, would it be possible to get a business card from you?"

Prospect: "I don't have one with me but will bring one when I come back."

Then the person walks away, knowing very little about you, your company, your solution offering(s), or how your company is assisting other companies similar to theirs. The salesperson is left knowing nothing or very little about the individual's current environment and situation, potential challenges, and needs, as well as if there is any potential sales opportunity.

Also, in the time of the interaction, there probably was not a strong enough impression left on the individual to come back and spend additional time with the salesperson to learn more, or even to remember the salesperson's name should they be contacted within the next few days. That is, if the salesperson was lucky enough to be able to catch the person's name in the introductions and/or from the person's name tag.

The all-too-often "initial" conversation (described above), which takes approximately the same time as a quick advertisement, has left the salesperson with very little information and has not progressed any potential opportunity forward, and the individual (prospect) walked away not learning anything about the salesperson, the company, or the solution offering(s).

QUICK ADVERTISEMENT AND CASUAL CONVERSATION

Once a quick advertisement is designed and committed to memory, one might be surprised how easily it can be revised to fit many opportunities, such as:

- Introductions at work-related social events where people ask what it is that you do.

- Trade show and industry events at both the booth area and social events.
- When meeting multiple individuals at prospects'/customers' offices.
- When individuals join a meeting already in progress and the salesperson would like to introduce themselves.
- Should the individual from the prospect/customer with whom the salesperson is meeting communicate to colleagues that the salesperson will be in their office if they would like to stop by with questions, etc. Should someone stop by, the salesperson usually has only a brief time to introduce themselves before continuing with the meeting.

Utilizing a quick advertisement in the aforementioned situations provides an opportunity for each person to know *who you are, what you do, what company you represent*, and *what your company provides* to individuals/entities.

The salesperson may be pleasantly surprised when trying to contact and follow up with individuals to whom they were introduced or spoke with briefly how much easier it is for individuals to remember who the salesperson is due to the quick advertisement.

The quick advertisement can also be utilized in personal and social settings.

Think back to when you might have been attending a social event where you introduced yourself or someone else introduced you to other individuals, and then someone asked, "So what is it that you do?"

Oftentimes when this situation occurs, many people will simply say something like, "Sales, computers, education, distribution, etc.," leaving the person with very little information and directing the conversation back to the person asking the question to follow up with additional questions if they would like to learn more details.

I recommend trying this approach next time you are in a social setting and introducing yourself to individuals.

Utilize a shortened version of the quick advertisement as your introduction, and see how it engages and attracts more interaction with the person(s) to whom you have just been introduced, and how much easier the conversation progresses.

Information provided in a quick advertisement introduction can provide individuals a few additional information points, such as your profession and how long you have been in the industry. I have found it also helps to include some personal points of information (hobby, family, etc.) as it provides a few additional topics and makes it much easier for people to continue with the conversation, as well as enticing them to continue the interaction.

Besides, you never know what contact you may encounter at a social setting that may assist and benefit ongoing sales efforts and your career.

I was working for a company providing inventory resource management for the education market and had been trying to set up a meeting with the administration of a particular school district in Colorado for some time to provide information about the company's solution offering(s) and explain what we had been able to provide to their neighboring school districts. But I had not been able to schedule an actual meeting with the administrators and move the opportunity forward beyond initial conversations, even though there was a good chance the solution offering(s) would help them if I could just get the opportunity to meet with them.

After months of attempting to schedule a meeting, it just so happened on a particular weekend I was helping a rodeo colleague provide a riding and team roping seminar in Colorado, where about thirty individuals were in attendance.

During the two-day seminar, I assisted many student riders and ropers, who were at different levels of experience and skill level with their riding and roping techniques.

Early in the first day of the seminar, an individual was struggling to be able to catch the practice steer (model replica of a steer setting on the ground where students could practice roping on foot rather than horse-back), which had been set up for each person to practice and improve their roping techniques in a more controlled environment and for the in-structors to provide them immediate feedback.

After working with this individual throughout the first day, the per-son was beginning to catch the practice replica model steer. By the end of the second day of the seminar, this person was roping from their horse and had, for the first time, actually ran and caught a live steer from horse-back while in the arena.

This person was ecstatic about the progress she had made and was very grateful for all the efforts and attention provide to her during the two days of the seminar.

At the conclusion of the last day of the seminar, there was a potluck dinner held for the students and their families, which provided an oppor-tunity for everyone to interact with each other in a social setting rather than focusing on the training.

During the dinner, this particular individual who had caught her first live steer from horseback came up to me with her spouse and began thanking me repeatedly for all the assistance. During the conversation, the individual's spouse asked me what I did (when not providing roping and riding lessons), which provided an opportunity to deliver a quick commercial.

Upon completion of the quick commercial introduction, I asked the person what she did and she stated she was the superintendent of the dis-trict with which I had been attempting to contact and schedule a meeting.

Any guesses as to the chances of getting a meeting with the district cabinet at that point?

I contacted the individual the following Monday, and within 3 days, I had a meeting scheduled with the district cabinet, which ultimately re-sulted in the district signing a substantial contract.

Lessons from this experience:

First, the benefits and impact of being able to deliver a quick commer-cial in an appropriate situation.

Second, one never knows who they might meet or when they will get an opportunity to sell (or at least make an impression on someone who may know someone who can assist with a sales opportunity). It is not always *what* you know but *who* you know...or who knows you! Lastly...never underestimate the impact or significance someone can have on someone else's life.

It has been said, "If you can change someone's day...you just might change their life!"

If it were not for helping the person and having the opportunity to assist her first, I might have continued to encounter difficulty making entry into the sales opportunity.

COMPANY'S CUSTOMER LIST

When starting with a new company or a new territory, acquire an existing customer list as soon as possible.

Oftentimes when a salesperson joins a new organization, there is an assumption from individuals within the company that the new salesperson automatically knows who their customers are, where they are located (city, state, etc.), and have the appropriate contact information.

In addition to the company customer listing, the salesperson will also want to obtain a list of customers/prospects for their specific sales territory or region (this can usually be acquired from sales management or the information technology department).

Request to receive lists (e.g., company customers and territory/region customers, prospects, etc.) in an electronic format (preferably in a spreadsheet) allowing for sorting, filtering, etc., as well as adding additional information.

Once the list(s) is obtained, then perform the following:

- Review the list(s) with sales management and/or coworkers (who are knowledgeable about the customers), acknowledging and identifying specific customer types: references, large customers, large prospects, geographic location, etc.

- It will also be helpful to obtain (or create) a report containing the following information. Most companies' computer systems can run a standard or custom report to obtain this information. However, if this functionality is not available, then you can also create a list with as much of this information as can be obtained from various sources, such as prospects' and customers' website(s).

EXAMPLE OF FIELDS/CATEGORIES

1. Company name.
2. Address (mailing and physical including zip code).
3. City.
4. State.
5. Current Standard Industrial Classification (SIC) or industry.
6. Identify existing solution(s) to be targeted for possible replacement. This information is especially important for preparing marketing campaigns, RFP responses, etc.
7. Current solution(s) the customer has purchased and utilized from your company.
8. Specific customer and prospect identifier, such as gross sales figures, number of sites, number of users/employees, etc.). Inquire as to what identifier(s) your company currently utilizes for identifying customers and prospects to assist with determining what identifier(s) should be utilized.
9. Account ranking indicator(s). This allows and provides a methodology for stratifying the customers and prospects into groups or categories for sales and marketing focus and targets. Also, this allows for grouping accounts by categories, such as high-value target accounts, strategic accounts, large sales opportunities, etc.
10. Identify important contact roles and positions, such as C-level: CEO, CFO, CIO, decision makers, etc.

11. Relevant contact information for roles and positions mentioned in item 10.
    a. Office phone.
    b. Office e-mail.
    c. Office mailing address, etc.

LEARNING FROM CUSTOMERS

It is extremely valuable to identify current company references and long-term customers to learn why each one of them initially purchased from the company and continue to utilize the company's solution offering(s). This also presents an opportunity to learn about areas of success and any "measured and reported" results, such as increased effectiveness and efficiency, increased revenue, increased customer satisfaction, decreased costs, etc.

Initial calls to longtime customers and company reference accounts should be considered "warm calls" as they currently have a relationship with your company, its solution offering(s), and its people. As opposed to prospecting "cold calls," in which the individual on the other end of the call may have no idea or information about you, your company, or its solution offering(s).

Established customers and reference accounts have a tendency to be more willing to meet with the company's salesperson and be more open and honest when speaking or meeting with existing vendors regarding their satisfaction level and results. Oftentimes, if a salesperson explains they are new to the company and/or industry and that their management team has identified specific individuals as "experts in what they do," the individuals being recommended are usually willing to assist in sharing information about their company and industry.

REFERENCE CUSTOMERS AND CONTACTS

When reviewing the existing customer account list for references, the salesperson should consider criteria and elements, such as:

- Large, high-profile customers (national/international) who play an important role within their industry/market.
- Large and/or high-profile customers within the salesperson's specific sales responsibility (territory/accounts).
- Individuals working within existing customer accounts who are widely known for participation within their specific industry (organizational or group officer, published in industry magazines, recognized advocate or speaker), viewed as an industry or functional expert, and therefore sought out for their opinion.
- Attempts should be made to contact and meet, if possible, each individual being utilized as a reference for you and your company's solution offering(s). This provides an opportunity to establish a relationship with reference contact(s), allowing regular communication regarding prospect calls and the situation and circumstances surrounding these call(s).
- Reference accounts and those individuals utilized for reference calls should be highly regarded as they are extremely important to the success of a salesperson. In a way, they are an extension of a salesperson's team but with the freedom of communicating to the prospect in a different and more direct manner than the salesperson. A salesperson can explain and show the potential purchaser(s) what and how the solution offering(s) provides value and benefits. However, the reference account offers and provides their experience of having been through the process and has firsthand daily knowledge of the outcomes and results recognized. Since the reference account and individual have been through the phases (sales, implementation, installation, training,

support, etc.), they are viewed by the prospect as very knowledgeable and credible.

Potential purchasers also have a tendency to view references as a neutral party and therefore seem to be more willing to exchange and share information with them regarding their decision, such as current status, decision and implementation timing, and plans or concerns in regard to moving forward with the company's solution offering(s).

Why do potential purchasers view references as important and crucial? Because most of us would like to avoid making a poor decision!

The pressure to make a correct and appropriate decision may be amplified and under scrutiny, depending on the number of people the decision impacts, the length of time the decision impacts, and the amount of investment that is requested to complete the purchase.

In many cases, the person(s) or committee making the decision will be evaluated by the level of success received from the decision, as well as the associated results.

Therefore, references assist potential purchaser(s) in building, or solidifying, confidence in their decision. They ensure the company can perform what is being claimed and can successfully complete the implementation, and provide ongoing support and services.

MANAGING DAILY SALES ACTIVITIES

As expressed earlier, one of the most important commodities a salesperson has is *time*. Therefore, managing this most precious commodity in both a professional and personal capacity is extremely important.

Here are some of the areas salespeople will spend time on during the day and should be managed appropriately:

1. Prospecting. This is critical for keeping the salesperson's pipeline/ funnel active with newly identified opportunities. Utilizing a prospecting document will assist in managing this process.

PROSPECTING DOCUMENT

Prospect Account Name	Prospect Account Number	Current Solution(s) Utilized	Contact Prefix	Contact Name	Role/ Job Function	Email Address	Company Size/Sales

Number of Employees	Mailing Address	Mailing City	Mailing State	Mailing Zip	Physical Address	Physical City	Physical State	Physical Zip

Company Website (URL)	Company Phone	Contact Phone	Contact Extension	Account Notes	Assistant Name

2. Cultivating current sales opportunities with calls and meetings, ensuring forward movement of identified, targeted, and forecasted opportunities. Utilizing a customer document will assist in managing this process.

CUSTOMER DOCUMENT

Account Name	Account Number/ID	Product(s) Utilized	Company Annual Spend	Contact Prefix	Contact Name	Role/Job Function	Email Address	Company Size/Sales

Number of Employees	Number of Sites	Mailing Address	Mailing City	Mailing State	Mailing Zip	Physical Address	Physical City	Physical State	Physical Zip

Company Website (URL)	Company Phone	Contact Phone	Contact Extension	Account Notes	Assistant Name

3. E-mail. It is recommended to set specific times throughout the day to check e-mail. This reduces the chances of getting caught up in the eternal e-mail vortex, thus having it utilize more of the day than planned and take away from those sales-related activities that allow for closing opportunities and achieving goals.

   Today's technology devices (cell phone, tablet, laptop, etc.) allow you to quickly view and respond to e-mail. Setting and scheduling specific times throughout the day or before and after meetings will allow salespeople to focus on those activities that generate sales and individual achievement goals. Another recommendation is to set up e-mail settings to prioritize messages based on specific criteria (prospects/customers, internal company, etc.).

4. Forecasting and strategizing. This involves continually building, maintaining, and managing a sales pipeline/funnel. This is an ongoing process usually identified and recorded in some form of electronic application, such as CRM, spreadsheet, etc. This process allows the salesperson and sales management to understand where each salesperson, territory, and account stands in reference to sales activities, actions, and quota. It provides information, such as number of sales opportunities, where each is in respect to the sales cycle, potential sale amount(s), close date, actions and activities, etc.

5. Customer satisfaction issues and resolutions.

6. Follow up on status of current implementation(s).

7. Ongoing reference(s) communication.

8. Scheduling travel (flights, hotel, etc.) for upcoming prospect/customer meetings, conferences, etc.

9. Marketing (developing targeted campaigns focused on prospects and customer type(s), groups, categories, specific solution offering types, geographic area, etc.).

10. Expense reporting (timely reporting of expenses and reconciliation of expense reimbursements).
11. Offer duties as needed/assigned.

As you can see from the list above, there are many things competing for a salesperson's time on a daily basis. Therefore, it is critical to be able to prioritize and manage these activities to meet the goals of the salesperson and the company.

CUSTOMER RELATIONS MANAGEMENT (CRM) PHILOSOPHY

In today's world, it is quite common for companies to utilize some type of Customer Relations Management (CRM) application. It is important for a salesperson to make sure to inquire about, understand, and utilize this application based on the sales management and company's philosophy and policy.

Although the term Customer Relations Management (CRM) is a fairly common and widely utilized term, it can have different meanings to different individuals depending on *what* and *how* it is utilized within their company.

It has been my experience that companies utilize various applications for their CRM purposes, as well as utilizing the information in varying degrees. Many companies utilize a commercially offered CRM solution. However, the elements and areas (features and functionality) utilized within each company, as well as how the CRM solutions information is used within each company, can be as unique as the individual companies themselves.

Some companies have elected to design or customize an application to be used as their contact database or utilize a portion of an existing application, such as accounting and/or billing solutions or spreadsheets. In some cases, companies customize an internally designed and developed application.

CREATING A CONTACT (CRM) DATABASE

If the company does not currently utilize a CRM solution, then I recommend creating a contact database containing pertinent customer/prospect information to be utilized for quickly accessing information that is critical to the overall success of the salesperson.

It is worth the salesperson investing time to create a database containing prospect/customer information. In today's world, much of the prospects' and customers' company information may be public information, depending on if the entity is a public or privately held company. Organizational information can also be located utilizing resources, such as Internet searches, company websites, industry journals and publications, magazines, etc.

Compiling information in an electronic format allows filtering and sorting of designated information, such as company name, contact name, state, city, role/position, company revenues, number of company locations, number of employees, etc.

In the event a salesperson is not provided with a CRM database and has limited time to create one, there are some alternative methods available to obtain the information in a relatively quick manner:

1. Utilize a free contact database application available on the Internet.
2. Subscribe to a commercially offered contact database solution.
3. Outside assistance (family, friends, etc.).
    - Produce a list of company names, including information, such as contact name, role, state, city, etc., and then engage additional assistance from individual(s) accessing the Internet to locate missing companies' information (company website, etc.).
    - Hire someone to complete the contact information through an established agreement, such as pay-per-company or pay-per-contact information (company name, contact, address, e-mail, phone, etc.).

It is vitally important for a salesperson to have access to prospect and customer information.

If this information is not provided by the company, then it is the responsibility of the salesperson to accumulate and have access to the contact information.

Salespeople may be surprised at the number of individuals they will encounter and work with over their career and how many of these individuals may be associated with the same company or industry over their entire career. Establishing these types of contacts provides the ability for individuals to assist each other during their careers, as well as assist in staying informed about the industry, other prospects/customers, competition, etc.

It is advisable to keep the contact database current, allowing for planning and scheduling action items and sending out promotion information, industry and/or seminar notices, thank-you notes, holiday and birthday cards, etc.

SUMMARY

In the sales profession, *time* and *timing* are two very important elements—possibly the two most precious commodities a salesperson possesses.

Learning the history of your company is one way to build credibility. Focus on learning the most significant events that have allowed the company to grow, expand, and achieve the level of success.

Just like it is important to build relationships quickly with prospects and customers, it is also important to build relationships quickly with individuals that the salesperson will be working with inside their own company.

Getting started with a new company or even with a new or additional solution offering can be a busy time. So, whether the person is a new employee learning a new company and solution offering(s) or a current employee tasked with learning a new solution offering(s) being introduced, focus on learning the most important elements first.

If the solution offering provides multiple application modules or a suite of solutions, make sure you can explain the most important values and benefits for each application/module.

Utilize a quick advertisement to explain to individuals what your company's solution offering(s) provides to purchasers in a brief and concise manner.

The quick advertisement can be developed and learned in a short time frame. Once completed, it can be easily adapted to different situations when speaking with prospects.

One never knows who they might meet or when they will get an opportunity to sell. It is not always *what* you know, but *who* you know...or *who knows you!*

When starting with a new company or a new territory, acquire an existing customer list as quickly as possible.

It is valuable to identify current company references and long-term customers to learn why each one of them initially purchased from the company and continues to utilize the company's solution offering(s).

Potential purchasers also tend to view references as a neutral party and seem to be more willing to share information with them regarding their decision.

There are many things competing for a salesperson's time on a daily basis. Therefore, it is critical to be able to prioritize and manage these activities to meet sales objectives and goals.

In today's world, it is quite common for companies to utilize some type of Customer Relations Management (CRM) application and philosophy. It is important for a salesperson to make sure to inquire, understand, and utilize this application based on the sales management and company's philosophy and policy.

LESSON 10

SOLUTION KNOWLEDGE

One of the questions often asked within a company and sales management is how much knowledge of the solution offering(s) does a salesperson need to have to represent the company and the solution offering(s) and be effective in successfully completing sales opportunities?

LEVEL OF EXPERTISE

In most cases, a person does not have to be an expert with years of formal education and training in order to utilize and explain the use (value and benefits) of a company and solution offering(s).

I do not completely understand the properties of electric current, nor do I completely understand the technology involved in CDs/DVDs; however, this would not preclude me from being able to describe values and benefits of each one.

The point is that we do not have to be experts in electricity to utilize electricity. Most people have the capabilities required to walk into a room and activate a light switch, and most people have the ability to utilize a CD or DVD player even though they may not fully understand the technology.

It has been my experience when it comes to having knowledge and information about the company and the solution offering(s) being represented, some is good...more is better.

However, there seems to be a delicate balance between a salesperson having a certain level of knowledge to be effective and needing to know everything about the company and its solution offering(s).

If a salesperson is representing solution offering(s) involving lifesaving elements, the salesperson should confirm with their sales management that they have the appropriate level of knowledge and training to provide advisement and recommendations.

Since the majority of salespeople are not dealing with lifesaving elements, they do not need to know everything about the company's solution offering(s) before contacting prospects/customers and initiating discussions. Therefore, the questions become *"when"* does a salesperson have enough knowledge about the company and its solution offering(s) to begin reaching out and contacting prospects/customers to discuss potential interest, and *"how"* is this required level of knowledge gained?

It has been said that more sales opportunities have been put at risk due to a salesperson not understanding the sales cycle, elements, and processes rather than not being familiar or having gained complete knowledge of their company and its solution offering(s).

COMPANY SALES TRAINING

Historically, it was customary for companies hiring new salespeople to have them spend time at the corporate headquarters, going through a company-designed training program sponsored by the company's training department. Then, the salesperson would spend time with another sales representative from the company or an individual from sales management (supervisor) observing *"how"* they interacted and *"what"* they communicated to the prospect(s)/customer(s).

The sales hiring and training process is changing. A newly hired salesperson and the corporate office may not be located in the same geographical area, and therefore the training may be conducted either at a company branch location or virtually utilizing the Internet (web sessions, etc.). The company may also require new employees to go through a series of company-specific online video certifications, trainings, etc. There are also some companies who prefer to perform a combination of office (on-site) training along with virtual training.

Most companies today feel that if the salesperson has gone through the information on the company website, attended the on-site or virtual training(s), completed any required certification(s), and spent time with a company salesperson and/or the sales management, then the salesperson is ready to begin contacting prospects/customers and representing the company and its solution offering(s).

One recommendation is after the salesperson has completed the required company training, they spend time simulating selling and communicating the company's product offering to their friends, family, pet(s), etc., just to be comfortable talking about what the company and the solution offering(s) provides. This may seem somewhat trivial or elementary, but I have learned from experience that being able to clearly, concisely, and confidently express information (value, benefits, selling points, etc.) about the company and its solution offering(s) will be beneficial when initially speaking and/or meeting with prospects and customers.

Once the salesperson has a level of comfort explaining high-level selling points about the company, its solution offering(s), the value proposition, and how the offering has assisted other companies, then they should contact customers (references in their territory) and schedule a meeting. This will provide an opportunity to learn more specifically *how* the customers are utilizing the solution offering(s) and *why* they selected the company and its solution offering(s).

This will provide several benefits.

1. Builds relationship with customer(s) for ongoing business opportunities (references, add-on sells, etc.).

2. Hearing why the customer selected the company and its solution offering(s).

3. Understanding what level(s) of success the customer initially experienced and currently experience with your company and its solution offering(s).

4. Gaining additional information and understanding about the industry and company's involved in the industry.

5. Provides insight as to specific customer and industry issues and challenges, along with an increased understanding of the future direction and needs of the industry and prospects/customers.

6. Allows gaining and building "success stories," which can be leveraged and utilized when speaking with other prospects/customers and assisting in developing questions in regard to how customers are addressing these same areas. People enjoy hearing stories of another customer facing the same situation they are currently experiencing and how they were able to address and resolve their issue(s).

7. Begins to build or add to a "questions database," which can be utilized when communicating with other prospects/customers.

8. The meeting may result in individual's providing referrals (company and contact), thus allowing the salesperson to make contact with the referred person and reference the individuals who provided their name.

LEARNING VALUE AND BENEFITS

If a salesperson is joining a company (or learning a new solution offering), they should spend time focusing and learning *why* the offering affects a prospect's/customer's business. This can be done even from a high-level (macro) summary, such as improving effectiveness or efficiency, increasing profits, decreasing costs, etc., as opposed to focusing on each feature (micro) or every element/component that is in the offering and the activity it performs. Do not misunderstand. If a salesperson has the time and is able to learn each element of the company's solution offering(s), doing so will allow the salesperson the ability to be an expert within their company. However, should the salesperson have this "expert" level of knowledge, they should be strategic as to how it is utilized as their role is to sell, as opposed to dedicating time as a trainer and/or support contact.

Oftentimes when starting with a new company (learning a new offering), the information to the salespeople may be provided by the company's training department, which is accustomed to providing training to customers and as such, they are accustom to going through the *entire* training delivered to customers. They are comfortable routinely going through each element (field, aspect, etc.) of the solution offering rather than providing information in regard to the high-level summary of the "values and benefits."

Again, it is certainly desired, and maybe appropriate, to learn each and every element of a solution offering(s), but depending on the time frame of when this information is needed and when it is expected to be communicated to potential purchasers, the salesperson may have to begin by learning the value proposition and benefits at a high-level and then learn specific aspects gaining incremental knowledge and understanding of further elements over time.

When prospecting and having an initial dialogue with a potential purchaser(s), the salesperson may only get a few minutes to communicate and describe the value proposition, value(s), and benefit(s) of the solution offering(s). The prospect(s) often prefers to have the salesperson communicate the value and benefits of the solution offering(s) at a high level, and then as interest and curiosity continues they can begin to learn more about the individual components, elements, and aspects of the solution offering(s).

ENOUGH TO GET STARTED

In most cases, the salesperson (new position or solution offering) is probably more prepared than they think, but it is common for salespeople to have some consternation when first calling and meeting with prospects and customers.

To assist with addressing reservations, the salesperson should make sure they can state the company's and solution offering's value proposition and value(s) and benefit(s) provided to the potential purchaser(s), such as:

1. As a 'Distribution' (purchaser's market/industry) and technology-focused and driven organization, (Your Company's Name) offers a total resource management solution with the ability to extend your distribution resource reach and scope beyond the company's four walls and buildings, resulting in saving time, money, and resources for the company while providing extended opportunities for future revenue growth and overall company goal achievement.

2. With our company's focus on 'Distributors' (potential purchaser's market/industry), (Your Company Name) can provide your company a fully integrated, centralized, and web-based resource management solution. Our solution(s) will allow your company to accommodate growth, improve efficiency and effectiveness, and embrace the latest technology, including mobile and handheld devices, therefore maintaining its leadership role within the industry and reducing overall company cost(s).

MAKING ONESELF BETTER

Salespeople should join groups/associations that are involved in the industry they are selling into to keep apprised of the current issues, trends, and news about the industry. You can also monitor and participate in industry-focused websites and blogs and subscribe to electronic and printed information (e-magazines, etc.) covering news and events in regard to prospects'/customers' industries. Being able to ask and discuss industry issues, trends, and events will provide credibility and assist in becoming an adviser and resource for prospect and customers alike. It also allows for the salesperson to ask specific questions to the potential purchaser(s) as to their opinion and/or how their company is going to address upcoming issues, trends, regulations, events, etc.

———————

SUMMARY

It has been said that more sales opportunities have been put at risk due to a salesperson not understanding the sales cycle, elements, and processes rather than not being familiar or having gained complete knowledge of their company and its solution offering(s).

Meeting with customers will allow learning *why* they selected the solution offering(s) and *how* they are utilizing the offering(s), along with successes.

To build confidence...practice, practice, practice...allowing the delivery of the company's and solution offering's value proposition, value(s) and benefit(s) in a brief, clear, and concise manner.

Being able to discuss industry issues, trends, and events will provide credibility and assist in becoming an adviser and resource for prospect and customers.

LESSON 11

VALUE PROPOSITION

A value proposition is a key element when discussing and communicating a company's solution offering(s) and what it offers to potential purchaser(s). A value proposition is a representation of value provided and delivered; summarizing the total of benefits a vendor proposes a consumer will receive in return for the customer's associated payment or other value transfer.

> **Value:** An amount, as of goods, service, or money considered to be a fair and suitable equivalent for something else, a fair price or return.

> **Proposition:** A plan suggested for acceptance; a proposal. A subject for discussion or analysis.

A simple way to look at the value proposition a company and its solution offering(s) provides is to communicate the value(s), benefit(s), and result(s) that are possible to be gained by the company and/or user(s), such as improved effectiveness, efficiency, profitability, etc., and the perceived worth (value) placed upon receiving the proposition being offered and provided.

Salespeople who offer and provide a value proposition(s) to potential purchaser(s) tend to be focused on addressing and positioning a "long-term" solution offering(s), in which the emphasis is on value(s) and benefit(s), therefore affecting and improving the overall purchaser's goals.

Salespeople represent solution offering(s) with varied sales cycle lengths from days, weeks, months, or even years. Those who are involved with lower-cost, higher-volume transactional sales may find themselves competing mainly on one or two elements, such as price, volume/quantities, shipping/delivery, etc.

These sales opportunities historically involve less expensive consumable items, where the item is purchased "as is," providing a lower entry investment where utilization occurs in a relatively short period of time. These types of sales opportunities are focused around high transactional volume of a "product" offering, as opposed to a "solution offering(s)" requiring a longer sales cycle, involving a larger monetary investment, and the longevity and overall impact of the purchasing decision.

Example:

Convenience stores found across America sell products, relatively low-priced items available and targeted at individuals who have a need for immediate or short-term consumable items (beverages, snack food, petroleum products, etc.). These types of businesses may be conducting hundreds of transactions within a 24 hour time span. The transactions being completed do not require formal decision criteria, committee or group meetings, an RFP, or presentation/demonstration in order for the consumer to make a purchasing decision.

SELLING VALUE VERSUS PRODUCTS

You may be thinking...Value versus Products...what is the difference?

One difference is the mind-set and perception in the way(s) they are presented and positioned to potential purchaser(s).

A value proposition is expressed as a high-level, high-value con-sumer experience that solution offering(s) have on a purchaser(s) as it relates to their overall expectation of success. A product may represent a singular unit or item that impacts a subsection or smaller piece of the purchaser's expectation(s).

VALUE SELLING = RELATIONSHIP SELLING

A relationship is defined as...the state of being interrelated; connect-ing or binding participants in a relationship.

Transactional sales opportunities are focused on low price, high volume, and high inventory turnover. Relationship sales are focused on longer-term and more involved interpersonal interactions for solution offering(s) that usually have a higher price associated with the overall sales opportunity(s).

Most consumers view products as low price, quickly consumable items (e.g., business office products, sticky notes, writing utensils, etc.). As a result, it is probably unlikely a company is having multiple calls with multiple vendors, resulting in multiple visits and providing presentation(s) for the company's next purchase of sticky notes. This would most likely not be the best utilization of a company's executive or purchasing com-mittee's time.

For standard everyday product purchases, most companies regard "products" as those that are typically low priced and quickly consumable. Therefore, they are usually purchased by companies based on some set of criteria primarily involving elements such as lowest cost, quickest de-livery, cheapest shipping, and least amount of time invested. Therefore, entities view most "products" as those items that need to be purchased and acquired in order to continue conducting business on a daily basis.

On the other hand, when selling and providing *"value solutions,"* it is imperative for the purchaser to understand and perceive the impor-tance and perception of what the value (solution offering) "represents" to the purchaser(s) and the entity. Therefore, the solution offering(s) (e.g., software solution, conceptual idea, tangible good, etc.), is not as important as *"how"* the offering and value is presented and perceived by the purchaser(s) and the *"overall value"* perception in the purchaser's mind.

It is the responsibility of the salesperson to develop, position, and deliver their solution offering(s) as a *"value proposition,"* not as a "product to the purchaser."

SUMMARY

A *value proposition* is a representation of value provided; summarizing the total sum of benefits a consumer will receive in return for associated payment.

It is the responsibility of the salesperson to develop, position, and deliver their solution offering(s) as a *"value proposition,"* rather than a "product to purchaser(s)."

This conceptual approach and mind-set will assist salespeople in differentiating their company's *solution offering(s)* from the competitor's... products.

LESSON 12

PROSPECTING METHODOLOGY

The elements and activities associated with "prospecting" are probably as old as humankind itself.

Imagine being one of the first persons on planet earth. What activities would be needed to survive? Some answers are locating shelter and/or a living facility, obtaining nutrition/food/water, securing safe locations from potential predators and/or enemies, and finding companionship. It became imperative for these individuals to *"locate and find"* essential elements to survive and thrive in the environment.

The element of prospecting for sales is equally important to the ongoing survival of salespeople and companies. Therefore, it is important to always be looking for new and/or additional sales opportunities.

In order for a salesperson to survive and thrive in a sales career, it is imperative that some type(s) of prospecting, either by the individual salesperson or the company, be conducted in an ongoing manner.

The activity(s) of prospecting is one of the key elements of selling, for without this process, the sales cycle and selling process never really has a chance to get started...or completed.

Without someone such as a prospect or customer being curious and interested in a salesperson's solution offering(s), the likelihood of moving through the sales process to a successful completion of a sale is remote.

Therefore, without the activity of prospecting, there will be little to no sales completed, resulting in...no implementation, services, or training... no revenue for the company...and no commissions for the salesperson!

To avoid this situation, it is imperative for a significant and continual amount of time to be dedicated on a regular (daily/weekly) basis to prospecting. Ensure enough time, energy, and resources are focused on looking for new and/or additional sales opportunities.

HOW CAN PROSPECTING BE ACHIEVED?

What are some of the ways prospecting activities can be completed?

The act(s) of prospecting can be done in many different ways, as well as with many different combinations, of which this book will just address a few.

1. Prospecting conducted by the salesperson (cold calling, etc.).

STRATEGIC CALL PLANNER
Account Name:
Date:
Goal:
What is the goal of the communication/interaction?
Progress:

What information is needed to move the opportunity forward?
What next step(s) are being pursued/sought?
Opening:
What information is going to be shared to build curiosity and interest?
What Value Proposition, Benefit(s), Quick Commercial is going to be utilized?
Environment Information:
What is needed to qualify the opportunity?
What is needed to determine decision criteria?
What is needed to determine potential challenges to the opportunity?
Opposition and Challenges:
Anticipate and prepare for opposition/challenges...how will these be addressed?
Competition:
Is there competitor(s) involved in the opportunity?
What activities/actions are needed to address competitive situation?

2. Assistance from the company (sales leads activities, generation of sales leads, inside sales assistance, etc.).

3. Third-party or outsource assistance (paid services for lead, complementary vendor assistance, etc.).

4. Marketing leads generated by company activity (website, seminars, trade shows, etc.).

5. Networking within industry groups, complementary industries and solutions, etc.

6. References. Leveraging customers for additional prospects who may have interest in the solution offering(s).

When considering prospecting methodologies, there are a few key elements to consider:

1. Locating the individual(s) within an organization who may be curious and interested in your company's solution offering(s).

2. Locating individuals who are not satisfied with their current solution, current system features, or functionality and are looking for ways and methods to improve their situation.

3. Locating individuals who have the ability to make and approve purchasing decisions.

4. Locating individuals "inside" or "outside" the prospect's company who can potentially assist with introductions to appropriate decision makers within the company.

5. Never underestimate the influence or power of what just "one" person within an organization, market, or industry can provide.

THE INFLUENCE OF ONE

This allegory portrays the power and influence of what just *one* person can do for another or even for a group.

Think of this in regard to the power and influence of what *one* person can do for your sales pipeline...the result is the *"Influence of One!"*

When thinking about the importance and power of how just *one* person can make an impact on prospecting, I am reminded about a story of a high school football team that had won two consecutive state high school football championships.

After winning two consecutive state championship football titles and going undefeated in the third season, this team found themselves in the state championship playoff game, where they were down by two touchdowns at halftime.

The team headed into the locker room at halftime with their heads and hopes down because they realized the possibility of coming back on this particular team would take a Herculean effort. The other team was also undefeated this year.

The head coach gathered the team in the locker room, and when all the players had assembled around him, he stood looking at them for a few seconds...seeing long faces and eyes looking down in presumable defeat.

He then asked a couple very simple but important questions.

"Is there a player here who can cause just *one* defensive turnover?"

"Is there a player here who can get *one* interception?"

"Is there a player here who can run for just *one* touchdown?"

Players who had been previously looking down at their shoes, anticipating receiving a stern diatribe as a result of their poor performance and lack of execution and focus, began looking up. One player declared, "I can cause *one* turnover!"

Then another player spoke up with growing enthusiasm, stating, "I can make *one* interception!"

Another player yelled out, "I can make *one* touchdown!"

Each player suddenly realized he could do just *one* thing to help his team, and if they all did just *one* thing to help the team, they had a chance to come back and win.

All of the sudden, the mood in the locker room changed from that of defeat to that of optimism as players started yelling out with more and more enthusiasm what *one* thing each could do to help the team. The enthusiasm and optimism became contagious.

The team suddenly realized they could not only come back and score on the opposition, but they could actually win this game simply by each player doing just...*one* thing!

The team took the field for the second half of the game energized, motivated, and confident. The result of each player thinking they needed to do just *one* thing to help their team resulted in not only overcoming the two-touchdown deficit but going on to win the championship game!

The point...do not underestimate the importance and impact of locating *one* opportunity and successfully completing the sales process and continue to duplicate the prospecting effort over and over!

As a salesperson, if you should ever find yourself falling behind in sales and sales quota...think about the *Influence of One* and begin by locating one prospect and then another, and like the football team, the enthusiasm, optimism, and momentum will begin to improve the chances for success.

UTILIZING AVAILABLE INFORMATION WHEN PROSPECTING

Make sure to utilize today's technology and availability of information to learn more about potential purchasers as information is becoming more readily available (company website, social media sites, etc.) and utilize Internet search engines to research additional information on contacts, company officers, executives, etc.

BUILDING A PROSPECT LIST

Upon realizing the importance of prospecting to a salesperson's success level, how should a salesperson go about creating and building a prospect list(s)?

Following are activities for creating prospecting list(s):

1. Identify "quick strike" opportunities utilizing known information on existing customers to create profiles. Then, examine results for opportunities where companies may not be utilizing your entire solution offering(s), and approach these accounts, confirming interest level for adding functionality, such as additional modules, additional users, additional sites, etc.

2. Inspect the sales territory/region profiles, and categorize accounts identifying the *top 10-20* quick strike targets for completing new and/or additional sales opportunities quickly.

3. Categorize the territory based on specific criteria, such as Standard Industrial Classification (SIC) code(s), company size, geographical location, industry growth, and industry direction.

4. Examine the accounts in a sales territory/region, evaluating and noting high probability sales opportunities, therefore potentially closing the opportunities in the shortest amount of time. This is often referred to as looking for "low-hanging" fruit—those sales opportunities that have the highest probability of closing quickly due to some set of circumstances.

5. 80/20 Rule. Keep in mind that approximately 80 percent of the sales revenue and associated commissions will come from approximately 20 percent of the territory accounts. Identify and put a strategy in place for addressing the 20 percent.

6. Utilize **CARE** methodology for prospecting and profiling sales opportunities:

    C = Customer's...current environment (situation/circumstance).

A = Application(s)...solution offering(s) being utilized (from both your company and the competition). If utilizing a competitor, what is their willingness to evaluate making a change?

R = Reason(s)...for investigating options and reason for a change.

E = Example(s)...proof of results that have been accomplished with other customers.

7. Utilize **SYSTEM** methodology:

S = Solutions...what does your solution(s) offering provide to address their needs and goals?

Y = whY...should they select your company over other options available?

S = Successes..."proof sources" and references acknowledging successes.

T = Technology...utilize and leverage today's technology to engage prospects.

E = Effort...work smarter and provide extra effort to win each sales opportunity.

M = Memorable...make a positive impression with individuals within an opportunity.

BREAKING DOWN PROSPECTING INTO SMALLER TASKS

Oftentimes, what appears or seems like a daunting task can be divided (broken down) into tasks (smaller pieces), allowing the overall project to appear more achievable.

Consider how an author might go about completing the task of writing a book. It is probably unlikely that the author would simply sit down with 200 plus blank pages, begin writing/typing, and complete the book in a single sitting.

More likely, the author begins writing/typing "one" word, which leads to "one" sentence, which leads to "one" paragraph, and then "one" page. The author then continues to focus on repeating this effort, completing multiple words, multiple sentences, multiple paragraphs, and multiple pages until the task of writing the book is achieved.

PHONE MESSAGE(S)

In today's fast-moving, information-packed world and availability of information it is very important to be able to provide communications that pique the potential purchasers' curiosity and interest in order to have them act on the information.

Prospects and customers receive a number of phone calls and messages throughout the day, and therefore, it is imperative to be able to deliver a message that stands out and separates the salesperson from other messages, providing a reason for the individual to respond to the call.

Here are a few recommendations in regard to phone messages.

Many of today's phone systems allow the caller the option of going back and listening to the message and revising/amending it before leaving it with the intended recipient. This provides an opportunity to leave a voice message, listen, and then either record again or deposit message.

Another method of practicing leaving voice messages is for the salesperson to call their home phone or cellular phone and leave a message, allowing them a chance to listen to the message and evaluate if they would return the call.

This is also a good way for the salesperson to hear how their voice sounds to others and if they are leaving all the pertinent pieces of contact information, as well as pace/speed and speech patterns (*ahs, ums,* etc.).

One thing to listen for specifically is rushing the information toward the end of the message. As some individuals approach the end of the message, they increase their speed, sounding like an auctioneer. This forces the listener to go back and listen to the message, sometime multiple times, in order to clearly understand the information. Make sure to make it *easy* for the person to return the call. Speak clearly and at a pace as if an individual is writing down the number if you were actually speaking to them on the phone, keeping in mind it is a good idea to repeat the phone number(s).

It may seem obvious if the salesperson would like a return call to provide pertinent information in the voice message. However, I have received many phone calls where the individual left out information needed to respond or return the call. The following are the pieces of information to be included in a voice message to a prospect:

1. Salutation/Greeting.
2. Caller's name.
3. Caller's company name.
4. Many of today's phone systems include date and time of the message, but it is courteous to let the individual know what day and approximate time the voice message is being left.
5. Brief description and/or reason for the call and message.
6. Salesperson's contact phone number(s). If utilizing a cell phone (and depending on reception), you may want to repeat the phone number a second time, allowing the listener another opportunity to hear and write down information and phone number.
7. Conclusion: "Thank You, have a great day, looking forward to hearing back from you, etc."

When leaving voice messages, make sure the environment around your phone is appropriate. If background noise is too loud, it can affect the ability to leave a message that can be clearly understood.

Make sure to speak in your natural speaking voice as if you were actually speaking to the person.

Most of today's phone messaging systems allow the listener to go back a specific number of seconds (e.g., 10 seconds, 20 seconds, etc.) while listening to a message and even slow the message down to hear the information. But what is the probability that a busy executive or person with purchasing responsibility is going to go through additional effort to return a salesperson's call?

To assist in making the phone message interesting and increase curiosity for the prospect, consider including some of the following items:

1. Your company's name and why the contact may know or have heard of your company, such as that your company is a recognized leader in the industry, utilized by *x* percent of the industry, etc.
2. What your company and its solution offering(s) provides to other customers in the industry, such as allowing customers to be more effective, more efficient, cut costs, increase profit margins, etc.
3. Provide a brief description of a known industry problem(s) and how the solution offering(s) solves the problem(s).
4. Provide a name of a current customer in the prospect's area and explain how your company's solution offering(s) is assisting them.

The following is the structure of a phone message for prospects:

Good morning, (Mr./Ms. Their Name). My name is (Your Name) with (Your Company's Name).

Today is Wednesday at approximately 10:30 in the morning. (Your Company's Name) is the industry leader and specializes in assisting distribution companies with their enterprise resource management needs. We are currently assisting several other companies in your industry to address the recent required compliance changes. Recently, (Your Company Name) helped (Name of Reference Company) address and resolve the compliance issues, allowing them to be in compliance prior to the regulatory deadline saving them time and money.

I would like to schedule a time to discuss if this new regulation compliance is an issue with your company, and if so, how your company is planning to address the regulatory change.

Again, my name is (Your Name) with (Your Company Name,) and I can be contacted at (Your Phone Number).

Thank You, and I am looking forward to speaking with you soon.

BECOME INTERESTED IN PEOPLE

A long time ago, a person told me, "If you want individuals to be interested in you...then 'first' be interested in them!" The importance of this statement became very clear as I began my sales career.

When speaking and communicating with prospects and wanting them to become interested in you, your company, and your solution offering(s), then you should first show interest in them and their company.

Prospecting is a common way for salespeople to initiate the first contact by investing time and effort into individuals and potential sales opportunities.

One approach is to invest time and resources getting to know prospects, such as stopping by their office for introduction(s), learning more about the individual(s) and their companies. When doing this, let them know the visit is not about trying to sell them anything "today" but just an opportunity to put a name with a face and to get to know the company and its individuals, as well as what they do and the product(s), service(s), etc., they provide for their customers.

This provides an opportunity for individuals to get to know the salesperson and for the salesperson to learn more about the individual(s) and the company. Investing in building relationships, credibility, and trust early in the relationship pays dividends when it comes time for prospects and customers to make purchasing decisions.

Another important aspect of prospecting is obtaining information about the potential purchaser(s). To assist with this effort, get in the habit of asking good and appropriate questions that provide more information about the individual(s) and the prospect's business. One way of doing this is to ask questions directed at learning both business-related and personal information about each person with whom you communicate, such as:

1. When attending work-related (trade shows, etc.) or social events, learn individual's first and last names and their company's name and locations.
2. What role they perform for the company.

3. What their company provides to their customers (if not known).
4. Where they grew up, where they live, and some personal information (schools/college, family, kids, etc.).
5. What they like to do away from work (hobbies, etc.).
6. Contact information and/or business card(s).

There are certainly additional topics to discuss; however, these are examples of areas individuals enjoy talking about and are easy for them to discuss while establishing and building a relationship.

Most individuals are willing to speak and discuss what they and their company provide for other individuals and/or companies.

Individuals spend a large percentage of their lives at work and are usually willing to speak about the contribution(s) they provide to their organization.

Furthermore, most individuals are at least equally interested in talking and discussing activities outside of their work, such as family, kids, hobbies, interests, etc.

Have you ever noticed that when someone is asked, "How are you today?" or "How are you doing?" they will usually respond with a similar and somewhat predictive response, such as, "Am well, how are you?" or "Am having a good day, and how is your day going?"

Why do individuals respond in this manner? It may be for a couple of reasons:

1. It is common courtesy in our society to respond in some fashion, and therefore, it is how most individuals are taught to respond.
2. Because someone has shown an interest in knowing how they are doing, feeling, etc.
3. When someone engages us, in return, we also engage.

It is similar in prospecting. Becoming interested in the individual(s) and the company you are contacting provides an opportunity for them to become engaged in a dialogue with you. Besides, it makes the idea of prospecting more palatable if you actually have a genuine interest and curiosity in the individual(s) and companies being contacted.

When conducting prospecting activities, it is beneficial to make some form of *connection* with each individual the salesperson communicates at a prospect's company. In some cases, you may speak with one or two individuals (secretary, assistant, etc.) prior to reaching the appropriate contact or decision maker.

This *connection* can stem from common and shared knowledge, such as work associates, friends, interest/hobbies, physical location, and geography, among others. Contacting individuals without making some type of *connection* leaves the salesperson in a position of being simply another written message or phone call the potential purchaser(s) will receive. Having someone (secretary, assistant) within the prospect's company reinforcing or reminding the contact to respond to your communication will separate you from the other messages received. Without making some type of *connection,* the salesperson may find their communication (calls, e-mails, etc.) being ignored or deleted...along with other sales representative's messages.

Therefore, it is helpful for the salesperson to attempt to establish a *connection* in order to be memorable to each person contacted.

LEARNING WHAT IS IMPORTANT TO PEOPLE

Think about where, when, and how people meet. People come together around common interests, and most people like to surround themselves with what they enjoy, such as groups of people, activities, hobbies, etc. They also decorate their homes and work space with items relating to their interest(s).

People also enjoy sharing their interest(s) with others by outward displaying meaningful items for others to enjoy. It is rare to find an individual who has their office decorated a certain way and is not willing to discuss the objects and items displayed.

If objects and items displayed are also of common interest to the salesperson, they should make sure to let the individual know. It can be surprising how quickly the salesperson may be accepted as a person with a common interest, rather than just another salesperson who wants to sell something.

Again, how is this interest established? By the salesperson being interested in them...first!

SUMMARY

Prospecting is vital to the ongoing success and achievement of a salesperson's goals and ongoing career. It is important to determining a way to make this activity productive and enjoyable.

It is important to be able to provide communications that pique the potential purchaser's curiosity and interest in order to have them act on the information.

Establish a *connection* in order to be memorable with each prospect you encounter.

If you want people to be interested in you and your solutions, first be interested in them.

When calling prospects and customers, I find it helpful to ask one of the following:

"Did I catch you at a bad time?"

"Did I catch you in the middle of a project?"

"Do you have a few moments?"

These types of questions allow the person an opportunity to either continue with the call or to reschedule at a more convenient time.

Make sure to utilize the *CARE* and *SYSTEM* methodologies.

Should you find yourself falling behind in sales goals or quota, think about the *"Influence of One"* and begin by locating *one* prospect and then another, improving the chances for success.

LESSON 13

MARKETING METHODOLOGY

Marketing is defined as the commercial functions involved in a company's global message about the company and its image. It is the act or process of buying and selling in a market.

Whenever an individual or company attempts to make itself or its solution offerings more attractive to another (company, person(s), entity, etc.), the effort is usually conducted through some form of marketing technique(s).

MARKETING HISTORY

When considering the methods and media/mediums that have been utilized over time by entities to convey the company's solution offering(s), ideas, concepts, etc., many of the following have been utilized:

1. Storefront signs.
2. Traveling and door-to-door salespeople.
3. Word of mouth (referrals, etc.).
4. Newspaper and print (magazines, etc.).

THE BUSINESS OF SALES | STEVEN M. MONKS

5. Billboards.
6. Radio.
7. Television.
8. Mail (letters, postcards, etc.).
9. E-mail.
10. Internet and websites (e-magazines, blogs, etc.).
11. Pop-up advertising on the Internet.
12. Social media and social websites.
13. Trade shows, conferences, seminars, etc.
14. Social events.

Potential purchasers have been and will continuously be bombarded by marketing and advertisement(s)...*anywhere and everywhere*...as well as involving senses, such as look, listen, touch, smell and taste. Therefore, making it even more imperative that a company's marketing message be noticeable, appealing to and incorporating multiple senses, memorable, and instills enough curiosity and interest to result in the prospect(s) conducting some action toward gaining more knowledge and information about the company and/or its solution offering(s).

PERSONAL AND INDIVIDUAL MARKETING

It seems to be human nature that when an individual(s) is seeking something, such as prospects, customers, friends, employment, etc., they do specific things to appear more attractive. This is accomplished with *marketing* techniques.

Think about some of the marketing techniques used by individuals in an attempt to gain something they would like to attract in their lives. When individuals utilize marketing techniques, they address areas such as personal grooming and clothing, vehicles, homes, jewelry and accessories, and even social groups and occupations to attract or gain acceptance of others of a certain group of individual(s). The reason for individuals appearing and acting a certain way is to attract and become part of (or join) other individuals or groups. Our own personal marketing (appearance to the world), along with our marketing message (actions and mannerisms), is what is utilized to market and attract a certain person(s) or group.

Business entities are really no different when it comes to marketing. They are also attempting to entice and attract individuals and entities by promoting their company and their solution offering(s), as well as continuing success with their customer base or a certain group of individuals/entities involved within their niche markets.

The overall goal for most entities is to be in business to help people and entities.

Therefore, how does a company go about informing individuals and entities about what it can provide in the way of assistance to individuals, groups of people (companies), and other entities? The company utilizes *marketing* techniques!

OVERALL MARKETING STRATEGY

The company and salesperson's overall marketing strategy(s), objective(s), and goal(s) should be:

1. Identifying and adding new accounts (opportunities) into the sales pipeline (forecast).
2. Moving existing accounts (opportunities) forward in the sales process and forecast pipeline.
3. Building and strengthening relationships with target accounts.
4. Fostering relationships with strategic accounts.
5. Improving relationships with prospects.
6. Identifying existing customers as reference accounts.
7. Exploring new markets, industries, and new territories.

Make sure to continue to leverage existing customer account information, such as what issues, challenges, and problems have been resolved and what other accomplishments customers have recognized by utilizing your company's solution offering(s).

MARKETING LIMITS...OR NOT

The overall marketing plan for each salesperson can have one (or more) campaigns being delivered and utilized at the same time and/or in conjunction of one another.

To that extent, marketing campaigns can be presented in many ways (letter, phone calls, e-mail, postcards, and giveaways containing company logos and/or message, such as hats, shirts, bags, cups, mugs, etc.).

There is really no limit to what a salesperson and the marketing department can imagine when it comes to marketing campaigns, although there may be financial limits to implementing these ideas. Each year during trade show season, marketing departments are busy exploring and developing new ideas to grab individuals' attention.

Some marketing campaigns are designed to provide a piece of the overall marketing message at regular intervals over a period of time. This type of marketing is referred to as "drip marketing."

One example would be a marketing campaign that sends prospects a small replica of a railroad train car each month with the company's logo and a portion of the marketing message presented on the side of each railroad car. This could also be accompanied by correspondence (letter, postcard, etc.) further explaining the value(s) and benefit(s) provided by the company's solution offering(s) to the prospect. Over the six months of the marketing campaign, the prospect receives one railroad car per month, ultimately completing a train (containing the six different railroad cars: locomotive, box car, tanker car, caboose, etc.). The intent of this is to have the train be displayed in the prospect's office, thus completing an ongoing message and marketing campaign that is seen daily and reminding the receiver of the value(s) and benefit(s), along with creating interest and incentive to contact the company.

This also provides an opportunity for a salesperson to contact prospects to confirm they received the latest train piece, and letter message, and *why/how* it may pertain to their company.

Even though this particular campaign is scheduled to continue over a six-month period, the salesperson and company may also be conducting concurrent and additional targeted marketing campaigns highlighting additional and/or different value and benefit points during the same time.

OVERALL MARKETING PLANS AND OPTIONS

What would some of these additional marketing plans and campaigns look like?

The following is a small sample of the types of marketing plans and options that might be utilized. This is just a small representation of various options available.

These may be completed utilizing one or multiple types of media, separately or in conjunction with one another, such as e-mails, letters, postcards, website(s), Internet link(s), Internet sessions, etc.

Campaigns designed and focusing on:

1. *All company accounts* (prospects and customers) targeted by corporate marketing delivering overall marketing and branding message delivered through various methods. This is a periodic campaign(s) executed once a month, once a quarter, or at trade shows, seminars, etc.

2. *All company accounts* (prospects and customers) targeted by the corporate marketing department providing periodic (monthly, quarterly, etc.) information targeting a *specific solution offering.* This may be utilized if the company offers specific modules, individual (separate) applications, or a particular business functionality (accounting, warehousing, payroll, purchasing, etc.), or operational functionality, such as hardware, software, mobile devices.

3. *Current customers* (adding or expanding functionality, modules, etc.).

4. *Prospects* (building interest and curiosity) in specific functionality or usability.

5. Leveraging existing marketing materials designed to *target specific roles/titles/individuals* within a prospect and/or customer.
6. Scheduling targeted and specific *marketing events*: trade shows, seminars, webinars, Internet sessions, podcast, etc.
7. Utilizing and leveraging *proof sources*, such as testimonials, case studies, Return on Investment (ROI), publications, articles, etc., and converting this information into marketing campaigns, preferably including an ROI model(s) for each of the company's solution offering(s).
8. Developing a *list of industry challenges/issues* and then *providing resolutions/answers* to each of these, utilizing the company's solution offering(s). Create campaigns focusing on addressing each area of the solution and communicate the message(s) over time.

Again, this list is just a few ideas to encourage thoughts and can be utilized in conjunction with other ideas to provide information and promote interactions, discussions, and meetings with prospects.

MARKETING POINT OF VIEW

Marketing campaigns have varied levels of targets, objectives, and success, but the ones that seem to be the most effective are ones that seem to promote the company's solutions from the purchaser's/user's position and view, as opposed to the selling company's point of view.

WHAT DOES THIS MEAN?

Some marketing materials (website, brochures, etc.) consist of a lengthy list of features and functionality of what the solution offering(s) provides. They leave it to the potential purchaser(s) to figure out how they would utilize the features and functionally to improve their processes and businesses. This assumes the potential purchaser(s) will connect the dots and determine how they could utilize the solution offering(s) and come to the conclusion of what the solution would do for them and their company.

When thinking about marketing for a company's solution offerings, consider providing value (benefits) and resolutions to specific (known) issues and challenges rather than listing the features and functionality of the solution offering(s).

MARKETING INVOLVING SALESPEOPLE

How should a company determine what the value and benefits of their solution offerings' features and functionality would be for potential purchaser(s)?

They should work with the sales departments and those individuals who interact with customers/prospects daily to determine current challenges, issues, needs of the target market, and how the solution offering(s) addresses and provides resolution(s).

Once this is determined, there are numerous ways organizations can utilize marketing techniques to attract individuals and companies to their company and solution offering(s).

Companies may utilize their own internal marketing department, utilize an external third party, or use a combination of both (depending on size and scope of marketing campaigns) to assist them with communicating the marketing message to targeted individuals, entities, and market(s).

ATTRACTING BUSINESS TO YOUR COMPANY

The world begins introducing marketing techniques to each of us at an early age, utilizing a myriad of media, such as television, radio, electronic devices, Internet, e-mail, mailings, billboards, newspapers, magazines, window advertisements, etc. Therefore, by the time an individual reaches young adulthood, they will have been exposed to thousands of marketing advertisements focused on attracting their money, time, effort, etc., to a company's solution offering(s).

So, how can salespeople work collectively and collaboratively with their company's marketing department to create individualized marketing campaigns focusing on attracting potential purchasers to their solution offering(s)?

One of the best ways is to attempt to be as creative and imaginative as possible (within budget parameters) and to attempt to differentiate the company's solution offering(s) not only from competitor's, but from other marketing and advertisements currently battling for the purchaser's/customer's attention and financial spend.

Today, there are entities that continue to use the same marketing methods they have used for years (focusing on providing features and functionality listings), and many of them continue to achieve a level of success with this approach.

However, if the company you are representing is still utilizing the same marketing methods, I would encourage exploring and expanding into some new and innovative techniques to create differentiators for the company and its solution offering(s).

When considering marketing techniques, concepts, and ideas, think about ways to differentiate and potentially involve some newer technology. Consider what the music industry has done to get their message across to consumers, utilizing such methods as making their product available on television, radio, mobile devices, tablets, laptops, cellular phones, etc. The music industry is embracing technology, making it easier, adaptable, and available for consumers to access their product almost everywhere. Therefore, their products have become ubiquitously available.

What methods are available to communicate the messages of your company and its solution offering(s)?

MARKETING TECHNIQUES

We have all been doing some form of marketing for a large part of our lives, trying to look a certain way, act a certain way, and portray a certain image to others, which is similar to what companies are trying to accomplish.

The ways marketing can be accomplished are almost infinite, and therefore limited only by a person's imagination. Historically, marketing techniques have focused on those activities and/or concepts that affect the greatest number of individuals within the company's target audience(s), resulting in a favorable Return on Investment (ROI).

Example:
- Number of marketing targets (individuals/entities) = 10,000.
- Investment per contact = $1.50.
- Marketing campaign investment = $15,000.
- Responses generated from campaign (utilizing national average of 1-2 percent) = 100-200.
- Estimated sales close (10 percent close rate) = 10-20.
- Average sells contract amount = $5,000.
- Estimated return on advertising campaign investment = $50,000-$100,000.

Therefore, it is important to consider what method(s) and medium(s) could be utilized to provide the most potential exposure and access to targeted contacts in the specified target market(s) within an appropriate investment point. This equation is commonly referred to as *"cost-per-contact."*

This overall marketing concept and methodology focuses on utilizing today's technology and methods to make a positive impact on the largest number of targeted prospects/customers while controlling the investment required, thus reaching targeted consumers and allowing the company to maximize marketing outcome goals (results) for each campaign.

Marketing methodologies and techniques can be as different and varied as the results each campaign produces. The methodology largely depends on the marketing philosophy and budget size of an entity, but the reality is that for most entities to continue to remain in business and be successful... they need customers, and marketing and marketing techniques can dramatically impact their success.

SPECIFIC AND TARGETED TYPES OF MARKETING CAMPAIGNS

When it comes to marketing campaigns, salespeople should think in terms of *"multiple streams of selling."* This means that salespeople should consider multiple methods and techniques for providing exposure to materials and how this information can be delivered to target market(s). Salespeople should be thinking *who* and *what* companies can benefit from receiving these materials.

The following examples take into account designing and targeting campaigns for both prospects and customers, either together or with separate campaigns.

1. *Company/Territory top accounts*...this can be determined by a specific number of accounts or by a percentage of total accounts, where the accounts are determined by some criteria (revenue size, SIC code, number of users, etc.). Campaign(s) are focusing on building and/or furthering the relationship within the accounts with decision makers.

2. Evaluate and categorize the sales territory, identifying *"prospect"* accounts based on current competitive solutions. Then, create strategic campaigns focusing on replacing all/most of the incumbent vendor's solution(s).

3. If the salesperson's company offers multiple solution offerings, then segment the sales territory *prospect* accounts by their current solution and create campaigns specifically targeted for moving accounts to *"one"* of your company's solution offerings.

4. Segment the sales territory *customer* accounts by current solution(s) and create campaigns specifically targeted for *adding* and/or expanding new/existing functionality.

5. Provide *group meetings* where the salesperson has the opportunity to meet with prospects and customers, resulting in *one-on-many* and engaging multiple companies at the same time. These can be conducted by some set of criteria, such as:

- Regional, state, city (area within a city), etc.
- Industry or market.
- Utilization of the company's offering (overall customers/ prospects if offering multiple applications).
- Utilization of company's specific offering (applications, modules, hardware, software, mobile devices and apps, etc.).

AVAILABLE MARKETING MATERIALS

When looking at the various ways for salespeople to potentially locate, access, and produce marketing ideas and material(s), there are a few places worth exploring:

1. The company's marketing resources repository. These are company-created informational materials (print and electronic) with targeted messages designed for large audiences (national, international, regional, and local), as well as targeted events, such as trade shows, conferences, seminars, etc.
2. External resources (created and available from a third-party sources and/or suppliers). These materials may come from a contracted outsource or even third-party articles, publications, customers, vendors, etc.
3. The salesperson creates materials themselves by designing and developing ideas and concepts that incorporate information available from items 1 and 2.

One of the main objectives of a company's marketing department is to create and communicate information regarding the company's image and branding, along with its solution offering(s), resulting in creating interest from potential purchasers. The marketing department may also receive information from other company departments, such as Research and Development (R&D) regarding new and/or improved features and functionality to solution offering(s).

MARKETING RESOURCES

It will be beneficial if the salesperson stays up to date and informed of marketing plans being proposed and delivered from the corporate office.

1. Stay apprised of the marketing "collateral" available and utilized, such as: company website, brochures, articles, testimonials, case studies, white papers, Internet strategy (Internet sessions, webinars, podcast, etc.), and social media.

2. Stay informed of what marketing "methods and strategies" are being utilized to market to prospects and customers (websites, e-mails, direct mailings, trade shows, industry events, geographic events, etc.), and what the company's philosophy is regarding marketing and advertising communication from the corporate office and the frequency (weekly, monthly, quarterly, etc.).

3. The salesperson should evaluate methods and strategies for utilizing and leveraging corporate office marketing material(s) into their *regional/territory marketing* campaign(s).

4. Evaluate the option(s) of utilizing company marketing and advertising material(s) and customizing for specific "targeted accounts" and/or "territories/regions." This allows for delivering specific and targeted information to prospects/customers while appearing as a knowledgeable resource and building credibility through information provided.

5. Inquire as to what industry communications (publications, websites, e-magazines, etc.) the company is currently utilizing and what type of information is being delivered, and then strategize how to leverage these communications.

6. Salespeople should ask customers how they can become more involved in the prospect's/customer's industry (attending industry events, speaking at or participating in industry events, contributing to industry publications, etc.).

7. Stay informed as to what the company's marketing department is planning for "new marketing" materials (promotions, trade shows, seminars, geographic events, etc.) and the time frame for

planned releases of new or existing marketing and advertising information.

PROOF SOURCES

Proof sources, such as testimonials, customer case studies, white papers, technical documents, Return on Investment (ROI), etc., to potential purchasers can be beneficial and powerful evidence assisting in reducing decision maker's risk. When proof sources are provided, it allows decision maker(s) to continue to move forward with the sales cycle, taking the next step(s) while continuing to build trust in the salesperson, the company, and its solution offering(s).

Providing proof sources can also be beneficial for a company to design and create a means (spreadsheet, webpage, etc.) where prospects can enter and/or provide their own company data (numbers/figures) and then view the results based on their selected input information, such as calculating a Return on Investment (ROI), etc.

If an interactive proof source is designed and created, it should be easily deployed and used. It should require a minimum of information that is readily known by the user, and the input fields should be self-explanatory (or have an explanation provided). The ROI information form reflects the expected result when utilizing the company's solution offering(s).

Proof sources that are designed, implemented, and utilized correctly can be a powerful and useful sales tool because they allow the user(s) to utilize *their* individual and specific data. The information and results are customized to the user/prospect.

If your company does not currently have some form(s) or type(s) of prospect and customer information models, such as an ROI model, etc., you should consider working with the sales and marketing department(s), along with existing customers, to gain the type(s) of information important to prospects. The resulting marketing/sales models produced can be utilized to allow potential purchaser(s) to become interested in what they can expect to achieve by utilizing the company's solution offering(s).

RETURN ON INVESTMENT (ROI) MODEL
(Prospect to provide (enter) underlined information)

PROSPECT'S CURRENT INVENTORY STATUS

Current Inventory Value	*$4,000,000*
Number of Inventory Items (Estimated)	*10,000*
Average Inventory Item Investment	$400
Total Number of Customers	*200*

COST OF INVENTORY LOSS/SHRINKAGE

National Average Annual Inventory Loss/Shrinkage	4.0%	
	Annual	**5 Year**
Prospect's Inventory Loss/Shrinkage (Number of Item Lost Annually)	400	2,000
Cost of Item Loss/Shrinkage	$160,000	$800,000

SAVINGS FROM SOLUTION OFFERING LOSS REDUCTION

Item Loss Reduction (percentage)	50.0%	
	Annual	**5 Year**
Savings	$80,000	$400,000

ADDITIONAL SAVINGS RECOGNIZED (NOT EXPEDITING INVENTORY/CUSTOMER SERVICE/ETC.)		
Per Customer	*$50*	
	Annual	5 Year
Saving per customer multiplied by the total number of customers	$10,000	$50,000

SAVINGS WITH NEW SOLUTION OFFERING		
	Annual	5 Year
Savings from Inventory Loss Reduction	$80,000	$400,000
Saving from not expediting Inventory/Customer Service/Etc.	$10,000	$50,000
Total Estimated Savings	$90,000	$450,000
Initial Investment for New Solution Offering	$50,000	
Annual Investment (Annual Fee) = 15% of initial investment x 5-years		$37,500
Prospect's Savings/ROI over 5-Years	$40,000	$412,500

TRADE SHOW RECOGNITION

It does not seem to matter what industry or company a salesperson may represent—most companies have an annual trade show circuit(s) and/or conference season(s). Each year, promotional companies and marketing departments around the world seem to focus on discovering some new or modified eye-catching promotional item (gizmo) in attempt to attract individuals to their trade show booth (or area, event, etc.).

The amount each company spends on trade shows, conferences, seminars, and marketing ideas and items varies as widely as the availability of promotional items themselves. It seems that each year, some item becomes the popular trade show item(s) for that season/year. The item piques people's interest and gets people talking about it, where they got it, the name of the company (displayed on the item), and the function the company performs. This creates interest and gets individuals discussing where they can get the item, which drives interest and traffic to the company's booth/area/room. This provides an opportunity to learn more about the company, its solution offering(s), and what can be provided to potential purchasers and/or their company.

This seems to provide some degree of pressure on each company to determine and obtain what will be the big conversational item for public display at trade shows, conferences, seminars, etc.

PROMOTIONAL ITEM(S)

The overall goal of a company's marketing department, as well as of individual salespeople, is to provide appropriate information about their company and its solution offering(s) in a manner and format that is engaging and builds curiosity and interest. The goal is to result in some action (discussion, phone call, research, etc.) from prospects in regard to what the organization has to offer and can deliver to those individuals and entities within selected target market(s).

One effective marketing strategy is to present a current "known" industry problem/challenge/issue/need affecting target market(s), and provide specific examples as to how the company's solution offering(s) addresses and resolves the specific problem/challenge/issue/need. This can be completed for multiple known or identified issues and challenges where the problem is presented and then how the solution offering(s) address and resolve the issues and challenges for the target market. This has much more of an impact on the audience than simply listing the features and functionality contained within the solution offering(s) and relying on the audience to figure out how to utilize them in resolving their issues and needs.

When marketing departments and salespeople are designing and developing specifically targeted marketing campaigns, they should be thinking about each one of the campaigns from the perspective of what it is that the company's solution offering(s) provide that addresses (resolves) the prospects issue(s)/challenge(s). Presenting the known challenge(s)/issue(s) and then showing how the vendor's solution offering(s) can successfully address the challenge(s)/need(s) differentiating and separating the offering from competitors.

TRADE SHOW EVENTS AND CONFERENCE ATTENDEES

If you have ever attended a trade show or event consisting of booth area(s) you have probably observed salespeople around their particular booth containing some form of backdrop with the company's name and a table filled with company brochures, free items, gifts, candy, etc., along with some type of container to collect business cards (some type of information card), or some type of electronic device to scan attendees' information (name, company name, position or role, etc.), which enters them in to a drawing for a free gift.

The drawing and electronic scanners allow vendors to easily and quickly gain attendees' contact information and interest level for populating a database for sharing information with salespeople and allowing for follow-up after the completion of the trade show/event.

Attending many trade show events, I have witnessed attendees walking through the booth area more focused on gathering "free stuff" than on what vendors had to offer as solutions. These individuals appeared interested while helping themselves to free item(s) and stating, "I will be back to speak with you later." Then they walked away prior to the salesperson gaining any significant information about them, their company, or their current environment (situation, needs, issues, challenges, etc.) and then did not return to the booth. I decided to try an alternative approach.

A NEW MARKETING IDEA

The idea was called a "Cowboy Yo-Yo"...a $1.00 marketing idea... worth thousands...in *interest!* It stemmed from a game I played as a kid growing up around the rodeo environment.

The item was built by taking a piece of 3 foot soft nylon rope, 3/8 of an inch in diameter that can be found at almost any hardware or home repair store. A hole was punched through a tennis ball or baseball size sponge ball (approximately 2-4 inches in diameter), the more colorful, the more attention it attracts. Then, the nylon rope was threaded through the hole in the sponge ball, and standard knots were tied at each end of the nylon rope. The sponge ball was positioned next to one of the knots at the end of the rope. When completed the Cowboy Yo-Yo looks like a 3 foot nylon rope with a sponge ball attached at one end.

While standing around the booth area, I held the rope in one hand with the ball hanging at the other end of the rope toward the ground. Then, I quickly flipped the ball up in the air just a few inches with my hand holding the rope knot. With one quick upward motion of my hand, a loop was produced, allowing the rope to encircle the sponge ball and creating a knot in the middle of the nylon rope. This resulted in tying a knot in the rope utilizing just one hand.

As I began doing this, people at the trade show started coming around to watch. After watching a few times, they would ask if they could "give it a try."

What is the goal of a trade show...to get people (prospects) to come up and speak with you!

This seems fair...they approached me asking a question...could they give it a try? Of course they can...all they need to do is simply answer a few of my questions.

Within minutes of utilizing the Cowboy Yo-Yo, attendees at the trade show began talking to me, as well as each other...quickly making this item the buzz all around the trade show. By the end of the two-day show, I was known as the..."Cowboy Yo-Yo Guy."

Attendees brought over additional individuals to have them watch and attempt to complete the task. Also, while attending social events at the show, people came up to me to discuss the Cowboy Yo-Yo, wanting to know where they could purchase one and where I had acquired mine (several people asked if they could buy the one I was using). I could have sold several of the Yo-Yos. People expressed that they were going to go back to their offices and try to locate these or build them for an activity at their next company (departmental, etc.) meeting.

For a period of time after the show, when I was contacting and following up with attendees regarding their interest in my solution offering(s), I would mention that I was the "Cowboy Yo-Yo Guy," and you would be surprised how many people would take the call because they remembered seeing or hearing about it at the trade show. Many of these follow-up calls resulted in scheduling meetings with purchasers to discuss the solution offering(s)—as well as a request to bring along the Cowboy Yo-Yo.

The moral of the story is...that this simple marketing strategy was inexpensive but had a *big* impact on individuals, which set me and my company apart from the other vendors and sales representatives at the trade show.

Small confession: the attendees at the trade show did not know that the salesperson in front of them, dressed in a suit in a city convention center, had practiced and played this game as a cowboy growing up.

When it comes to opportunities to get in front of an audience and promote the company and its solution offering(s) I would recommend considering thinking outside of the box and trying something different and unique to attract people to your booth.

Do not overlook the salesperson's abilities, background, and experiences to see if something can easily and inexpensively be utilized to differentiate the company and its offering(s).

EVENT MARKETING ADVERTISEMENT

Some companies elect to be more selective and focused on the type of marketing events (conferences, trade shows, seminars, etc.) they will attend and/or to which they will send people (sales, sales support, etc.) depending on budgets. Reductions of marketing events being attended, combined with the reduction of company's personnel, make it even more critical to maximize the impact of the message on attendees/prospects.

Many of the marketing events (e.g., trade shows, conferences, etc.) have keynote speakers planned for general sessions and then also have mini sessions (breakout sessions) based on topical content, such as job functions, industry, material type(s), etc., and often ask for volunteers from the industry who have experience and are knowledgeable to lead these sessions. One strategy that can be beneficial for your company/salespeople is to be an actual participant in the event. One approach is to have your company's customer(s) volunteer to present or lead a topic of discussion.

When your customer(s) volunteer for an event, the salesperson should assist or copresent with the session/topic. The intent is not to be able to provide a sales presentation during this particular breakout or mini session, but rather to provide topical information along with the customer who volunteered as an expert on the subject. This also provides an opportunity for the presenter and the salesperson to explain how the topic of the session was addressed and resolved by utilizing the salesperson's solution offering(s), while subtly delivering the salesperson's and company's message in front of prospects who may not pass through the trade show floor area. Another benefit is that presenters and copresenters also have an opportunity to attend other breakout sessions, as well as planned social events (receptions, dinners, etc.). This allows additional contact with attendees, as well as an additional conversation topic, such as whether they attended the breakout session, a request for feedback, etc., which leads to a conversation about how their company is addressing the session's topic.

Example:

A particular event focuses on distribution organizations, and one of your customers volunteer to lead a breakout session on the topic of inventory control. The goal of the session is to provide information about the importance of inventory control and how the customer addressed and resolved inventory control issues/needs with the assistance of your company's solution offering(s).

The salesperson attends the session to answer audience questions and to provide additional information. This provides an opportunity to gain an introduction to individuals interested in the importance of inventory control and provides audience members' names to follow up.

The result is an opportunity to have a one-on-many interaction with people interested and involved in the subject matter and provides leads for the salesperson.

Another benefit is that in most cases, those individuals volunteering to be a presenter/speaker at an event may have their registration fee(s) waived or reduced. In certain cases, the company whose solution offering is being represented may assist in offsetting expense(s) for the customer to attend and volunteer to present at a session. Each company should check with their business/legal counsel regarding business rules and ethics prior to scheduling a customer-assisted event.

Creating an opportunity to be in front of several individuals at an event is more advantageous, valuable, and profitable than setting up a booth and hoping attendees will stop by to hear what you and your company have to offer.

PROMOTING COMPANY IMAGE

Let us think about how well-known companies market themselves, their brand, and their image.

While traveling through any large city across America, one sees advertisements of well-known national companies. Think about what image automatically comes to mind and how you can recognize the company by its brand and image, even without words indicating the company's name.

Staying with this theme, think about when someone within the industry in which you work mentions the company name or sees the company's logo. What image comes to their mind?

Do you think there is a clear-cut image and branding that allows them to know, understand, and remember what the company does and provides?

If individuals from your industry see your company's name and logo and there is not a company image and/or branding that comes to mind and they do not know what your company provides, then there is an opportunity to address and make improvements to the marketing message.

As company leadership and salespeople attend public events, they should be aware of and evaluate other companies' marketing, advertising, and branding. Which marketing messages are eye-catching, create interest, and are memorable, and *why*?

Is it the ones with the most print, most pictures, and unique logo, or is it an eye-catching image causing people to stop and take a second look? Also, evaluate other marketing campaigns. Are some so busy and confusing the viewer thinks, *This is difficult to figure out what the message is, so I will move along to the next one?*

Some of the top companies' messaging utilizes a mixture of consistently repeating their image (logo) along with memorable messages. This creates and presents a consistent image experience in users' minds while conveying the message as simply as possible. The image and message need to be unique and interesting in order to stand apart (and above) other companies. Think back to some of the most memorable marketing advertisements and promotions and consider why they were so memorable, and then try to incorporate that type of advertisement into your company's message.

The salesperson and the marketing department should strive to provide a unique and memorable marketing message experience to set their company and solution offering(s) apart from the sea of other marketing messages barraging prospects in today's world.

MARKETING DIFFERENTLY

It has been said, "Companies who take a completely different approach to marketing in their industry will stand to achieve the greatest success."

There's another saying that applies well to companies' marketing strategies: "Dare to be different; otherwise, you too will be one within the masses that had a great story to tell but no one to listen."

In today's world, it is especially important to deliver a marketing message differentiating the company and its solution offering(s).

THINKING ABOUT "WHY AND HOW"
PEOPLE PURCHASE

To a large degree, individuals make purchasing decisions based on some level of emotional involvement and then supplement and support the decision with logic. If a salesperson can get the potential purchaser(s) emotionally involved and emotionally vested in the solution offering(s), the possibility for a successful sales outcome increases. Therefore, it pays dividends to be creative and original when approaching marketing strategies as the ability for creating emotional involvement appears in various forms.

SEPARATING YOUR MARKETING MESSAGE

How can a salesperson and their company reach potential purchasers?

Take one or two days and keep track of the number of marketing messages you encounter in just a few days. Then, think about the traditional methods of marketing and how the company is marketing to their target audience(s). Since we are constantly being barraged by marketing messaging from organizations, what can the company do to differentiate and separate themselves, along with their marketing message, from the crowd?

Think about utilizing slogans or sayings that tie together your company's image, branding, and solution offering(s), such as "Every sol-U-tion we offer...includes 'U' in it!"

CUTTING TEETH ON TECHNOLOGY

Marketing and sales organizations should be considering ways to utilize available technology as today's society is becoming more familiar with embracing, utilizing, and depending on the latest technology.

Kids are literally cutting their teeth on technology. Look around at any large public family gathering, and you will see kids using a cellular phone. Children are riding around in strollers, playing with (sometimes chewing) on their parent's cellular phone.

If they are handed a cellular phone, grade school kids know what is required to access the icon for pictures on the phone and how to move from one picture to the next and change the size and picture attributes (portrait, landscape, etc.) when viewing the phone's photograph gallery/album.

As time moves forward, consumers are becoming more comfortable and accepting of technology. Salespeople and companies should keep this in mind when considering marketing campaigns. Most young adults today grew up being digitally native. Most grew up utilizing computerized toys, games, tables, laptops, cellular phones, etc.—even electronic crayon(s).

MARKETING AND MOBILE DEVICES

Mobile applications are exploding in today's world, making it easier and quicker to access and collect information. These applications are making it easier to accomplish tasks for companies and society. Marketing and salespeople should explore methods to utilize and exploit this information bonanza as the trend is likely to continue.

It has been said that many future opportunities for companies will be in the content, applications, and mobile devices environment(s). These are areas where companies should consider spending time, energy, and resources as these are what users/consumers want. Therefore, they are areas companies should be trying to leverage and integrate with their solution offering(s), such as cellular phones, Internet applications, etc.

MARKETING PERCEPTION

Salespeople should view the sales cycle and sales elements similarly to how farmers look at growing crops. If one is in the farming industry, decisions need to be made early on as to what crops (seeds) will be planted in what fields and what fields should be utilized for each crop based on some form of decision criteria, as well as what materials and resources are going to be needed for each crop (field). Then, each field needs to be properly prepared and conditioned prior to planting of seeds. Then, the proper machinery needs to be utilized to plant the seeds, ensuring they have the best chance to grow. Next, the proper elements are required to ensure the seeds can grow, such as water, sunlight, and nutrients. During the growing cycle, some crops may need additional elements to ensure they can make it to harvest, which happens when the time and conditions are right based on environmental factors and criteria.

The farmer plans, prepares, and is required to complete elements of crop growing several months in advance of harvesting and recognizing the fruits of their labor.

Similarly, it is important for salespeople to condition and prepare their sales territory and determine what solution offering(s) should be offered to what potential purchaser(s) based on some criteria. Then, they must conduct marketing campaigns, planting seeds to potential purchasers, and offer supporting proof sources to ensure the interest level continues to grow until the conditions and timing are appropriate to complete the sales cycle and contract agreement.

Like the farmer, the salesperson should understand the action items needed to plan, prepare, and strategize are sown many months (or in some cases, longer) prior to having the sale come to fruition depending on business environmental factors and criteria.

DIFFERENT VERSUS SAME

Some company's are producing marketing materials representing the perception that their solution offering(s) is *similar* to what the competition provides and therefore, are offering the same type of solution offering(s). While, on the other hand, the sales department is out promoting the perceptions of *why* and *how* their company's solution offering is *different* and better than any of the competitors.

Companies in very popular and competitive markets offering similar solution offering(s) are utilizing a marketing methodology to create separation and differentiation in the marketplace. So, rather than producing marketing materials "commoditizing" their offering, where they look and act like others in the industry, they are separating their company and their solution offering(s) by marketing and promoting themselves by differentiating the product(s)/service(s) they provide. Some of these companies are not just selling a solution(s) that can accomplish a task, but rather a solution(s) that can improve lives or make people safer. They are incorporating emotion into why their product should be purchased.

By looking and acting like the competition, the perception of the company is that the solution offering is a commoditized solution, and therefore should be competing in the same environment with other competitors that may not be at the same price point or that may not offer the same functionality and features, let alone the same value and benefits. If a company does not want to have their solution offering commoditized (considering the same as competitors), they should consider redefining their solution offering branding and nomenclature. This can provide the perception the solution offering(s) are unique, providing higher quality and better results and involving emotion, resulting in a more effective and desirable solution.

UTILIZING MARKETING TO CHANGE THE RULES

One approach to separating and differentiating a company from the competition is to change, create, or revise the use of terminology and naming (nomenclature) as opposed to utilizing pseudo industry terms, and thus commoditizing and diluting the value and benefits of a company's solution offering(s). Think about how national fast-food chain restaurants introduce new items on their menu. Even though their new offering may contain similar ingredients, look similar, and have a similar result when utilized as their competition, they determine a marketing strategy and naming convention that fits into their branding image while separating it from the competition.

Take time to consider how your company's existing solution offering(s) interact with the company's branding and naming convention. Also, look at how any newly developed and/or offered solution(s) naming conventions is going to fit into the existing solution offering, along with the company's branding image.

Consider evaluating your company's current solution offering and brand messaging to determine if prospects are commoditizing the solution offering(s) based on the branding, naming convention, and industry terminology utilized in marketing materials. Then, determine what changes may be made to assist in differentiating the company and its solution offering(s) resulting as innovators and leaders in the industry.

Do not be apprehensive about exploring the opportunities to create, redefine, and reestablish your branding and naming convention to differentiate your solution within your industry. When a company begins to utilize and emphasize its solution's specific naming convention with prospects and customers, the company may be surprised how individuals will also begin to utilize the same naming convention. This differentiates and separates the company's solution(s).

When prospects and customers begin utilizing the company's new naming convention and branding is when the company begins to truly gain buy-in from prospects and differentiation from competitors. Then, when the competition tries to gain access to your customers, they will be viewed as a "commodity solution" and grouped with "all the other competitors."

NEW MARKETING CONCEPT

In today's competitive marketplace, companies are looking for ways to increase market share, customers, and profitability while staying within their financial budget(s) and delivering exceptional solutions and services to their customers.

One new marketing concept is for vendors that provide solutions that complement each other's solution offering(s) to work together, combining their marketing and sales efforts at events. This marketing and sales approach may become more prevalent moving forward where complementary vendors will collaborate to provide conferences, seminars, and prospect/customer meetings (based on geography, solutions, etc.), as well as potentially sharing lead generation and mentioning complementary solution offering(s) within each other's sales representation(s).

This marketing strategy allows for multiple vendors to come together to provide seminar(s)/meeting(s) to mutual prospects and customer base(s), utilizing the value and benefit of each of the vendors to draw in attendees. This leverages the synergy of the interest level(s) of the vendor's solution offering(s) and allows the attendees to see and hear about each of the vendors and their solution offering(s).

The result is that rather than each vendor marketing and advertising just their solution offering(s) to those individuals who may be interested in a specific solution, an opportunity is provided for each vendor to participate in sharing and offsetting proportional costs associated with the seminar/meeting while receiving the benefit of reaching multiple prospects and/or customers, providing a "one-on-many" opportunity and exposure to new prospects who may not be familiar with the solution offering(s)... for a fraction of the investment of conducting a seminar on their own.

The benefit to the attendees is that they learn, view, and inquire about multiple vendors' solution(s) and how these solutions may work or integrate together to make more of a complete business solution/system for their company, such as mobile technology and application providers, computer hardware and software applications, etc.

Each vendor's sales personnel are potentially exposed to new prospects along with the benefit of learning and being able to provide high-level information about their complementary counterpart's solutions (sales crossover and cross-training) to drive interest in each other's solution offering(s).

CREATING PRESENTATIONS
AND DEMONSTRATIONS

There seems to be two schools of thought in regard to which department should create, design, and develop an organization's sales presentation and/or demonstration of the company's solution offering(s). One thought is the marketing department should create the sales presentation(s) and demonstration(s) to insure consistent image, branding, and message delivery of the information provided to potential purchasers. Companies that have this philosophy often think the marketing department should be responsible for creating and delivering RFP, RFQ responses, and proposals.

Another thought is for the sales presentation and/or demonstration to be created, designed, and developed by the sales department, utilizing information provided and/or supplemented by the marketing department. This approach allows the individual salesperson to create and design the presentation to show the value and benefits as they pertain to potential purchaser(s) needs, challenges, issues, and goals.

When the marketing department is responsible for creating the sales department's presentation and/or demonstration, the result can be a presentation of comprehensive materials that can be overpowering and provide copious information about *every* area of the solution offering(s), which may not be of interest to a prospect. The reason for this copious information is that the marketing department tries to produce a "standardized" company presentation that is "all encompassing" to "any and all" prospects. Therefore, the presentation is designed and developed trying to include every scenario a purchaser(s) may have interest. This approach is understandable however, salespeople should review and customize the presentation/demonstration to fit the situation and time frame(s) allowed by each prospect.

Please note: If the company has a "standard" and/or "official" company presentation that is to be utilized, then make sure to obtain proper approval and/or permission prior to altering (customizing) the presentation/demonstration for prospects.

The risk of a salesperson not customizing the presentation for audiences is that the salesperson spends time delivering information (features/functionality) the audience may not be interested in seeing or hearing. By spending time on items not of interest to the audience, the salesperson risks the chance of audience member(s) "disengaging" as they have little interest in the information being delivered. Should this happen audience members can suddenly have 'something' to do which requires their attention because the presentation/demonstration appears to be a data and feature listing of the solution offering(s), and not focused on their particular needs and goals.

If the salesperson works with an organization that provides a "standard or official" company presentation, I would recommend reviewing the information and determining what value and benefits, as well as, features and functionality that provide appropriate information for the audience and can be delivered effectively given the time frame allotted.

I also recommend going one step further and customizing (annotations, transitions, animation, etc.) the presentation to reflect your presentation style, effectively making it *your* presentation. By doing this, you will feel much more comfortable delivering the information, and the audience will know it, and will appreciate it!

MARKETING CAUTION

Salespeople should be careful when sending out marketing messages, such as e-mail, letters, etc., to confirm the message(s) are not violating any company policies and/or legal rules and restrictions.

It is also advisable to provide gender-neutral correspondence and voice mails when uncertain of the gender of the contact. Be careful when addressing individuals as Ms., Mrs., or Mr. unless it is known for sure. People prefer to be addressed by their correct gender, which can be tricky with some first names, such as Chris, Kim, Gerry, Robin, etc.

I worked with a guy named Kim, and he had been communicating with a prospect through e-mail as a result of a marketing campaign. When Kim found out he was going to be in the prospect's city for another meeting, he sent an e-mail asking if the prospect had time to meet while he was in town, as he would like to stop by and introduce himself. The prospect happened to be a male who suggested they should meet at a popular local restaurant. Just prior to the meeting time, the prospect sent a text to my coworker, letting him know he had arrived at the restaurant and was the good-looking guy sitting at a table next to the fireplace wearing a dark suit with a blue tie.

The prospect was somewhat surprised when my coworker Kim walked up to the table and introduced himself as the person he was meeting.

They were both good sports about the slight confusion, but it's a good reminder and lesson for salespeople to know who they are meeting.

TEXTING

It is estimated that over eight trillion texts are sent annually (approximately two hundred thousand texts are sent every second), making texting more common and acceptable as time goes on. Be cautious of utilizing texting as an official form of communication until a prospect and/or customer text you, which informally signifies this is an acceptable form of communication. However, this form of communication will continue to be more accepted and possibly preferred as society becomes more comfortable with technology.

One of the risks with texting is that the person receiving may misinterpret the "meaning and demeanor" of what is being communicated. Abbreviations utilized may not be understood as intended.

As an example, receiving a text message stating, "Whatever," can be interpreted a couple different ways (e.g., it does not matter because there is no preference, or what has been stated is not believable or true).

SUMMARY

Marketing activities are important to the success of a salesperson, and no matter who provides it or how it is provided, it is necessary to reach quotas, achievements, and goals. It is critical to perform activities that are going to drive interest in and curiosity about the company and solution offering(s).

The numerous marketing techniques and methods are almost infinite, being limited only by imagination and budget.

Salespeople should market their solution offering(s) from the purchaser(s)/user(s) position rather than the seller's point of view.

When it comes to marketing campaigns, salespeople should think in terms of *"multiple streams of selling."* Salespeople should consider marketing methods and techniques for being able to provide exposure to target markets.

Marketing and sales organizations should consider ways to utilize technology as today's society is becoming more familiar with embracing, utilizing, and depending on technology. This trend is likely to continue.

Providing proof sources can be beneficial and powerful, assisting in reducing decision maker's risk(s).

Keep in mind, individuals make purchasing decisions based on some level of emotional involvement, and then supplement and support the decision with logic.

Do not under estimate the power of "simple" marketing concepts such as the Cowboy Yo-Yo.

Companies that take a different approach to marketing in their industry will stand to achieve the greatest success.

It is advisable to personalize information left with the potential purchaser(s). This can be accomplished by something as simple as handwriting information on the materials making it personalized to the individual.

A salesperson should develop a repository and database of customer testimonials, quotes, comments, and statements to support ongoing marketing efforts about the success recognized and achieved with the solution offering(s).

Dare to be different; otherwise, your company will be one within the masses that had a great story to tell but no one to listen.

Like the farmer, the salesperson should understand the action items needed to plan, prepare, and strategize are sown many months prior to having the sale come to fruition.

LESSON 14

CALL AND MEETING PREPARATION

It is unusual for every sales call and meeting to go the same (or even similarly). The unique environment and situation of each sales opportunity provides a salesperson the opportunity to utilize their skill set and techniques to analyze and strategize how to be successful in whatever situation and environment they encounter.

This is similar to competing in rodeo events around the country in that there are rarely two arenas the contestants compete in that are exactly the same. There are differences in arena size, ground, and weather conditions, as well as the event(s) livestock.

Therefore, it is the responsibility (job) of each of the rodeo competitors to figure out how to utilize the environment presented by each arena and animal(s) selected and then analyze and strategize the best way to apply their experience and skill set to compete successfully.

I was not always a proponent of conducting proper "formal" preparation for phone calls and meetings. In my early sales career, I was more of a shoot-from-the-hip and adjust-on-the-fly salesperson. This ability may still assist in certain situations when things may not be going as planned, but I have discovered there is a better and easier method that lessens the anxiety level considerably.

I have learned the benefits of being prepared and focused on what the objective is of each phone call(s) and meeting(s).

Earlier in my career, I seemed to always be busy and distracted by a number of things that needed to be completed within some time frame. Therefore, I would simply spend a few minutes (or seconds) preparing for prospecting calls and, in most cases, inevitably end up just dialing and hoping to adjust on the fly during the call.

As my career progressed, it became apparent that preparation is essential for maximizing the time and effectiveness of phone calls and meetings, as well as improving the chances of a positive and successful sales outcome.

Early on, it was apparent I did not quite understand and was not aware of the importance and impact the first impression of a phone call or meeting had on prospects and customers, as well as subsequent phone calls and meetings. Looking back, I believed that if a call or meeting did not go well, the prospect would provide another chance for me to improve, which is rarely the case. In today's fast-paced and busy world, a salesperson is fortunate to get *one* chance to meet and make an impression on a potential purchaser(s), let alone a mulligan (do-over) meeting to go back and present and offer what was intended. Therefore, communication preparation is critical and important, making it imperative that salespeople take time to prepare for calls and meetings.

IMPORTANCE OF FIRST IMPRESSIONS

Growing up, I had a friend who said, "You only get *one* chance to make a *FIRST* impression!" Later, I learned how prophetic this statement would become in sales and in my career.

It has been said that individuals make assumptions and form opinions of others within seconds whether on the phone or in person. Although as a society, we may have become more understanding and accepting, people still form immediate opinions of others based on their own individual experiences, and these initial opinions are made very quickly.

Now, there are times when individuals' impressions and opinions can be changed over time, as people can make an inaccurate assumption about someone. However, science has shown that most people will form an opinion, along with some assumptions, about another person very quickly, whether it is during an initial phone call or meeting. Therefore, it is imperative as salespeople that we do everything we can and strive to make a good and positive first impression on everyone we meet, but especially prospects and customers.

Whether people will admit it or not, there have been scientific studies that show we all seem to form some type of immediate opinion(s) and impression(s) of another based on our own experiences, culture, background, and upbringing. We then utilize this base experience as a pattern(s) when meeting and communicating with another for the first time. We take note of their voice (tone, volume, pace, etc.), mannerisms, and appearance (grooming, clothing, etc.). Science has shown individuals tend to accept those who appear to resemble those associated with their experience pattern(s), such as existing circle of friends, associates, coworkers, etc., more quickly than those who may not fit the experience pattern(s) as closely.

In giving this consideration...have you purchased something requiring significant investment from someone you did not like (for whatever reason)? If so, what are the chances that you would purchase from that same person again? Especially if it could be purchased from someone else who you may like more?

It appears that, if given a choice, consumers prefer to purchase and conduct business with individuals they like and who they feel share some form of experience(s) and connection.

Therefore, knowing individuals who the salesperson will be communicating (e-mail, phone, meeting) with for the first time will be forming an opinion and impression of them very quickly, it would stand to reason that the salesperson be as prepared as possible to make the best first impression on each individual encountered.

FIRST IMPRESSION

It is important to make sure to take advantage of the first opportunity and put your best effort and impression on display when meeting people. This is especially important for salespeople when dealing with potential purchaser(s).

It has been said, "Do not judge a book by its cover or a person by how they might appear."

Several years ago, as a member of a speaking group, I performed a speech titled "First Impressions."

This speech was motivated by, and the result of, the comment my friend had said many years before.

On the day of the speech, I approached the podium in front of the audience; dressed in a three-piece business suit (this was a several years ago). The business suit consisted of matching jacket, vest, and pants and was completed by a white dress shirt, undershirt, long necktie, socks, and shoes.

The first part of the speech focused and represented information regarding how research has shown how individuals will make assumptions based on another person's appearance.

After providing several minutes of compiled research data along with examples consisting of how people make assumptions about a person and product(s), I then went on to describe and provide information as to how our impression(s) and perception(s) may also contain flaws by providing some examples of individuals who might initially present us with different perceptions based their first impressions.

I then walked into the audience, picked up an empty chair, and set it down in front of the audience. I then stood on the chair, allowing the audience to be able to view me, head to feet.

At this point, I stated, "Some of you may have made assumptions about me as I approached the podium today based on how I appeared, but how would your perception change if I would have approached the podium as..."

1. Taking off the suit jacket, showing the sleeves of the shirt had been shredded, and asking if the audience's perception had changed?

2. Then continued, by taking the tie out of the vest, revealing the last several inches of the tie had also been shredded.

3. Then taking off the vest, revealing the shirt had been discolored with different color mark-a-lots that had been previously concealed by the vest. Again I asked the audience if their perception changed?

4. Then continuing, I hiked up my pant leg bottoms, revealing mismatched socks.

5. Then, I quickly untied and kicked off one of my shoes, revealing holes in the sock (one of which revealed the big toe).

So, I was now standing atop a chair in front of the audience with a shredded shirt and tie, stained shirt, and mismatched and holey socks.

I then asked the audience if their impression and perception of me had changed and if their impression and perception of the information provided earlier had changed.

Also, I asked if their impression and perception of the value and validity of the information provided would have been differently perceived and received if it would have been provided and delivered while at the podium looking like they view me now.

The audience appreciated the speech topic and performance, and as a result, this writer was rewarded with a "Best Speech Award," which was determined by the audience members' vote.

This speech provided a good opportunity to validate and confirm my friend's statement regarding the importance of making a good first impression to audiences and how a person can affect the perception and expectation of an audience.

THE W-6 IDENTIFIERS/QUESTIONS

One might think it would be intuitive for a salesperson to understand and gather certain information from prospects. However, you might be surprised by the number of times there is an interaction and communication between a prospect and a salesperson with little to no pertinent information gathered or exchanged in regard to the potential purchaser(s) situation, need(s), challenge(s), or issue(s) or appropriate information regarding the salesperson's solution offering(s).

I understand when interacting with a prospect or customer that there should be time for some customary pleasantries and light conversation, but depending on the time frame of the interaction, it is important for the salesperson to leave gaining knowledge of the prospect and/or their business, as well as the follow-up action(s) or activity(s) and time frame(s) to complete.

Therefore, utilize the W-6's as a way to remind a salesperson to gather information from those individuals who may become potential purchasers. These can also be utilized for recording and formalizing prospecting information and referring back to at a later date.

The W-6 Identifiers are: **W**ho, **W**hat, **W**here, **W**hen, **W**hy, and ho**W**.

If the salesperson can identify these elements for each sales opportunity, it will be easier to move the prospect(s) through the sales process and improve the chance of completing a successful sales opportunity:

❖ Who...such as *who* is the company the salesperson is meeting with, *who* will be involved in the decision criteria and decision making, etc.?

❖ What...such as *what* is their current environment and situation, *what* is the reason for considering a change, *what* is the decision-making criteria, *what* is the time frame for making any decision(s), etc.?

❖ Where...such as *where* is their office(s) located, *where* will the solution offering(s) be utilized, *where* will the presentation, demonstration take place, etc.?

❖ <u>When</u>...such as *when* will the decision be made, *when* would the company like to begin utilizing the selected solution(s), *when* would training and implementation begin, etc.?

❖ <u>Why</u>...such as *why* is the company considering a change (upcoming or impending event), *why* are they looking at making a change at this time, etc.?

❖ <u>hoW</u>...such as *how* will each vendor and their solution offering(s) be evaluated, *how* would the company like to have the proposal presented, etc.?

A salesperson should be thinking about the W-6 questions when preparing for an interaction with a prospect/customer. The W-6's should assist a salesperson in focusing on what information is important and required for qualifying the opportunity and provide information for moving the opportunity forward.

The following are some high-level business resource areas and describe how the W-6's can be utilized for presenting questions and gathering valuable information as it pertains to a potential sales opportunity, such as:

1. Inventory Management:
   - *What* does the prospect's company sell (solutions, products, services, etc.) and provide to their customers and their industry?
   - *hoW* does the company manage their business to insure product visibility, availability, deliverability, and supportability of their solution offering(s)?

2. Budgeting:
   - *hoW* does the company establish and set budget parameters for purchases?
   - *What* challenges are encountered during this process?
   - *hoW* does the company evaluate and determine what purchases will be made and *when* they will be made?

3. Accountability:
   - *Who* will be involved and responsible for making the purchasing decision(s) for the company?
   - *Who* will sign the contract once a decision is finalized?

4. System:
   - *hoW* is the current system meeting the company's needs and expectations?
   - *hoW* do employees and customers access and have visibility to the company's resources (sales items, inventory, services, etc.)?
   - *What* areas of improvement(s) would the company like to see in a new solution(s)?
5. Reporting:
   - *HoW* does the current system provide required and needed business reporting?
   - *What* additional reporting capabilities would the company like to have in a new system?
   - *What* issues does the company encounter by not being able to have timely and accurate reporting?
6. Staff and Personnel:
   - *What* changes would company staff and departments like to make to their current system?
   - *What* are the challenges, issues, needs, etc.?

I understand the high-level business and resource areas may be different for industries, markets, and companies you may be working with, but the intent is to understand from the example provided how to utilize the W-6's to structure questions to acquire important information from prospects. Gaining this information can assist in further qualifying the opportunity and allows for referring back to documented information while moving through the sales process.

GAINING PERTINENT INFORMATION

Preparation for prospect/customer phone calls and meetings can be as structured, informal, formal, and extensive as each individual salesperson would like (or need). The goal is not the worksheet document(s) themselves, but rather to gain and capture pertinent information from potential purchasers for understanding and clarifying information to be utilized for qualifying the opportunity and processing and strategizing the acquired information as you move forward through the sales cycle.

How the document is laid out or structured and how much of it is utilized is each salesperson's personal preference. This provides flexibility and allows for various questions/answers, gaining the information deemed necessary to qualify the opportunity and capture pertinent information.

I have accompanied other salespeople to meetings where they did not utilize any type of structured meeting process, such as W-6 questions, discussion items, goal(s) for the meeting, or action items for moving the sales opportunity forward. After spending the largest portion of the meeting making light conversation, the meeting time expired, and the salesperson left the meeting having little knowledge of the environment, the prospect's situation, or what opportunity there may be within the account.

Both individual's time could have been better utilized discussing and sharing pertinent information about their organizations and their personal roles within each. After spending an appropriate amount of time with light conversation, it is important to move to the reason for the meeting and to have a mutually beneficial information exchange, allowing both parties to end the meeting with more information than when the meeting started.

Having a structured format plan will improve the chances of leaving the meeting with information needed to qualify and move the opportunity forward.

It is also a good idea to utilize a structured document and/or format to ensure important questions and information are not left out, overlooked, or forgotten during an interaction. It is much easier to have the questions and information documented when leaving the meeting than to call back to gain information that was needed to qualify and move the opportunity forward. Besides, it also makes the salesperson appear more prepared and professional to the prospect(s).

Also, if your sales management team is similar to mine in the past, they are going to be aware of the meeting and are probably going to inquire as to information gained in regard to the sales potential, such as *who* is the company, *who* did you meet, *what* are they currently utilizing, *what* are they interested in purchasing, etc., along with requesting the salesperson make a forecast prediction regarding *what* solution offering(s) the account is interested in purchasing, *when* and *how* much. To avoid overlooking those questions which are going to be queried by sales management, or trying to remember details from each opportunity, it is much easier to have this information documented, as well as, being able to refer back to the information when needed.

Another manner for utilizing the W-6's for a salesperson is when meeting prospects for the first time, as answering the W-6's is an easy way to identify yourself while assisting in steering the conversation.

These areas help in identifying what individual(s) within an organization may want to know about the salesperson:

* ❖ *Who* is the salesperson (name)?
* ❖ *Where* is the salesperson from (company's name and city, state, etc.)?
* ❖ *Why* are they visiting the office (*what* is the purpose of the meeting)?
* ❖ *What* are the area(s) to be discussed (topics)?
* ❖ *What* is to be accomplished during the meeting?
* ❖ *When* will follow-up and next step(s) be completed?
* ❖ *hoW* will the follow-up take place (meeting, calls, e-mail, etc.)?

PLANNING DOCUMENT

The following activities and actions can be utilized for providing value to a prospect(s), as well as gaining valuable and pertinent information:

1. The opening of the conversation and/or meeting letting the prospect(s)/customer(s) know:
   a. Who you are and the company you represent.
   b. General purpose and reason for the communication/interaction.

     c. Quick advertisement delivering value proposition, including value and benefits statement(s).

     d. Ask permission to be able to ask questions and learn more about the organization. It is beneficial for the salesperson to *ask permission to ask questions,* as the initial question itself gets people in the mode of answering questions, and it is rare for someone to say *no* to the initial question.

2. Utilize W-6 questions for gaining information about the organization, as well as the contact(s). Confirm information that might have been gained from other sources (website, articles, etc.), prior to making assumptions about the organization's current environment and situation.

     • Continue utilizing W-6 questions to drill down further into specific issues, challenges, and problems that have been identified and can be addressed by the solution offering(s).

3. Identify and explain how other organizations have utilized the solution offering(s) to address similar issues, needs, and challenges that mirror the prospect's.

4. Gain permission and agreement to move forward with additional steps, providing additional information, follow-up phone call(s) and/or meeting(s), etc.

5. Inquire and confirm who else within the organization will be involved with the decision making, as well as who else may benefit by having additional knowledge and information about the solution offering(s).

6. Closing and wrap-up. State action items, along with follow-up item(s) and associated time frame(s).

7. Thank them for the information provided and their time spent for the information exchange.

W-6's DOCUMENT	
Account Name:	
Date:	
Name:	
Role/Position:	
Individual Contact Information:	Office Phone: Cellular Phone: Email:
W-6's Question Identifiers: (Examples)	1) Who...will be involved in the decision making process?
	2) What...is the decision criteria?
	3) Where...will the solution offering(s) be utilized, where are the decision makers office(s) located?
	4) When...will the decision be made (timing)?
	5) Why...is the company considering a change?
	6) hoW...will the decision be made (process)?
Top Issue(s)/Challenge(s)/ Goal(s):	

(Match with solution offerings Values and Benefits):	1) Business Process(es).
	2) Customer Service.
	3) Profitability.
	4) Etc.
Unique Account Information:	
(Formal and Informal Organization Chart):	1) Who is/are the decision maker(s)?
	2) Who is/are influencing the decision maker(s)?
Presentation Items:	
	1) Major points/issues/goals, audience member(s) and expectations, potential themes, etc.
	2) Unique business processes, procedures, forms, reports, etc.
	3) Etc.

HOW IMPORTANT IS A PLANNING DOCUMENT?

While on a flight after a meeting, I happened to be sitting next to an airline pilot, dressed in uniform, who was sitting in the passenger area of the plane flying back to Denver International Airport. Having flown regularly for many years and having much interest in airplanes and how they and airports operate, I felt this particular situation provided an opportunity to ask a few questions that had often been thought about in regard to the workings and operations of airplanes and airports.

After exchanging personal greetings and some initial light conversation, such as if he should be up front flying the plane, the weather for the flight, where he was from, how he felt about sitting back with passengers, etc., I realized the gentleman was quite friendly and talkative, so thought I would utilize this opportunity to ask some of my questions.

One question was, "Both the pilot and copilot seem to be very busy with paperwork, checking on instruments, adjusting knobs and settings, as passengers are being loaded onto the aircraft for takeoff, as well as when the aircraft is approaching an airport for landing. So, do pilots have all the required activities needed for takeoff and landing memorized, or do they utilize checklists (planning documents)?"

His response was, "Well, we certainly have all the necessary elements and activities for both takeoff and landing the aircraft committed to memory. However, we also perform takeoffs and landing procedures *by the book*. We have a checklist document that is utilized *'each time.'*" Then he went on to say they also had additional documentation that provided supplementary information about the aircraft should they need it for any reason or if something out of the ordinary was encountered.

The pilot's response to the question started me thinking. If it is important and essential for a planning document (checklist) to be utilized for pilots in charge of a multimillion dollar aircraft and many lives to help ensure the task is performed correctly and insuring nothing is forgotten or overlooked *each time*, it certainly could not hurt for a salesperson to have and utilize the same philosophy.

Utilization of a planning document (checklist) can allow the salesperson to be more prepared for a call and/or meeting and also provide helpful and supplemental information for those unexpected situations that may be encountered during a call and/or meeting.

BEING PREPARED FOR A CALL AND/OR MEETING

A few years ago, I had only been with a company for a short period of time and had been attempting to schedule an initial (introductory) meeting with a prospect in Texas. At that particular time, I was traveling to Texas every couple months. Each time I was making plans to travel to Texas, I would contact this particular prospect to check their availability for an introductory meeting and to learn more about their organization.

This process went on for several months. Each time a trip was planned to Texas, I would reach out to the prospect regarding their availability to meet.

Then one day, while in Texas conducting prospect and customer meetings, a meeting got cancelled, so I called to see if it would be possible for me to stop by for an introduction and possibly meet with someone from the company's management team, allowing for improving the probability of scheduling an additional meeting the next time I was in Texas.

I was able to reach the IT Director, and he said he had availability to meet in approximately an hour. I was excited about the opportunity to meet with this individual and strengthen the relationship with the prospect's organization.

When I arrived at the prospect's location just minutes prior to the meeting, I was able to review a meeting planning document that I had prepared several weeks prior in anticipation of meeting with the prospect. I took a few minutes to review the information that had been researched on the account and recorded in the planning document, enabling me to become familiar with management names, titles, and information that had been provided from their company's website, along with W-6 questions that would allow for gaining additional information about their company's environment, situation, needs, etc.

After quickly reviewing the information in the planning document, as well as reviewing what pieces of information were missing, I headed into the building for the meeting. I entered the prospect's building, introduced myself to the receptionist, and handed her a business card while stating the reason I was visiting them today.

The receptionist said, "Hello and welcome! We are glad you are here. Please follow me," and I was escorted down a long hallway that led to a door of a large meeting room that contained approximately twenty people.

As I walked through the door, the individual whom I had spoken with on the phone earlier in the day stood up, introduced himself, and shook my hand, stating, "We had another meeting scheduled for the next hour but decided to postpone that meeting so we could see your presentation instead."

Well, you might imagine my surprise, as the expectation for the meeting was a brief introductory meeting with one individual, and now I was getting an opportunity for an hour of management's time.

Remember the planning document reviewed just prior to the meeting? It allowed me to be better prepared by reviewing the information researched and captured on the company and also allowed me to be familiar with the management team and the products/services the company provided.

As a result of utilizing the planning document and appearing prepared, the meeting went well. Within the next few months, there were follow-up meetings, resulting in one of the largest sales opportunities completed that year.

So, would it have made a difference in the results if I had walked into the meeting unprepared and had not known the information and questions to ask prior to the presentation?

Similar to what the pilot explained earlier, I would like to think I certainly had the necessary elements and activities required for making this sell in my head. However, it never hurts to be prepared and perform sales procedures, *"by the book,"* or, in this case, *"by the planning document."*

PROSPECTING CALL AND/OR
MEETING OUTCOME(S)

There are basically four possible outcomes to a prospect/customer encounter.

1. *Interest Level*: "Little to no" interest from the prospect, in which the salesperson may want to reach out to additional individuals within the organization within a different department or organizational structure level. Then, if it is determined there really is not any interest at this time, the salesperson should ask permission to contact them periodically to see if their interest level changes, along with the opportunity to continue to provide information on the solution offering(s) and industry news updates. If agreed, the salesperson should put the account on a follow-up list to be contacted periodically (monthly, quarterly), as well as including on marketing events list(s).

2. *Extension:* Continuing the dialogue with follow-up conversation(s)/ meeting(s). There is a level of interest and they would like more information and have additional communication(s)/discussion(s) regarding the solution offering(s) to further explore the potential match and applicability of the solution offering(s).

3. *Progress:* Activities and actions for moving forward with additional steps in the sales process, such as scheduled meeting, analysis, presentation, demonstration, etc.

4. *Fulfillment:* This includes completion of add-on orders or smaller initial orders. These can be important for gaining access to an account and beginning (continuing) to build a relationship, allowing for additional access to information and individuals within an organization and acquiring additional knowledge for positioning larger sales opportunities.

SUMMARY

Individuals make assumptions and form opinions of others quickly, whether on the phone or in person.

You only get *one* chance to make a *FIRST* impression, so do not miss a chance to make a good first impression on potential purchaser(s).

The *W-6 questions/identifiers* are: *Who, What, Where, When, Why, and hoW.* The W-6 questions/identifiers can be utilized to gain information about prospect(s)/customer(s), company, people, environment, situation, and analysis.

Utilize a planning document to gain, capture, and plan for sales communications. The goal is to obtain and record pertinent information for qualifying the opportunity and then strategizing the opportunity moving forward through the sales cycle.

Sales call and meeting planning pays off in many different ways, from getting the information in a condensed and concise manner to continuing to accurately build the pipeline forecast and providing information to sales management.

Outcomes of prospecting include: Interest Level, Extension, Progress, and Fulfillment.

LESSON 15

NEEDS ANALYSIS... LEARNING WHAT IS IMPORTANT

Needs Analysis...making a salesperson smarter than a tree full of owls!

In an effort to assist and assure successful completions of sales opportunities, a salesperson needs to be able to identify, clarify, confirm, and learn those elements that are important to the potential purchaser(s). Here again, utilize the W-6 question identifiers to gain a better understanding of the environment and situation, such as:

❖ *Why* is the potential purchaser(s) interested in making a purchase?

❖ *What* do they want to accomplish by adding a solution offering(s) to their current business environment?

❖ *What* is the time frame for making a decision and completing the implementation/installation?

❖ *What* is the impending event and associated time frame?

❖ *What* is the purchasing motivation and decision criteria?

❖ *Who* will the decision be made (RFQ/RFP, presentations, etc.)?

❖ *Who* will be in charge of making the decision (individual, committee, group, etc.)?

❖ *What* anomalies and/or specific items and elements make this sales opportunity different and unique?

❖ *hoW* is the person(s) with the authority to sign a contract agreement?

I have attended meetings with my company's sales management when they began asking these basic types of questions in regard to sales opportunities that had been identified and forecasted for closing by a specified date.

If a salesperson is currently spending time, energy, and resources working with a sales opportunity, and depending on the sales stage, such as introductory, qualifying, meeting(s), proposal (RFP, RFQ), negotiations, closing, etc., the salesperson should have knowledge, such as *why* the prospect(s) is talking with the salesperson, *why* they are interested, *what* the purchasing motivation is, *why* they are considering adding or making a change to their environment, *what* their purchasing criteria is, *who* will be making the decision, and *who* has authority to sign a contract, among other items.

These pieces of information become more important as a salesperson begins to invest more of their time and company resources (additional departmental people, travel expenses, etc.) into moving the sales opportunity forward.

Salespeople can sometimes become overly optimistic in regard to the level of interest a potential purchaser(s) has in regard to their solution offering(s). This can be due to reasons, such as:

1. Salespeople by nature seem to be optimistic and therefore feel when an individual (prospect) expresses *any* interest in the

solution offering(s) it is automatically assumed there will be a high probability of closing the opportunity successfully.

2. Salespeople want to be known for doing a good job for the customer and the company.

3. There can be pressure from the sales management team to continue to grow the sales pipeline and forecast, leading to salespeople becoming overly optimistic when forecasting potential sales opportunities.

4. Sales management is aware there is a percentage of forecasted sales opportunities that may not close as predicted due to economic and industry factors, etc. Therefore, they may request each salesperson forecast a multiple over their assigned sales quota, such as 50-100 percent of quota (monthly, quarterly, annually).

PUZZLE SCENARIO

Many sales opportunities could be considered similar to a puzzle that the salesperson must solve in order to complete a successful sales cycle. The completion of the puzzle can be made easier with the assistance of the potential purchaser(s). However, sometimes it has to be resolved with limited assistance from the prospect due to a myriad of reasons, such as the prospect wanting to be equal and fair to all potential vendors, particular internal regulations, RFP and RFQ rules, etc. It seems the size of the sales opportunity often mirrors the size and difficulty of the puzzle to be solved, meaning that the larger the investment and the more individuals involved from the purchaser(s), the more difficult the puzzle may become to solve for the salesperson.

SALES PUZZLE CHALLENGE

Young kids' puzzles may consist of eight to ten large, colorful pieces with a fixed, wide puzzle border and easy-to-see images on each piece, along with a picture on the box cover showing how the puzzle should look when completed.

THE BUSINESS OF SALES | STEVEN M. MONKS

Adult puzzles can consist of 5,000 plus pieces and contain smaller and many similar-looking pieces. The coloring scheme can be much more subtle, and the puzzle border is contained within the actual puzzle pieces themselves. The box cover still provides an image of what the final completed puzzle should look like. Although the level of difficulty is greatly increased from the young kids' puzzle, the concept and techniques involved are much the same...the goal is to complete the puzzle (sale).

This simple puzzle illustration points out different levels of sales opportunities that can be encountered, but it can also be more difficult than first thought.

Consider the following when it comes to the puzzle and sales opportunities.

- What happens to the level of difficulty if the five thousand piece puzzle's border pieces are removed before starting? Traditional wisdom would say to begin with the puzzles border pieces.
- What would happen to the level of difficulty if some of the internal puzzle pieces were removed prior to beginning the process?
- What happens to the level of difficulty if the puzzle is put into a plain box with no picture of how the finished puzzle looks?
- What happens to the level of difficulty should the puzzle pieces be put into a different puzzle box, resulting in trying to put the puzzle together while working from an incorrect picture of the outcome?
- Lastly, what would happen to the level of difficulty if all the pieces had to stay in the box and the assembler had to pick one piece of the puzzle out at a time? If it did not fit to earlier removed pieces, then the assembler has to return it to the box and select another piece and keep repeating this process until the puzzle was completed?

As you can see, the level of difficulty and complexity can grow exponentially even when taking a familiar and simple process like putting a puzzle together when pieces of the puzzle (information) are removed from the overall picture or, in our case, the sales process.

Therefore, the individual assembling the five-thousand-piece puzzle is similar to the salesperson relying on their abilities to figure out a strategy enabling them to be able to analyze and break down the puzzle (sales process) into smaller sections (sales elements).

In keeping with the puzzle scenario, this could mean:

- Developing a strategy of dividing the five thousand pieces into smaller sections resulting in five puzzle sections of one thousand pieces.
- Displaying all the pieces of the puzzle on a flat surface with the color/image side facing up.
- Putting any straight edge border pieces together, forming an outline.
- Utilizing clues by viewing the picture on the puzzle box and locating specific area pieces.
- Grouping pieces with same or similar coloring together and working on each color section.

SALES ANALYSIS TOOL (SAT)

What tools and strategies can a salesperson utilize to assist in figuring out the sales opportunity puzzle?

One important element is for the salesperson to ask good and appropriate W-6 questions that allow potential purchaser(s) to provide substantive answers. Then, it is important for the salesperson to listen and record the answers provided.

It has been said that the secret to *talking* is *listening!* This is especially appropriate for sales as listening to answers provided will allow asking additional good and appropriate questions. Also, it is probably no coincidence that *"listen"* and *"silent"* have the same letters! After asking questions, the salesperson should be silent and listen to answers provided.

It is important for a salesperson to have analysis and qualifying questions written down prior to a phone or face-to-face conversation.

This will allow the salesperson to ask questions and then to listen and focus on the answers provided and will allow for further follow-up and/or clarification question(s), rather than focusing on what question they need or should ask next.

The Sales Analysis Tool (SAT) is designed to assist in identifying and communicating vital and key information in regard to sales opportunities. The idea behind the utilization of the Sales Analysis Tool (SAT) is for the salesperson to understand, acknowledge, and document what is *known* about the sales opportunity and, potentially more important, identify what they *do not know* about the sales opportunity.

The SAT provides a guide identifying the sales elements and factors that should be identified, clarified, and addressed/answered utilizing questions to identify the Circumstances, Issues, Impact, and Resolution/Options (CIIR) methodology, allowing the sales process to continue to move forward toward a successful completion of a contract agreement.

SALES ANALYSIS TOOL (SAT)	
Date:	
Account Information:	
1) Account Name:	
2) Industry:	
3) Location(s):	
4) Size (Employees / Revenue / Etc.):	

Contact Name:	
1) Role/Position:	
2) Contact Information:	Office Phone: Cellular Phone: Email:
Current Customer (Yes/No):	
1) Current Vendor(s)/Provider(s):	
2) Current Solution(s) Utilized:	
a) Your Company(s):	
b) Competitor(s):	
3) Current Environment(s)/ Situation(s):	
4) Current Reference (Yes/No):	
Decision Event(s):	
1) Reason for Considering Change:	
2) Impending Event and Timing:	
3) Issues/Challenges/Goals/Etc.:	
4) Existing Solution(s) Likes/Dis- likes:	

(continued)

5) Significant Influence(s):	
(Profit/Loss, Regulation(s), Etc.)	
Identified Project(s):	
1) What is the criteria:	
2) Time frame:	
3) Issues/Goals/Etc.:	
4) Budget Determined:	
5) Challenges to Success:	
6) Etc.:	
Formalized Project Criteria:	
1) RFP/RFQ:	
2) Needs / Requirement Documents:	
3) Etc.:	
Informal Project Criteria:	

1) Informal Organization Chart and Project Influencer(s):	
2) Individual Conversations/ Opinions:	
Next Step(s) and Timing:	
Can Your Company Win:	
What internal resources/people are needed to win:	
Overall Corporate Partnership Compatibility/Alignment:	
How does the corporate environment and philosophy align/match:	
Opportunity Risk:	
1) What is the probability (percentage) of winning:	
2) Why should your company win:	
Strategy Utilized to Win:	

The SAT tool is designed to be a working document, allowing the salesperson to record the known information about the sales opportunity and then continue to complete the remaining information items as they become known. This can assist in avoiding unknown factors and surprises along the sales cycle that may inhibit, delay, or derail the sales process.

Another benefit of utilizing the SAT is the information captured can also be utilized by other individuals within the salesperson's company (sales management, sales support, etc.) should individuals be brought in to assist with the sales process (demonstration, office visits, etc.). Having the prospect(s) information captured in the SAT document allows the salesperson to easily provide known information about the opportunity to internal individuals who are asked to be involved in any sales activities.

Some companies and sales management teams may have specific rules and/or policies in place where they want to have a certain amount of information about an account prior to scheduling and completing certain actions (corporate office visits, reference visits, presentations/demonstrations, etc.). Whether capturing sales opportunities information is required by the company and/or sales management, capturing account information can improve the chances of completing a successful sales campaign in an effective and efficient manner. In many cases, regardless of the size of the opportunity, the steps and elements required for completing the sales process are similar, so gaining and capturing the necessary information should also be similar. This information can assist and insure sales steps are not left out or overlooked, preventing a delay of the completion of the sales opportunity.

Depending on certain elements and conditions (investment amount, current relationship, etc.) surrounding each sales opportunity, the completion of the SAT document should be completed (even if the potential sales opportunity is a small initial or add-on order). This provides an opportunity for the salesperson to review and update information as this can always be referred to for identifying additional marketing and sales opportunities based on information captured.

The SAT document can also be utilized to insure steps of the sales cycle and process have not been forgotten or overlooked, therefore allowing the salesperson to have more confidence and reliability when forecasting opportunities. Since information has been documented along with what steps and elements have been completed, a better understanding of where and how each opportunity is positioned is provided.

Another benefit of the SAT is it prompts the salesperson to gain important information from prospects, allowing for a more expeditious and accurate qualification of the sales opportunity(s). Allowing the salesperson to either qualify the opportunity and add to the sales forecast, or realize additional information and analysis needs to be gained before forecasting. If for some reason the opportunity is not viewed or qualified as an opportunity, the SAT can assist in identifying this by prompting the salesperson to ask pertinent questions and capture the data allowing the salesperson to move on without spending time and resources.

The SAT will be of benefit should someone within the salesperson's company (sales management) inquire as to a specific account or sales opportunity as the salesperson can simply refer back to the completed SAT document and provide information as to *when, why,* and *how* the opportunity was qualified, continued, or disqualified, along with reason(s).

SAT OPPORTUNITY IDENTIFIERS

The following are some SAT Identifiers that should be gained and captured for sales opportunities:

1. Account information (name, industry, location(s), employee size, revenue size, contacts with roles and positions, etc.).
2. Existing relationship status (current customer, prospect, reference, etc.).
3. Current solution(s) or application(s) being utilized (your company's and/or competitors).

4. Decision event (impending event and/or reason for a change and associated timing).
5. Identified project (criteria, time frame, goals, and budget).
6. Formalized project criteria (RFP, RFQ, needs and requirement document(s), etc.).
7. Informal project criteria (personal opinions, individual conversation(s), etc.).
8. What is the possibility your company can win the opportunity based on known requirements and needs? Is any customization going to be needed?
9. What company resources are going to be needed to win the opportunity (sales engineer, sales management, implementation and training department, etc.)?
10. Corporate value alignment (company's culture and philosophy match).
11. Internal political influences (any interior adviser(s) or individuals who want the salesperson's company to win). Does the "formal" company organizational chart differ from the "informal" organizational chart, and who will be influencing the decision maker(s)?
12. Opportunity risk (what is the salesperson's and company's chances of winning the opportunity? Identify why the company's solution offering(s) should win).
13. Strategy to win opportunity. What sales strategy will be utilized to win the opportunity, and why will it be successful?

Some of the information elements and areas may not be known during initial communication with the prospect(s), however, these elements and areas should be explored, addressed, known, and documented in the SAT document as quickly as possible, providing supporting qualifying/disqualifying information.

WIN STRATEGY PLANNER

Account Name:

Date:

Compile Prospect's Decision Criteria:

Compare and analyze prospects criteria (Highest to Lowest) to your solution(s) offering (features/functionality/value/benefits).

Compare prospect's purchasing criteria to known competitor(s) strength(s)/weakness(s):

Assess Competitive Positioning:

How does your solution offering(s) match against known competitor(s) in this opportunity?

Determine and Select Win Strategy and Actions:

1) Focus on reinforcing the prospect's criteria that your solution offering(s) meets/exceeds.

2) Build additional value for areas...benefit(s)/functionality(s)/feature(s)...where your solution offering(s) is particularly effective.

3) Attempt to move up prospect's lower criteria where your solution offering(s) are effective.

4) Attempt to minimize (reduce) purchasing criteria that may not be an area of strength/effectiveness.

SAT SAVES TIME

There are times when a prospect/customer interacts with a salesperson, expressing some level of interest in the functionality the company's solution offering(s) can provide, and because salespeople have a tendency to want to believe that if someone expresses interest to us that it means...not only do they want to purchase this functionality, but they want to purchase it from *us*!

Sometimes in the salesperson's eagerness to get the sales process started and completed in the shortest amount of time, they have a tendency to skip some of the sales process steps, as well as the gathering of pertinent information, and just move forward to the proposal and contract signing stages. Do not be surprised if there is an urge to do this. Over my career, there have been times, usually smaller add-on opportunities with existing customers, when the sales opportunities have presented themselves and closed quickly without going through each of the sales cycle steps.

However, I want to share with you that there have been many more times when I thought winning the opportunity was almost a foregone conclusion, and therefore, it would be okay to skip steps of the sales cycle and move forward, providing a requested pricing proposal or even a contract. Feeling confident about the opportunity, I even added to the sales forecast, therefore making sales management aware of the sales opportunity...only to hear back from the prospect that they made a decision to move forward with another vendor and then having to explain to sales management why this forecasted deal was not going to close.

Then having the uncomfortable experience of going back through the situation with sales management explaining why the deal was not won, I realized there had not been enough information gained and understood about the potential opportunity. Therefore, in an attempt to close the deal quickly, there were sales cycle steps skipped. The lack of information came back to haunt me.

Just to be clear...the SAT document and information contained does not have to take a long time to complete and in many cases is completed over time, although it is preferred to be completed as quickly as possible. However, if the SAT information is gained and completed, it will save the salesperson time, resources, and potentially the experience of having to explain a lost sales opportunity to sales management.

It has been my experience that if an individual contacts the salesperson requesting a pricing proposal without the willingness to provide and exchange information, the salesperson should be cautious and question the reason(s) for this proposal request. It is unusual for a unsolicited individual to call and not be interested in exploring and discussing the value(s), benefit(s), feature(s), etc., or willing to share much about their needs, challenges, etc., prior to requesting a price quote. So, one might ask, why would an individual do this?

The answer may have us going back to our early adult days when searching around for the best price offering. Another option is that a vendor and solution offering has already potentially been selected; however, they are in need of a competitive pricing proposal.

If you represent a company whose solution offering(s) is not known for being the least expensive option in the industry, then it is imperative to be able to provide reasons and evidence why any additional investment is outweighed by the value and benefits provided by the solution offering(s). So, even though the investment may be slightly more than the competition, the solution offering(s) provides the value(s) and benefit(s) needed, resulting in a better option.

As a sales professional, you will probably run across companies who are going to purchase from a competitor for a myriad of reasons (friends with competing sales representative, local support, perceived lower cost, etc.). Some of these companies that have made their selection of a competitor require receiving multiple competitive pricing proposals before they can complete their purchasing decision with the selected vendor.

Therefore, the company calls a salesperson requesting a proposal and provides just enough basic information to receive a proposal, so they can fulfill their requirement of receiving competitive proposals before moving forward with the selected vendor.

Salespeople should be cautious if contacted by an individual who is not interested in providing answers to the SAT inquiries and just interested in receiving a pricing quote/proposal. Should this situation be encountered, be aware of potential motives and be cautious regarding providing pricing without adequate information, as without it, the chances of winning the opportunity are remote.

HIGH-LEVEL INFORMATION

When exploring and ascertaining prospect's decision criteria, a salesperson should strive to gain as much information as possible regarding what is important to the potential purchaser. If the purchasing entity is utilizing a committee to make purchasing decisions, then it is important to understand *both* the *company's* (purchasing committee) purchasing criteria, as well as, the *individuals* on the committee's purchasing criteria.

The following are some high-level criteria purchasers may consider:
1. Does the "standard" solution offering(s) meet all their needs, and if not, what percentage is met?
2. Ability and flexibility to customize the solution offering(s) and associated service(s) to individual company specifications.
3. Is there an upcoming or impending event that may affect the solution offering(s) implementation or timing?
4. What is the vendor's reputation and impact to the prospect's industry?
5. What is the solution offering(s) stability/dependability?
6. Customer service reputation and ongoing support (local, regional, national, etc.) and hours of operation.
7. Pricing (flexibility, payment, and finance options).
8. Implementation, installation, training options, and timing.

The earlier a salesperson can reveal decision criteria, the better the possibility of being able to affect (revise), as well as reposition the criteria to better address (fit) the available feature and functionality areas of their solution offering(s).

This also provides an opportunity to reprioritize criteria where the salesperson's current solution offering(s) may not be as strong or as effective as other areas. Thus, it allows repositioning the solution offering(s) strengths toward the top of the criteria priority list while lowering the priorities of any lesser strengths (functionality) of the solution offering(s).

COMPARING "SALES" TO "PURCHASING" ELEMENTS

The following comparison reflects the differences in elements and steps in "purchasing" versus "sales."

OVERALL "SALES" ELEMENTS

When reviewing elements most commonly recognized and associated with successful sales opportunities, the list contains most, if not all, of the following:

1. *Marketing:* Information focused on generating curiosity and interest (features, functions, benefits, etc.).
2. *Prospecting:* Strategic campaigns focused on contacting targeted purchasers based on some established criteria, such as current solution(s), demographic(s), geography, industry(s), etc.
3. *Relationship Building:* Establishing communication (phone calls/meetings) and building credibility, trust, and willingness for potential purchaser(s) to continue dialogue(s).

4. *Value Proposition:* Solution offering addressing issues/challenges, willingness to look at alternatives, proof sources (case studies, white papers, Return on Investment, etc.).
5. *Analysis:* Identifying current environment and situation. Utilizing formal/informal process querying techniques to identify and clarify items, such as issues, challenges, and needs, along with what is currently working for the purchaser(s), what is not, and why, etc.
6. *Performance/Presentation:* Opportunity to present/demonstrate proposed solution offering(s), including value(s), benefit(s), feature(s), and functionality.
7. *Negotiations:* Proposal items, such as pricing, RFP, RFQ, payment and contract items, etc.
8. *Closing:* Completing and signing of contract agreement.
9. *Implementation:* Including installation, project management, initial and ongoing training, and professional development, along with associated time frames.
10. *Follow up:* Ongoing dialogue during sales cycle, implementation, and installation.
11. *Reference:* Regular communication(s) regarding the company's success(s) and sharing the success story with others, along with recommendations for other prospects to potentially contact.

OVERALL *"PURCHASING"* ELEMENTS

The *Purchasing* elements/steps and timing utilized by a purchasing company may be different, and it is the responsibility of the salesperson to determine how the elements and steps of the sales cycle are aligned with the purchasing process.

The following are traditionally the high-level elements/steps a purchasing entity completes when making a decision.

1. *Acknowledgment of issues,* including needs, challenges, etc., and the interest to solve/resolve.
2. *Curiosity* to explore potential solution alternatives and options.

3. Formal/Informal determination of *purchasing criteria* elements.
4. Approving a plan to research and *explore solutions* and resolutions (RFP, RFQ, etc.).
5. Willingness to communicate, *meet and evaluate* (presentation/demonstration) provider's solution alternatives.
6. *Negotiation(s)* with selected provider(s) on factors such as pricing, implementation, training, references, etc.
7. *Decision.* After evaluating qualifying solution alternatives based on purchasing criteria, one of the following options is selected:
   a. Selecting your company and its solution offering(s).
   b. Selecting a competitor's company and its solution offering(s).
   c. No decision, no change. The prospect(s) decides to stay with the current situation, potentially attempting to re-solve problems internally (change in processes or proce-dures, etc.).
8. *Completing paperwork* with selected vendor (contract, etc.).
9. Implementation/installation items (timing, individual(s)/depart-ment involved, training, etc.).
10. Ongoing *support and relationship* with vendor selected.
11. *Future needs* moving forward.

SAT QUESTIONING

One way of gaining and confirming information from a potential purchaser(s) is to simply...ask them questions.

It is also important to gain and understand individuals' feelings and attitudes toward potentially making a change (or addition) within the organization.

One technique to assist individuals understand why the salesperson is asking questions is to position the question(s) by saying, "If I worked for your company and was out selling to prospective companies utilizing your company's financial resources to research and analyze opportunities, what type of information would be expected to be provide back to your company?"

By repositioning, in terms of their company and their sales representatives, it allows individual(s) to better understand why the salesperson is acquiring information needed to better understand the opportunities environment (situation, needs, issues, goals, etc.). This shows that the salesperson is simply doing what they would want their own sales representatives to do with their prospects/customers. This can assist in having individuals view the questioning in a different light and thus allow individuals to be more willing to assist in providing information.

The salesperson should also be cognizant of the reservation and potential concerns an individual(s) may have regarding making a change to their organization. At a high level, some of the concerns regarding changes may revolve around impacting: overall continued company success, their specific job function, integration with existing processes and procedures, ease of doing business, customer service, etc.

Having the SAT questions prepared and written down prior to communicating with each of the individuals within an organization accomplishes:

1. Maximizing the time spent with each individual by having the questions prepared, allowing for moving smoothly and quickly through the process.
2. Focusing on the individual and their answers rather than focusing on formulating the next question(s).
3. Allowing the salesperson time to ponder what questions to ask prior to communicating with individuals and to consider how the respondents can provide answers to the questions in a manner without concern(s) they may alienate themselves from the rest of the decision makers and their company.

Keep in mind, the SAT information is only as good as the questions asked and the accuracy of the information received. Some potential purchaser(s), or purchasing committee members may have their own agenda and purchasing criteria, which may vary from the overall company or committee criteria.

In some cases, the purchasing criteria may be set by an individual or small group of individuals and then evaluated by a larger committee. Therefore, the personal opinion of each of the individuals may be different from the committee's, especially if they did not participate in producing the project and decision criteria. However, they have been selected to participate as a member of the evaluation and final decision committee.

Just be aware that certain individuals who are questioned may not have the same agenda and goal(s) as the committee they are involved with and may have different objectives. If the salesperson feels this may be the case, consider triangulating information to confirm and better understand particular individual's objectives and if they are different from the overall project committee's criteria and goals.

It is also important for a salesperson to be aware and understand any informal and political structure that may be present within a prospect's organization. This involves the company's *inner circle* of influence on decision makers. There may be times when the decision criteria is determined and decided by the informal political structure and individual's personal goals prior to determining the company's needs and purchasing criteria, which are to be addressed by a new solution offering(s).

There may also be times when an individual's personal goals and/or *inner circle* influences may become actual committee decision criteria, whether the overall committee prefers them or not. So, it is beneficial for the salesperson to know and understand how the committee determined the project decision criteria.

The salesperson should note in the SAT document any political or *inner circle* associations and influences on the committee/decision maker(s) that may impact the project's final decision and outcome. The salesperson may find out the official organization chart and structure may differ from the political and *inner circle* of influence on company decisions.

Many years ago, I had a seasoned salesperson explain to me about the informal (*inner circle*) organizational chart and its potential influence on decision makers.

His statement was, "Not saying that you have to believe in the influence of a prospect's inner circle or informal organization chart, but it is happening whether you believe it or not!"

It is better to gain insight into any informal *inner circle* so the salesperson can understand it and prepare appropriately rather than ignoring it and having it affect the outcome of the purchasing decision and successful completion of the sale.

Example:

Several years ago, I had been working with a small group of individuals within a prospect in Minnesota that represented a large opportunity for my company. The end of the year was quickly approaching, and I felt a face-to-face meeting would be appropriate and assist in moving the opportunity forward toward closing by the end of the year. The group of individuals with whom I had several communications over the past several weeks encompassed the company's senior management team. Therefore, I thought it would be advantageous to get all the decision makers into a meeting room, providing an opportunity to share and exchange information needed to complete and close the opportunity.

This particular company was owned and operated by a single family with the majority of the management team having the same last name as the company's name. Grandpa was the chairman of the board, the eldest son was the CEO and president, and the eldest son's offspring were all involved in managing and operating the company. There were also a few department managers (accounting and purchasing) involved in some of the phone conversations leading up to the meeting.

Over a few weeks, I had conducted several phone calls, speaking with each of the senior management team individually and gathering information needed to prepare for the meeting. All of the senior management team seemed open and eager to find a solution and implement it as quickly as possible.

However, during a couple phone calls, one particular individual, who was the accounting manager, did not seem as willing and eager to move forward with the proposed solution offering and its implementation timing. This individual seemed to be resisting and pushing back on resolutions, as well as inhibiting progress and information needed to move forward.

I was still optimistic about the opportunity and its possibility of closing before year-end. A meeting date was secured, and the forecast close date was moved up. I informed my sales management team that this large opportunity would probably close by year-end. I continued to move forward, preparing and focusing on the needs and requests of the senior management team, and diminished the concerns of the accounting manager, who did not seem to be in favor of moving forward with the suggested project.

The meeting was held at the prospect's location, and each of the individuals who I had previously spoken with entered the meeting room. After introductions and light conversation, the meeting commenced.

During the meeting, most of the attendees had positive attitudes toward the project and openly shared and exchanged information regarding the possibilities. However, the accounting manager continued to voice their reservations and concerns about the project and as a result caused disruption to the meeting.

At the first scheduled meeting break, I took the opportunity to take one of the VPs, with whom I had good phone conversations over the past several weeks, aside. I stated my concern for the one individual who was causing disruption in the meeting. I asked if he could provide some guidance as to how to address the situation, as well as potentially utilize his position in the company to suggest this person not be as disruptive and allow the meeting to continue to move forward.

After stating the concern, the VP looked at me, grinned, and said, "Oh, that's our sister, and since she is married, she doesn't have the same last name as everyone else attending the meeting!"

Immediately, I knew I might be in trouble since I had focused most of my time and energy on individuals within the company with the same last name, thinking that since they were all part of the senior management team, they would override any negativity and push back provided by the accounting manager.

My concern about the accounting manager was validated about a week after the meeting when one of the VPs contacted me to let me know they would not be moving forward with the project at this time. During the conversation, I discovered the accounting manager had a direct line of communication to the chairman of the board (her grandfather) and voiced her concerns regarding the decision that might be made by her siblings. The chairman sided with his one and only granddaughter, and the decision was made to not move forward with the proposed opportunity.

Now, I had the experience of going back to my sales management team and explaining this sales opportunity had been delayed and why, and removing it from the forecasted year-end close opportunities.

This was a tough but valuable lesson as it taught me the importance and impact the "informal organizational chart" (inner circle) can have on an opportunity. Therefore, it should not be ignored or overlooked.

Make sure any type of informal organization (inner circle) information discovered is recorded in the SAT documentation information.

POSITIONING SAT QUESTIONS

When asking SAT questions, it can be beneficial to present them in a neutral manner, therefore avoiding having individuals queried concerned about how their answers and/or information shared may affect or reflect on them.

For instance, "I have heard from other companies in your industry that they are experiencing difficulty with <u>(state issue).</u> Are you and your organization experiencing the same type of issues/challenges?"

Stating the question in a *neutral* manner tends to make the person answering feel and realize they may not be the only person experiencing the issue/problem being queried. Saying it has been heard from other individuals and companies can make it easier for the person to feel more comfortable sharing their situation (needs, challenges, goals, etc.).

The following are examples of SAT questions a salesperson may ask at different organization levels within a sales opportunity.

SENIOR MANAGEMENT LEVEL SAT QUESTIONS

- *hoW* do you feel the current solution(s) are performing for the company?
- *What* area(s) of the current solution(s) would you like to improve, and how would you like to improve them?
- *What* functionality or area(s) of the solution offering(s) works well for your department(s) and why?
- *What* functionality or area(s) of the current solution offering(s) is not working well and why?
- *hoW* do area(s) of the current solution offering(s) that are not working well affect the organization?
- *hoW* do the current solution offering(s), process(es), and procedure(s) affect you and your department's personnel?
- *What* current and future challenges and needs do you see your organization facing (regulations, reporting, etc.), and how should a solution offering(s) address these challenges?
- *What* areas of the organization do you see being improved with a new solution offering(s)? Do you see any area(s)/department(s) not being positively affected by a new solution?

- *What* individual(s), department(s), committee(s), and group(s) are responsible for making company purchasing decisions?
- In your opinion, what would a new solution offering(s) be able to perform for the company, and what would be the most important decision-making factors?
- Have you heard of other companies in your industry that are concerned about <u>(specific issue)?</u> Are you also concerned about this issue, and if so, how is your organization planning to address it?

DEPARTMENT MANAGER LEVEL SAT QUESTIONS

- *Who* (names and roles) is involved in making purchasing decisions for the department and/or organization?
- *Where* are they located (same building, different location, remote, etc.)?
- *hoW* do you feel the current system is performing, and how do you and your department feel about making changes to the current solution environment?
- *Why* are you and the company considering a change now?
- *What* are the way(s) you and your department are looking to improve the system to positively affect the department and company, and how will the results be measured and evaluated?
- *When* and *what* is the time frame(s) for making a decision(s), and is there an upcoming event(s) that affects the decision and implementation timing?
- Other companies and departments like yours have shared that they are struggling with <u>(specific issue).</u> Are you and your department also finding this to be a difficult area? If so, how do you currently (plan to) address this issue?

INFORMATION TECHNOLOGY (IT) LEVEL SAT QUESTIONS

- Who (names and roles) is involved in making technology purchasing decisions for the organization?
- Where are they located (all in the same building, another location, remote, etc.)?
- What is the current technology being utilized by the organizations (servers, laptops, tablets, mobile devices, etc.)?
- What is the current environment (infrastructure), and what is the reason for considering a change?
- What do you like and dislike about the existing system?
- What is the company's short-term and long-term technology plan and direction?
- What is the current budgeting process and procedure for new purchases?
- What is the time frame for making a decision(s) and is there an upcoming event(s) that impacts the decision and implementation timing?
- hoW do you feel about making any changes to the current environment?
- If the decision was yours to make, what decision(s) would you make in regard to purchasing a new solution/system for the organization?
- I have heard other company's IT personnel state they are concerned about (specific issue). Is this a concern for you and/or the organization, and what are the plans to address the situation?

BENEFIT OF AN INTERIOR ADVISER

Salespeople need to be aware of the importance and value of having an individual(s) within the *"prospect's company"* assisting them to promote (subtly sell) *internally* to their coworkers and peers, and that the salesperson may want to spend additional time with these individual(s) to make sure they have a good understanding of the value and benefits of the solution offering(s).

If a salesperson is fortunate enough to have an *interior adviser* (someone assisting them within the account), the salesperson should assist the adviser to make sure they understand the value and benefits, allowing for promoting the solution offering(s) within their company.

Salespeople should also keep in mind the *interior adviser's* role within their organization. Most of these individuals are not sales professionals, so the salesperson needs to provide informational items and assistance, such as value propositions, brief overviews, proof sources, etc., allowing them to easily and subtly promote the company's solution offering(s).

There are also times when salespeople miss a chance of having an *interior adviser*. Even though an individual(s) within the prospects organization may be willing to assist, they may not feel they possess enough knowledge about the solution offering(s) to feel comfortable promoting and talking internally to their coworkers about the value(s) and benefit(s) of the solution offering.

Oftentimes when this situation happens, these individual(s) are not willing to ask for assistance on how to promote ideas to their coworkers. Therefore, it is the salesperson's responsibility to be looking for *interior advisers* but also providing information and guidance as to what and how to discuss with their colleagues.

It has been my experience that an *interior adviser* will become very informed and knowledgeable in regard to the solution offering(s). They may view this as an opportunity to become the prospect company's pseudo "internal expert" on the solution offering(s), and therefore become instrumental in the decision-making, purchasing, and implementation processes.

SAY IT ANOTHER WAY

Sometimes when salespeople ask SAT questions, the answers provided might be the "company line" and fairly vague, resulting in not providing any real specific answer. I recommend politely asking the individual to restate their answer, *saying it in a different way*, indicating the answer was not clearly understood.

Salespeople may be surprised by simply asking an individual, *"Please, say it in another way."* The individual will not have time to "rewind and recalculate" the canned answer, and therefore will actually say what they meant to say originally.

Please keep in mind that this technique should be utilized in a strategic and polite way as the salesperson would not want to risk irritating the individual by requesting they do this for multiple answers.

SUMMARY

Sales opportunities resemble a puzzle that the salesperson must solve in order to complete a successful sales cycle.

Salespeople need to be able to identify and clarify elements that are important to purchasers and utilize the Sales Analysis Tool (SAT) and W-6 indicator questions to gain a better understanding of the environment, situation, needs, and goals.

The SAT and identifiers assist in identifying vital information, allowing confirmation of what information is *known* and what information is *not known* about the sales opportunity.

Utilize the Circumstance(s), Issue(s), Impact(s), Resolution(s)/Option(s) (CIIR) questioning methodology to assist in uncovering/discovering potential opportunities.

When ascertaining a prospect's purchasing decision criteria, strive to gain as much information as possible regarding what is important to *both* the company's (purchasing committee), as well as, each individual on the committee in the event there is not a common goal.

During the SAT questioning process, identify those individuals who may assist as an *interior adviser,* as well as, identifying individuals who may have a particular interest in the purchasing decision, such as who gains if you and your company are awarded the contract, and who gains should another company (competitor) be awarded the contract.

The *"Sales"* and *"Purchasing"* elements and timing can be different, and it is the salesperson's responsibility to determine how to coordinate and align these elements and steps to complete a successful sales opportunity.

Salespeople should be aware of the existence and impact of the "informal" organizational chart and *inner circle*.

Individuals within a prospect's company seem to migrate to the salesperson who they feel appears to be the most willing and easiest to work with, as well as by how much they are willing to assist them during the sales cycle.

Reducing risk for potential purchasers will improve the chances of them moving forward, so salespeople should consider ways of reducing the risk for prospects, allowing them to move forward and complete a successful sales opportunity.

One of the key elements to a "sales victory" is not necessarily defeating the competition, but rather defeating the competition's strategy. One way of completing this is to gain and capture important information using the SAT document and W-6 indicator questions during the sales cycle.

LESSON 16

MULTI-DIMENSIONAL SALES SPACE (MDSS) TECHNIQUES

The mantra for performances and presentations should be "the audience *ALWAYS* comes first!"

Salespeople should consider and view each opportunity to perform for an audience, whether an individual on the phone or in person in front of an audience, as an honor and privilege. Most individuals in today's world are busy, and just like a salesperson; their time is the most valuable commodity they have. Therefore, whenever individual(s) are willing to take time out of their schedule, it should be recognized and appreciated.

When the sales cycle reaches a point for a presentation/demonstration, it should be viewed and approached by the salesperson as an opportunity to have a multi-dimensional dialogue and information exchange between the prospect(s) and the salesperson.

The opportunity for a salesperson to present to a prospect(s) should be viewed as a performance, in which each of those involved play an important role. The definition of a performance is the act or style of performing a work or role before an audience.

Viewing the presentation/demonstration opportunity as a "performance" provides a mind-set for the salesperson and individuals assisting to utilize their skill set and area(s) of expertise in a creative, educational, and memorable experience for the audience members.

EVOLUTION OF THE SALES PERFORMANCE

Multi-Dimensional Sales Space (MDSS) supports the ideas of utilizing current technology and incorporating various multimedia into the company's image and solution offering(s). This provides a unique, interesting, and engaging way to differentiate and separate from the competition along with creating an image and emotion(s) drawing prospects toward your company and solution offering(s). Depending on your age, you may have seen, witnessed, or even participated in the evolution of presenting from transparencies and overhead projectors to today's numerous presentation tools. Historically, companies liked to standardize on one presentation method when providing presentations/demonstrations to prospect(s). However, more recently, some companies are allowing salespeople to utilize alternative presentation tools if the salesperson feels it is more effective and within budget parameters.

Given that there are more available and valuable presentation tools in today's world, salespeople may be missing an opportunity to gain an advantage or at least to separate themselves from the competition by not utilizing the same presentation tools as their competitors. Salespeople and their company should investigate currently available presentation tools, allowing them to present and position their solution offering(s) in the best possible environment. Another potential missed opportunity for salespeople is to investigate and incorporate some of today's technology when performing and presenting their solution offering(s). I am not advocating using *current* technology just to utilize *current* technology; however, if it assists in making a positive impression in regard to how the solution offering(s) is perceived by the prospect(s), then it should be considered.

If a salesperson's company mandates certain presentation/demonstration tools be utilized, then continue utilizing what the company requires. However, keep in mind that if the competitors are utilizing dated technology and you are able to incorporate current technology, it will set you and your company apart, making the company's offering(s) look current, as well as memorable.

Example:

A few years ago, I worked with a computer software applications company that provided Enterprise Resource Planning (ERP) applications. One of the benefits was that all the applications were web based. The prospect had narrowed the vendors down to the top three and invited each to present on the same day. During the day of the vendor presentations, the organization's Internet server went down, and therefore, there was no Internet connectivity to the meeting room. The other two selected vendors were not able to present their solution. However, one of my sales team members simply took out his cellular phone and utilized its browser functionality to connect to Internet, and we moved forward with the presentation. Think this had an impact on the audience? You bet it did!

It not only supported and highlighted the design and development of the software applications, but it also provided the prospects with the comfort of knowing that if their Internet server(s) were to go down, they could continue utilizing the solution offering(s) and continue conducting business through the use of their cellular phones, which each had at their fingertips.

The fact that we were the only vendor who could present that day played a large role in my company's sales team being selected and the sales opportunity completed successfully.

PRESENTATION STRUCTURE OUTLINE

1. Introduction and Salutation:
   Introduction of yourself and any team members (providing names, role/position, and some brief additional information, such as something personal: length of time with the company, family, hobby, etc.). State something that allows the person to connect with the audience, such as that the sales team members are golf enthusiasts if many of the audience members are also golf enthusiasts. Depending on the number of audience members, it can also be beneficial to provide the sales team's business cards, allowing audience members to have and refer to it for names, as well as having contact information.

2. Opening:
   Make sure to deliver an attention-grabbing opening. This can be completed in various ways, but it should gain the audience's attention. A few years ago, I attended a trade show. When one of the keynote speakers was introduced, he stood just offstage and out of sight. When his name was announced, he came running across the stage and did a cartwheel and then launched himself into the air, completing two consecutive back handsprings and ending up at the other end of the stage with his arms raised in the air to indicate his completion, like gymnasts do at the end of executing a routine. The audience responded with rousing applause. This was an example of an attention grabber!

3. Presentation Body:
   The following information contains recommended areas for the body of the presentation. However, information gleaned from utilizing the SAT document should be utilized to decide what areas and elements should be addressed for each audience and situation:
   a. Provide a high-level overview, including the overall main points and information summary to be provided, consisting of information about your company, along with the selected main and major points determined by an RFP or SAT document. The number of items presented may be determined

by any specific time frame allotted to present and address the overall purchasing criteria.

b. Further address each of the main points and purchasing criteria in more detail (beginning by addressing the largest impact, challenge, and need first and then the next most important, etc.).

c. Address additional (remaining) purchasing criteria and elements by order of priority.

d. Address items and elements uncovered as part of the SAT document and while speaking with individuals from the organization.

e. Address additional functionality that is available but might not be needed by prospect until a later date.

f. Discuss potential scheduled functionality that will be forthcoming and is determined to be beneficial to the purchasing decision.

4. Questions:

Address questions and/or clarification(s) items presented during the meeting. I recommend also having the salesperson (someone from the sales team) write down questions, preferably in an area where the audience can see (whiteboard, etc.) and then marking each one completed as addressed, or if additional action needs to be executed, such as follow-up, research, etc. This lets the audience members know the identified action items, who will follow up on open items, and how they will be informed of answers (e-mail, phone call, etc.).

5. Call to Action:

- Identify follow-up actions, who is responsible for responding, how they will respond (e-mail, phone call, etc.), next step(s), and timing for identified actions.
- Provide an activity(s) for the audience members to do following the presentation to reinforce your message, such as watching a video, visiting a website, etc.

6. Closing and Conclusion (utilize wraparound style):

- One way of concluding the meeting is utilizing the wrap-around style. This allows for connecting the ending of the presentation back to the beginning.
- This works well with a theme performance and presentation where the ending of the performance is connected to something said or done at the beginning of the performance, therefore completing the story full circle and reinforcing the message, leaving a strong, compelling, and memorable impression on the audience.

7. Prior to leaving the meeting:
   Return any of the prospect's equipment (projector, whiteboard, etc.) utilized for the presentation, as well as any materials that were provided and left behind in the room. This eliminates or reduces the chances of a competitor picking up the information in the event there are multiple vendor presentations provided. It is advisable to offer to clean up the room, as well as assisting in resetting the room (tables and chairs) if rearranged for your presentation meeting.

8. Thank-You:
   Follow up the meeting with thank-you notes to the audience members. Depending on the number of audience members, a personal note or phone call is preferred. However, if the number of individuals prohibits this, sending an e-mail providing a brief summary of the meeting along with your contact information will allow for follow up questions/comments.

CREATING MENTAL WALKWAYS

One of the salesperson's goals during the presentation should be to intellectually and mentally construct an emotional connection spanning where the potential purchaser's organization is currently with their solution and where the salesperson's solution offering(s) will allow them to move to by implementing the solution being proposed.

The goal(s) should be to create and construct scaffolding, providing mental and intellectual walkways where the potential purchaser can conceptually walk along with what the salesperson is presenting. This allows the audience the support of the scaffolding through proof sources, references, stories, etc. This technique allows the audience members to mentally see and understand the transition from where they are today and where and how they can easily get to where they want to be, utilizing the salesperson's solution offering(s).

MAIN POINTS—THREE TIMES

It has been said that individuals who are not familiar with a certain concept, idea, or element may need to hear it at least *three times* in order to remember it.

Due to the fact that there may be individuals in the audience who have other things on their mind (professional, personal, etc.) during the presentation, causing them to reduce focus and/or drift off at some point (checking e-mail, phone messages, etc.), it is important to communicate and share the top three to five points in each presentation and important area(s) multiple times during the presentation. One way of doing this is through the use of stories, allowing the audience another chance of hearing the information again as main points are reinforced.

PEEERC (PERFORMANCE-EXPLAIN-EXPAND-EXPLORE-REVIEW-CONFIRM)

I recommend utilizing the PEEERC (pronounced: PERC) presentation philosophy, allowing the audience multiple opportunities to absorb the information communicated and hear the main message at least *three* different times.

If you listen and observe radio and television commercials, they will say the name of the company or solution offering and contact information (phone number and/or website) at least *three* times.

This information is usually delivered toward the beginning, again in the body of the commercial/advertisement, and again at the closing. Some commercials and advertisements will even provide this information more times, depending on the time frame of the information delivered.

The benefit of the PEEERC information supported by stories is that the audience gets to hear and view the most important points and elements of the presentation multiple times and in various ways, helping to make the information more interesting, engaging, and memorable.

PEEERC

Performance = Presentation.

Explain = High-level overview point(s) or criteria (acknowledging importance).

Expand = Value and benefit(s) and provide examples with stories.

Explore = Ask audience member(s) how capabilities will or could be utilized within their organization.

Review = Summary communication regarding information presented, such as overall points, and/or section and area points.

Confirm = Ask audience members how they see themselves and/ or their organization utilizing the solution offering(s) presented.

This lesson of presenting the most important points and portions of a presentation multiple times was learned after experiencing the following situation.

Early in my career, I was presenting a computer software solution to a prospect. I had just completed delivering a presentation to the prospect focusing on addressing all of their purchasing criteria.

Toward the conclusion of the presentation, I asked the audience if they had any questions. An individual from the audience raised her hand and asked if the company's solution offering(s) would provide them with a specific functionality. This particular functionality was one of the top five items on their criteria list, and therefore was listed as one of the major points to be covered during the opening of the presentation and I had spent several minutes on this particular topic. Even though this major point was covered during the opening (top five criteria) and closing (summary) of the presentation, either the audience member had been distracted and missed the information, or the information had not been presented in a way that was clearly understood.

After the meeting, I drove back to the airport to fly home. I was listening to the radio, and a song came on that was familiar and started me thinking, *why are songs so easy to remember and stick in our minds?* To which the answer was they utilize a familiar structure of telling a story along with a repeating chorus, allowing the listener to hear the chorus line multiple times, and therefore, making the song quickly and easily learned and memorable.

After this incident, I began communicating and presenting the top 3-5 points addressing the most important and critical areas of the purchasing decision criteria at least *three times*. I utilized story lines (stories) to address the major points and then supported this message by communicating these multiple times (chorus) through various methods (additional points and stories, visuals, sounds, etc.).

GRAB ATTENTION EARLY IN THE PERFORMANCE

In today's society, it is common for almost everyone to have exposure and accessibility to twenty-first century technology, and as such, we are becoming accustomed to requesting and receiving information quickly (if not instantaneously). It is also common for almost everyone who attends a vendor meeting or presentation to walk into the meeting with items such as cellular phone, laptop, tablet, etc.

It appears society is becoming conditioned to be constantly provided information, whether it is work, social, or entertainment related (or a combination). Audiences have a tendency to lose interest quickly, and therefore, it is imperative to gain their attention early and to retain it throughout the presentation.

Walk through an airport today and observe all the different technology people are utilizing for work and entertainment (phone calls, watching movies, listening to music, playing games, etc.). It appears as if modern technology allows society to stay busy working and being entertained almost every minute of the day and night. Since society is becoming more accustomed to being bombarded by multiple stimulants, if attention is not captured early and kept throughout the performance, individuals may slowly begin to mentally drift away from the presentation as they begin to be distracted by other items, such as e-mail, phone calls, etc. Once the attention of an audience is lost, it can be difficult to reengage them, let alone get them up to speed on any missed information.

Incorporating current technology elements will allow changing up the presentation format and assist in keeping the audience's attention by engaging and stimulating their thought patterns.

BUILD CREDIBILITY QUICKLY

During the performance, it is important for the salesperson to establish and build credibility quickly. This provides a couple things:

1. Lets the audience members know the salesperson understands their business and industry.
2. Lets the audience members know the salesperson understands their company's environment and individual issues, which were discovered and/or clarified through communication utilizing the SAT document and W-6 questions.

The salesperson should appear to the audience as qualified and knowledgeable in the prospects industry, along with being an individual who can get actions completed within their own company—therefore being a customer advocate. One way of doing this is by communicating and displaying how the solution offering(s) is assisting "companies in their industry."

Another way of demonstrating this point is by providing general and specific industry statistics. This information can usually be found in professional industry websites, articles, and entities focused on national or global statistics. The ability to provide this type of industry knowledge and statistics puts the salesperson at a higher level, allowing audience members to view them as a consultant, resulting in building additional credibility, rather than being viewed as a salesperson looking for a sale and associated commission check.

An example of building credibility was displayed by a coworker (salesperson) who was in the education industry. The company we represented provided foreign language learning programs, among other offerings. This particular individual would begin each presentation by stating that she not only strongly believed in the program but knew firsthand of the value, benefits, and results because she had been through the program herself.

The program not only provided her the knowledge she needed to successfully complete the program, but after completing the program she was able to deliver a 20 minute speech using the foreign language she had been studying. Then she went on to explain how after completing the program she had also traveled to the country of the origin of the language and lived there for six months, reinforcing the language skills learned in the program.

This opening statement not only quickly built credibility for her, but it also provided the audience a comfort level that the she knew the program from personal knowledge, usability, and usefulness. Her story built instant credibility and connected with the audience members. Not only was she a salesperson for the program, but she had also been a user of the program!

Another way a salesperson can gain credibility quickly for both themselves and their company is through a referral by an existing customer.

PERFORMING VERSUS PRESENTING

Many of us may have experienced a salesperson presenting their solution offering(s) in a "monologue" fashion, in which they simply stood up in front of the audience and delivered the features and functionality they think the potential purchaser(s) might like to see.

I certainly understand there may be instances where time constraints, RFP requirements, and rules state that the presenter(s) is to offer the information from a script (by the prospect's decision committee) and the audience is to show up and simply observe the presentation. When this situation happens, there is a missed opportunity to get the audience members involved to explore and verify how and where the solution offering(s) is going to be best utilized.

The good news is that the times presenting from a provided script without some interaction with the audience are usually a small percentage, and even then, I would recommend trying to get the audience members involved in some manner (even if limited). A good way to do this is through utilizing a presentation theme where the performance itself engages the audience and reinforces values and benefits.

It is certainly best to have completed a SAT analysis utilizing W-6 questions along with having communicated with each audience member prior to the actual performance. However, there may be times when a salesperson only gets a chance to speak with a few of the members of the prospect's evaluation group/committee due to purchasing companies rules/regulations. If this is the case, it is important to take a few minutes at the beginning of the performance to ask some high-level questions in an attempt to gain some additional information before continuing with the presentation. Even a few minutes spent conducting a brief analysis with the audience will be beneficial and assist in directing the presentation.

THEME PERFORMING

One of the ways to make a salesperson's performance more enjoyable and memorable for the audience is to build their solution offering(s) around a theme that resonates with the potential purchaser(s), such as their industry, name, location, or if the salesperson knows the decision committee or group have a common interest, hobby, or activity.

A few years ago, I was working with a prospect and discovered that their senior management team was comprised of golf enthusiasts. Each of the management team not only played golf, but each also displayed various golfing items within their offices.

Therefore, a performance and presentation was developed and delivered around a golfing theme, utilizing presentation phrasing and examples, such as:

- Course description (representing high-level values of the solution offering).
- Individual golf course hole description (representing individual benefits, features, and functionality).
- Individual club selection (driver versus putter, etc.) and how each has a specific purpose (job function).
- The strategy of driving for show (distance) and putting for dough (money), and how providing excellent customer service will assist in keeping customers resulting in the company being more profitable.

The goal of the performance is for the salesperson to express their value proposition along with the value(s) and benefit(s) and how the solution offering(s) meets the purchasing criteria. Utilizing a theme provides an opportunity to separate the performance from what competitors present. In addition, it provides an opportunity to separate the salesperson's company and solution offering(s) and allows the performance to be memorable.

TELL STORIES

An effective way to structure a performance and presentation is to incorporate both a theme and stories. Who does not enjoy a good story?

Luckily, I have been fortunate to know some very good storytellers, and the gift of a good storyteller seems to be the ability to put the listener(s) in or at the scene of the story. This is the ability to not only make the story interesting, but to make it relevant and engaging and allow the listener(s) to appreciate the moment as if they were there.

Think back to a time when someone shared information that was easy to remember, making it easy to share with others months or even years later. One of the possible reasons is that the situation was familiar and relatable and the information included in the story made a "personal" impact on the listener. Think about moments you may remember from years ago, and why these memories are still easy to recall. Is it because those moments touched you personally, engaged you emotionally, and engaged a number of your senses? Some moments engage individual's senses so deeply they can recall the sight, sounds, smells, taste, and touch of an experience from many years ago as if it happened yesterday.

One of the keys to being an effective storyteller is having the ability to make the stories relatable, relevant, and memorable for the listener(s).

Good storytellers are able to share stories that the audience can relate to, resulting in some level of emotional, intellectual, and/or visual connection to the story.

STORIES CAN HELP MAKE SALES

You may be asking yourself, *Why are stories so important?* The answer is...stories can help make sales!

Stories can help make a presentation more interesting, enjoyable, and memorable for the audience members.

Therefore, keep a couple things in mind when preparing for a presentation:

1. The audience is taking time out of their schedule to attend, so thought and consideration should be given to making it as valuable and beneficial as possible.

2. Be cognizant of the fact that each audience member may have multiple things going on in their world, so salespeople should understand that although we think nothing else could be more important than what we have to say, that actually may not be the case for certain members of the audience. This makes it even more imperative for the salesperson to engage and involve the members of the audience early and often, thus reducing the potential for the audience members to become distracted.

One way of keeping the audience engaged is through the use of stories.

PERFORMANCE AND PRESENTATION PREPARATION

Delivering a performance and presentation that has not been properly prepared is similar to arranging furniture inside a house that has not yet been built. As a manager once explained to me, "If you do not know where you are going, any road will get you there!" Here are elements to be considered when preparing for a presentation:

1. Preparation details:
   - Provide a document to your main contact within the prospect's company requesting pertinent meeting information.

PRESENTATION PREPARATION DOCUMENT
Account Name:
Date:
Contact Name:
Meeting Location Address:
Meeting Time:
-Start:
-Conclusion:

(continued)

Please indicate/confirm the level of interest for the following items:
(List the top item/areas your company's solution addresses/resolves as it pertains to the prospect's goals/needs/situation)
Scale to be utilized: 5=Very Interested/Must See, 3=Some Interest, 0=Little Interest:
1) Business Process (Resource Management, Order Entry, Inventory Control, Etc.) = ____
2) Industry Suitability = ____
3) Technology Flexibility and Options (Cloud/On-Site/Portable Devices/Etc.) = ____
4) Custom Programming/Modification(s) = ____
5) Installation, Implementation, Data Services= ____
6) Training = ____
7) Customer Service = ____
Provide additional questions that support your solution offering(s) main value(s) and differentiator(s):
1) Level of importance of integration of new solution offering(s) into existing environment?
2) How important is selected vendor's reputation and future business direction and vision?
3) How important is selected vendor's industry/domain longevity and expertise?

4) How important is technology architecture (cloud/on-site/etc.).
5) How is the Initial and on going investment going to be evaluated?
6) What additional company (prospect) needs and goals should be addressed and shown?
Confirm presentation attendees (names and roles/responsibilities).

- When (date and time) the meeting is scheduled.
- Meeting location(s). Physical address to locate with Global Positioning System (GPS).
- Confirm the scheduled time for the meeting, including start and ending time.
- Equipment and items to be included in the meeting room (projector, speakers, whiteboard, flip-chart, etc.).
- Names, roles/positions, and contact information of individuals attending the presentation meeting.
- Provide presentation questionnaire for attendees.

PRESENTATION ATTENDEE DOCUMENT
Account Name:
Date:
Attendee Name:
Title/Role:
Responsibility:

(continued)

Their top 3-5 areas of interest to be shown (covered) in presentation:
1)
2)
3)
4)
5)

2. Review *prospect* developed and provided document(s) stating purchasing criteria requirements, such as an RFP, RFQ, etc.
3. SAT document (analysis document).
4. Request any prospect business documents to be utilized during the presentation meeting (sample(s)/example(s) of invoices, bill of lading, shipping labels, inventory sheets, etc.).
5. Performer(s) involved in the presentation need to remember they are familiar with the solution offering(s) while the audience members may not be familiar. Therefore, they should deliver the presentation by starting with building a foundation and framework.
6. Explore performance theme options.
7. Explore methods for engaging the audience during the presentation.
8. Provide stories relating to the audience's environment and situation, along with suggested and provided resolutions, such as how other customers have experienced the situation and resolved it using the solution offering(s).
9. If providing a team presentation, have the person(s) not currently presenting be the note taker and timekeeper, as well as monitoring the audience's involvement. I recommend working out nonverbal signals prior to the presentation, indicating

instructions such as slow down, speed up, clarify, etc. I have worked with sales engineers who would assist with presentations, and we employed nonverbal communications. For example, subtly touching an ear meant it was difficult to hear, subtly rubbing an earlobe meant it was time to pick up the pace and/ or move on to next topic/area, touching an index finger meant a quarter of the time had expired, pointing at a palm meant half the time had expired, and pointing at a wrist meant time had expired and it was time to wrap it up (or politely ask if additional time was available). Also, if someone raises their hand for a question and the presenter does not see that person, the person not currently presenting should let the presenter know there is a question from the audience.

10. Prospect's formal organizational chart alignment with the informal (inner circle) influences chart. This information should be noted in the SAT document.

11. Note and document expectations for next steps (proposal items, timing, budget issues, etc.).

12. Presentation follow-up:
    a. Thank You to attendees (handwritten notes, calls, or e-mails).
    b. Follow up on open or unanswered questions.
    c. Proof sources (references, case studies, white papers, Return on Investment, etc.).
    d. Proposal(s).
    e. Set stage for how proposal(s) will be submitted or presented (call, meeting, etc.). Also, it is advantageous to contact the prospect(s) *prior* to providing the proposal to arrange a time for reviewing submitted proposal document(s).

PRESENTATION PLANNING DOCUMENT

Account Name:

Date:

Information and Items:	Value(s) and Benefit(s) To Present	Interview Notes	Presentation Notes
RFP/RFQ Decision Criteria:			
Situation Analysis Tool (SAT):			
Review Other Account Information Documents:			
Review Documents Provided by Prospect:			
Presentation Equipment Required:			
Additional Company Resources Needed (individuals/refreshments/etc.):			

(If team presentation, determine who will present what information/areas)								
Presentation Theme:								
Introductions/Salutation:								
Opening:								
Body (focusing on most critical and highest priority elements):								
Summary:								
Questions/Follow Up Items:								
Call to Action and Next Step(s):								
Closing:								
Thank You(s):								
Additional Information and Items:								

PERFORMANCES AND PRESENTATIONS

After the salesperson determines what sales presentation elements should be provided and delivered to the prospect(s), how should the salesperson make sure the performance and presentation go as smoothly as possible?

The answer is *Practice, Practice,* and more *Practice*!

If you have ever attended an event where the presenter(s) were unprepared, nervous, or not familiar/comfortable with the message and/or material(s) they were trying to communicate, how did it make you feel? Were you uncomfortable, not only for yourself, but also for the rest of the audience, as well as for the presenter? Did it make it difficult to focus on the information being provided? Did you find yourself spending time focusing on the presenter's uneasiness and finding yourself looking for a way to disengage rather than exerting effort to gain/retain the message and information being provided? It took me a while to figure out, but in most cases, the audience prefers the salesperson to perform well (unless they want the competition to win).

Most people do not attend an event (movie, concert, theatrical performance, sporting event, etc.) anticipating the performance to be executed poorly, especially since they are investing their time. They have an opportunity cost associated with attending as they could be doing something else during the same time.

When this situation is encountered, it tends to leaves the audience feeling awkward about the experience and oftentimes apologetic toward the presenters and fellow attendees.

To help avoid this situation, it is recommended to make sure the salesperson is familiar and knowledgeable with the presentation materials and familiar with equipment utilized...and the way to accomplish this is to practice, practice, practice!

Until a salesperson is familiar with the presentation information materials and equipment, they should determine time(s) and method(s) to practice and provide mock presentation(s) prior to delivering it to the actual prospect(s).

It is unlikely that a salesperson will get a second chance for an RFP presentation to the same audience, therefore indicating the importance of the salesperson being prepared and delivering their best effort and performance.

COOKING SHOW–STYLE PRESENTING

One method for presenting is to utilize the cooking show concept. This is utilized on cooking shows, in which the finished product is presented to introduce interest about what is going to be completed during the show. Many times when a cooking show is being broadcast on television, the finished product is shown at the beginning of the broadcast, as well as just prior to a commercial break(s) to keep the audience interested and watching.

This same concept can be utilized during a presentation by showing the audience's top buying criteria item(s). As an example, if the prospect's top purchasing criteria and concern is order entry, and specifically how quickly and efficiently they can create orders in the system, then it would be advantageous to show this functionality toward the beginning of the presentation. Without showing the audience each feature and function of the order entry system, just simply show them how quickly and easily an order can be placed in the new system. Then, like the cooking show, go back and demonstrate additional features and functionality that are available and may be utilized to complete an order.

PERFORMANCE AND PRESENTATION PRACTICE IDEAS

The following are some ideas and recommendations for practicing performing and presentation techniques:

1. Practice in front of a mirror. This allows observing gestures, body language, speech, etc.

2. Video record yourself so you can observe and make any adjustments/improvements. Today's technology makes this exercise easily accomplished.

3. Deliver the performance and presentation in front of a neutral audience, such as coworkers, other members of the sales team, family members, friends, clubs, groups, etc. You may be thinking that some of these groups may not understand the particular solution offering(s) being presented. This is okay as it provides the opportunity for the salesperson to become more familiar and comfortable with the presentation material. Plus, it provides *repetition* of delivering the message and allows an opportunity for feedback on how the material was delivered. Besides, there may be individuals in the prospect's audience who may not be familiar with the solution offering(s) either. Practicing provides a good opportunity to hear feedback as to what areas were not clearly understood or did not seem to flow smoothly from value to value, benefit to benefit, topic to topic, feature to feature, etc. Practicing delivering the information will allow for adjusting the presentation flow and sequence, including the introduction, body, closing of the presentation, etc. Practicing will assist in reducing anxiety levels while anticipating delivering the presentation to an audience...when it really counts!

4. Additional tip: if it is not possible to video record a mock practice performance and the salesperson would like to know how they sound to the audience, they can utilize a cellular phone to record and listen. The salesperson may learn something about how their voice sounds, speech patterns, etc.

WILL PRACTICE GUARANTEE EVERYTHING GOES PERFECTLY?

Salespeople should not be concerned, even after practicing and preparing, if they still find themselves feeling anxious and nervous prior to delivering a sales performance to an audience.

I have delivered many performances and presentations, some good enough to secure a sale, and I can still find myself feeling anxious. No matter how much one practices, no one can ever predict what might happen during a performance and how audiences will react to the information.

Once, in the middle of the presentation, a loud alarm began ringing in the building, causing individuals in the audience to immediately abandon their chairs and begin ducking under the meeting tables. One audience member said, "Hurry up and get under the table with us." I responded, "What is happening?"

The response was, "That is an earthquake alarm, and everyone needs to get under a table."

Everyone in the room stayed huddled under tables for several minutes until the alarm rang again signaling all was okay.

Being huddled together under a table provides new meaning to "interacting with the audience!"

However, this is not something that would normally be predicted nor prepared for in anticipation of delivering a sales presentation.

MAKING A SOLUTION APPEAR CURRENT

One mistake salespeople make is to present and demonstrate their solution offering(s) in a manner that makes it appear antiquated or dated. This can be especially concerning if the prospect(s) is wanting to make a change in part to move away from an older solution that does not allow them to take advantage of or utilize more current applications and technologies to stay competitive by conducting business more effectively and efficiently.

PERCEPTION IS REALITY

Just imagine if a salesperson scheduled a meeting with you to show their latest and greatest solution offering(s) and they walked into your office, and began setting up an overhead projector, and produced a folder containing transparencies and colored markers to write on the transparencies. Likewise, if you were a prospect and the salesperson invited you into the corporate office for a meeting and then brought in a black and white television with a VHS tape player to show the corporate overview message.

How would this make you feel about working with this company and its latest and greatest solution offering(s)?

Unfortunately, even if the company did have the best and most appropriate solution, this "perception" might be difficult to overcome, resulting in questioning and viewing the company and its solution offering(s) as not being current technology.

As the evolution and pace of technology continues to rapidly increase, it is important for salespeople to continue to investigate methods to include and/or add current technology into their performance. Utilizing some of today's modern technology to show the offering will assist in providing the perception the solution offering(s) is current and up to date.

During my career, I have worked for software manufacturing companies where their solution offering(s) had been on the market for over five years, which in some industries and markets is considered and described as mature and in other industries and markets possibly dated.

One technique utilized when showing these solutions was to have and present additional technology, such as a handheld Personal Data Assistant (PDA) device, that could run the application(s). When presenting the solution offering, the audience would be presented with the PDA and explain how the application(s) could be utilized on the PDA device. Then, the device would be powered on and have it reflect the initial home (login) screen.

Since the device did actually run the application, the ability to show the device, turn it on, and explain to the audience how it would function provided the perception that the solution offering was more current than it might have actually been at the time. Then, I would pass the PDA device around to the audience members so they could hold the device and view the home screen, which looked exactly like the one being presented on the large screen in front of them. This assisted with providing the appearance that the solution offering(s) was utilizing current technology.

DOING WHAT HAS ALWAYS BEEN DONE

So, you might be asking, "Why would salespeople not be taking advantage of technology and attempting to incorporate more modern elements into their current presentations?"

There could be several reasons. The company has always done it this way, the company is looking and evaluating changing sometime soon, the salesperson could be uncomfortable showing and/or using some newer technology tools, or the existing method(s) has had success in the past, so why change?

Another reason is that the salesperson might not be thinking in terms of what could be utilized in making the presentation more interesting, engaging, and memorable for the audience.

A few years ago, I had only been with a company for a few weeks when the company received an RFP for a large opportunity. If won, the sales opportunity would be a significant sale for the company.

At that particular time, the company's policy was to have the marketing department prepare the RFP response, as well as design the presentation that would be delivered by the salesperson.

When the RFP presentation was sent to me, it incorporated a slide deck of approximately 150 computer presentation slides. Each slide numbered along with the total number (1 of 150), indicating to the audience how many more slides there was to go before the presentation concluded.

Not only was there an extraordinary number of slides in the presentation, but each slide had approximately 8-15 points crowded together with the font size so small, it was not legible unless the person was extremely close to the presentation screen. As if that was not enough, there were also screenshots of the application included on the slides, and the images were so small they were barely distinguishable.

Therefore, the audience members would not be able to clearly see and read the information.

It was quickly determined that the audience would become disinterested, disengaged, and possibly discouraged with the presentation provided, especially after viewing the first few slides and then knowing exactly how many more slides they would have to endure without being able to clearly view the information.

Realizing the reality of the situation, I asked the sales manager if we could try a slightly different approach to the company's standard presentation that had been provided.

The response was, "Steve, it is the company policy to deliver the same standard RFP presentation and information that is designed and produced by the company's marketing department."

It was further explained, "This standard RFP delivery approach allows others from our company, who may be asked to participate along with the sales team, to be familiar with the information."

After acknowledging the sound reasoning and approach of the development of the information and materials behind this way of thinking, I asked a very simple question, "Does our company win every RFP utilizing this approach?"

As you might imagine, the response to the question from the sales manager was, "Of course not!"

To which I responded, "Well, maybe it is a good time to try something different."

The sales manager stated he would need some time to think about it, and we would revisit the issue in a few days. After several more conversations and requests to try a new approach, the sales manager reluctantly agreed to consider the thought; however, I would need to present this new approach to him prior to the actual RFP meeting with the prospect, with the understanding that if he did not agree with the approach, I would default back to the standard company RFP presentation... to which I quickly agreed.

After spending several hours modifying existing information and creating new elements to the presentation, a meeting with the sales manager was scheduled just days prior to the RFP meeting. The new presentation was delivered, including elements such as slide animation and transitions, the company's website, customer video testimonials, mobile and handheld devices, projector, speakers, and a presentation theme.

Upon seeing this newly revised approach, the sales manager agreed this was acceptable and improved, and we would move forward with this new presentation for the RFP meeting.

The actual day of the RFP meeting, my company was the last of three companies to present in a single day. Each company received a two-hour time slot to present their company's solution offering(s). The vendor presentation order was determined by a random draw performed by the prospect's decision committee.

The first vendor presentation was scheduled at 10:00 A.M. to noon, the second was 12:30 to 2:30 P.M., and my company was scheduled from 3:00 P.M. to 5:00 P.M.

Therefore, by the time it was our turn to perform, the prospect's RFP committee had already had a long day and had been through two companies and four hours of presentations with only a 30 minute break between presentations.

The thought process behind designing and conducting the presentation was to make it a multi-dimensional information exchange including and involving different senses of the audience and involving several different elements and media to accomplish several goals in regard to the audience.

1. Utilization of a theme and storyline (similar to that of a movie), building curiosity and interest in regard to the direction and content.

2. Gaining the audience's attention and interest early. Knowing they have been sitting in a dimly lit room for an extended period of time viewing/listening to other presentations.

3. Getting them involved early in the presentation as it is more difficult to disengage or mentally drift away when involved in a conversational exchange.

4. Utilizing various multimedia and technologies to keep the audience interested (video, sound, animation, transitions, etc.).

5. Utilizing multiple technologies, audio and visual aids, laptops, handheld devices, and cellular phones to not only pique their interest, but also to educate them on the multiple ways the company's solution could address their current challenges and issues and meet their future needs.

This RFP presentation goal was not only to leave in the committee's mind that the solution offering(s) could meet their current needs, but also that my company understood the importance of utilizing appropriate technology to address these needs. Incorporating different technologies during the presentation supported the impression that the company could not only address their current requirements but also understood and embraced utilizing available technology moving forward.

As the end of our team's presentation time approached, the presentation was concluded by showing two brief video clips of existing customers offering testimonials of the impact the company and its solution offering(s) had on their organizations. This left an impression on the prospect that two of our largest and most well-known customers in the industry each spent time speaking directly to the prospect and sharing why they, and therefore the prospect, should choose the company and its solution offering(s).

At the conclusion of the two testimonials, I announced to the audience that we had reached the end of our designated time and thanked them again for their time and involvement. I asked if there were any questions before the sales team packed up and said our good-byes. One hand from the audience went into the air immediately.

The person in the audience politely thanked the sales team for our time and the information shared and then asked, "Why aren't all sales presentations like this one?" The room erupted with applause, resulting in the audience providing a standing ovation.

Now, it is not that rare to get a few claps or some applause at the end of a presentation. However, to receive a rousing ovation for a sales performance is rare, and in an RFP presentation, almost unheard of...let alone a standing ovation.

After the presentation was complete, many of the members of the audience came up and thanked the sales team for not only providing good information but making it interesting and for not being similar to the "other vendors" as they had just provided computer slide deck after computer slide deck, to the extent that it was difficult for the audience attendees to discern not only one slide and graph from another, but one topic from another, and one vendor from another!

Based on the audience's response, we left the presentation feeling optimistic about the information provided and our chance to gain the business. The result was that my company was rewarded a few days later with a substantial contract agreement. Moving forward from that day, the new style of presentation approach to RFP opportunities was utilized.

Was our company's solution offering(s) a better fit than any of the competitors? It is difficult to say, but one thing seemed to be very clear: we were memorable to the audience. They expressed their appreciation for the information and the way it was presented, which accomplished a couple items in the decision committee's minds:

- Our solution offering(s) met the majority of their purchasing criteria and requirements and would allow them to grow and add functionality when it was appropriate.
- Testimonials (references) had been presented via video recordings.
- Our pricing proposal was not the least expensive (actually, it was later shared that we required the most investment of the vendors selected and invited in for presentations).
- We were the one with the most impact. We were memorable, which made the competition forgettable!

One committee member shared with me after we had been awarded the contract and were beginning the implementation process, "It was difficult for the committee to figure out what the competition had shown or could provide because the committee members continued to talk about what your sales team presented and what it could provide. Each time we would discuss an area of the RFP criteria and requirements, someone from the committee would say something like, 'Steve's team demonstrated their company could do that,' and fairly soon the committee was only talking and discussing one company, which made the decision easy!"

MEETING AND PRESENTATION
INTRODUCTION(S)

It is my preference to have an individual(s) from the prospect/customer to present introduction(s) of me and/or the sales team. There are a couple reasons for this preference and method of introduction.

1. Having someone from the company provide introductions gives the appearance and perception that the presenting person/team has been invited into the company, and it is likely the salesperson has been working directly with the introducer, allowing them to provide some insight to the salesperson's/team's involvement, character, etc. This allows the audience members to engage more quickly as they now know more about the presenter(s).

2. Another benefit of having someone from the company provide introductions is that it is customary for one of the higher-ranking individuals within the company to conduct the introduction(s). Since it is likely some of the audience members are working with this individual, either directly or indirectly, the audience seems to more likely to cease actions (e-mail, phone calls, etc.) they were doing and focus their attention to the individual, allowing the salesperson each audience member's attention from the beginning of the meeting.

If an introduction(s) is provided by someone within the company, thank them for the introduction and provide some accolade(s) regarding the person, such as "they have been a delight to work with," "the company should be proud of the work they have been doing on this project," etc.

I again introduce myself and any team members, allowing the audience to hear the name(s) again and potentially provide any alternative names (nicknames) for any of the individuals on the presentation team. Several years ago, I worked with an individual who was on the sales team and had a name that was difficult to pronounce. Therefore, the audience appreciated being able to call him by his nickname.

It is important and valuable to customize each presentation to fit and meet each individual audience's needs. This allows the materials and delivery of the information to appear to be customized and unique to the audience.

Customizing the presentation to each audience's needs does not have to mean completely rewriting and redoing a presentation each time. It simply means altering those areas of the presentation to fit and meet the specifics of each particular audience. This allows for utilizing portions of the core presentation information and revising those areas, which addresses each particular audience's needs.

BEGINNING A PERFORMANCE
AND PRESENTATION

Getting started with a presentation can be difficult because of the different dynamics involved.

Audience members have a tendency to arrive at different times. Some will sit down, and some will walk around the room or walk in and out of the room. Some will start talking to other audience members, and some may be checking e-mail, texts, phone calls, etc. Then at some point, someone may walk in and announce one or some of the missing individuals are still in another meeting and will be a few minutes late.

Now the audience members are not sure if they should go ahead and begin or wait a few more minutes for people to arrive. A two minute delay turns into five minutes, which turns into ten minutes, etc., which puts delivering the information in the time allotted at risk, especially if a hard stop time (finite time) has been scheduled for the meeting.

Then, after waiting a period of time, someone from the audience will tell the salesperson to go ahead and get started.

Again, it is my preferences to have someone from the prospect/customer audience provide a brief introduction, letting the audience know why the meeting is taking place, as well as why they have been asked to join the meeting. However, sometimes during the delay, someone from the audience will say, "Let's get started!" to which the salesperson needs to begin the presentation on their own.

It is important to begin the presentation with a powerful opening, gaining the audience's attention and causing them to engage quickly. One way of completing this is what performers such as comedians do in their performances.

Performers and entertainers (comedians, musicians, etc.) practice and deliver the same (similar) performances for extended periods of time, changing minor portions of the performance. This allows them to keep the message sounding original, like it is the first time they were performing it. They want to have it appear to be spontaneous to the audience when in reality, they have it committed to memory and have performed it several times.

If you have attended or watched a stand-up comedian perform, they appear to just walk out on stage and begin telling humorous stories and observations and engage the audience quickly. Have you ever wondered why these performers are able to walk onstage and begin telling the audience stories without making a mistake, or why they have perfect timing and associated facial expressions and body language?

The reason is that they practice and commit portions of the material to memory, allowing them to slightly change the material based on the situation (audience, city, state, etc.). This enables them to deliver similar material and information when performing. So, why not take a page from other professionals and commit to memory the beginning of a presentation, ensuring it gets started with a planned and powerful opening?

When preparing for a demonstration, I encourage salespeople to think back to other presenters they have observed and consider what techniques were utilized to engage the audience. What techniques did the presenter do to make *you* and the rest of the audience members enjoy the presentation? As a general rule, most audiences will enjoy the same elements of a presenter (engaging, entertaining, informative, etc.) as you do when being part of an audience.

Therefore, it can be beneficial to make an effort to be observant of other presenters, their actions, and their techniques. What are other performers doing to engage the audience? Try to utilize some of these same techniques to develop and prepare for your presentations.

THE PRESENTATION AND MOVIES

Over the past century, most movies and songs have a reoccurring formula as to how they are constructed and written.

A popular song formula is verse, bridge, chorus, repeat. This familiar structure and format is what audiences are accustomed to and allows songs to be easily learned by the audience so they can sing along.

This can also be seen in movies. Whether they were produced many years ago or today, movie formula structure is basically the same. The characters of a movie are presented to the viewer and then further developed by letting the viewer(s) know specific characteristics about them. Then, as the audience becomes more familiar with the characters (character development), a conflict(s) is encountered that needs to be addressed and resolved, encountering some surprise(s) along the journey. The movie scenes are enhanced by providing certain scene settings and backdrops and are accompanied by music to further engage, involve, and embellish the emotional involvement of the viewers, therefore creating and emoting different moods and feelings from the viewers as the story unfolds in front of them.

In addition, the movie industry has experienced many technologic enhancements, providing opportunities, methods, and techniques to further engage and involve viewers through interaction, emotion, and an enriched movie experience, such as improved sound quality, larger viewing screens, computer graphics, and animation, along with 3-D and 4-D experience(s).

Why have songs and movies played such an important role in almost everyone's lives? Largely because they provide an avenue of entertainment for people, as well as an emotional connection, interaction, and experience.

Attending movies today is not just an activity, it is an *experience!* The movie industry has figured out ways to involve the human senses to enhance and enrich the entire experience, therefore making an emotional impact on the audience, reinforcing the message, and making it memorable.

This can consist of a cornucopia of stimulation on the audience's senses, including sight, sound, and, in some cases, 4D interaction. It has been said of most individuals that approximately 80–90 percent of information received and transmitted to their brain comes from visible stimulus, and that visual stimulation can be processed up to 50,000 times faster by the brain than reading regular printed text format.

It is also claimed that viewers are approximately 85 percent more likely to purchase after watching a video or program about a solution offering(s) video/program. So, now the reader knows why there are so many commercials and infomercials that continue to run throughout the day and night on television.

Therefore, salespeople should focus on delivering the overall sales presentation *"experience"* to the audience, utilizing techniques and elements that are known to be engaging and enjoyed by audience members.

MOVIE AND PERFORMANCE PREVIEWS

It is advisable for salespeople to allow and schedule additional time to set up prior to a meeting start time. However, there can be an awkward time between the salesperson arriving at the meeting location, setting up, and testing equipment, and then waiting for the audience members to arrive for the meeting.

So, what should a salesperson do with the time (5-15 minutes) between setting up equipment and waiting for all the audience members to arrive, other than greeting audience members as they enter the meeting room?

Why not utilize this time to advertise and market the company and its solution offering(s)?

This can be completed similarly to what is utilized at movie theaters. It can be something as simple as a 2-4 minute rolling (repeating message) advertisement consisting of a computer slide presentation, promotional video, or short movie/video containing high-level facts and figures about the industry, the company and its solution offering(s), etc., and accompanied by audio (narrator, music, etc.).

The preview(s) may provide the following:

1. High-level information about the industry, the company, and its solution offering(s).

2. Information to build curiosity and interest regarding what the company and its solution offering(s) can provide.

3. Information to build interest in the meeting (what may be shown and discussed during the meeting).

4. Information to keep the audience in the meeting room and engaged until the meeting commences. This decreases the chance of audience members leaving the room for another short meeting, phone call, e-mail, etc., allowing the meeting to begin on time and maximizing the salesperson's time sharing information.

Since this technique of marketing and advertising has worked for the movie industry for years, why not utilize it for your presentation?

Earlier in this writing, it was recommended that if the salesperson would like the audience to retain certain elements of their message, the information should be shared with members of the audience at least *three* times. This marketing and advertising technique can be one of those times for the audience to see/hear and absorb the company's information, allowing them to become familiar with the elements of the company and its solution offering(s).

COMPANY PRESENTATION POSITIONING

There may be times when a salesperson experiences a situation where multiple vendors are brought in to present their solution offering(s) on a single day or over a couple days. The salesperson may not get a choice as to when, or in what order, they will get to present their solution offerings.

There are certain strategies that can be utilized depending on the order a salesperson is delegated (or elects) to present. My experience has been that it is preferred to present last in a series of vendor presentations. However, sometimes a salesperson is dictated to be the first vendor to present. When this situation occurs, it is even more imperative for the salesperson to be especially memorable and make sure to have a bigger impact on the audience members.

The reason it is critical for a salesperson and the solution offering(s) to be memorable is it may be days (even weeks) between the time the salesperson presents to the decision maker(s) and a decision is finalized.

Therefore, without making a significant impact on the audience members and performing a memorable presentation, the salesperson risks the value proposition (values and benefits) becoming confused with another vendor, muddled, and/or simply forgotten.

Even though the salesperson presented how the company's solution offering addressed each decision criteria and their current challenges and needs, if the audience and decision maker(s) (committee) cannot remember which vendor provided what value(s), benefit(s), features, and functionality, many times they will select the vendor they do *remember!*

COSTLY LESSON TO LEARN

Several years ago, I responded to a prospect's RFP request and was subsequently contacted by a member of the decision committee. I was told that the committee had selected my company as one of the top three vendors and therefore was invited to the prospect's corporate headquarters to provide a presentation of my company's solution offering(s).

However, due to the prospect's scheduling constraints, the presentations would be spread out over a three-week period, resulting in the executive team members viewing one vendor's presentation per week. Then, the committee would reconvene the fourth week to make their selection decision.

The committee selected the order of vendors to present by alphabetical order by vendor name. Therefore, the company I was representing would be the first vendor to present.

After several attempts to be moved to the last company presenting, I was told if the company wanted to provide a presentation, I would need to go first, to which I agreed.

On the scheduled day of the presentation, my sales team presented to the executive committee, demonstrating how the company's solution offering(s) met each of the decision criteria (needs and challenges) and addressed questions and concerns.

Then, we anxiously waited another three weeks to receive the prospect's committee decision.

Three weeks after our presentation, I received a call from one of the committee members, who stated that the committee had selected another vendor. He thanked me for our time and effort in responding to the RFP and taking time to provide a presentation.

Wanting to improve the probability of winning the next opportunity, I asked the individual if they could provide some feedback on the performance and information provided, as well as the committee's reason for not selecting my company.

This person went on to explain some key features and functionality the committee especially liked and what this functionality was going to provide for their organization. The functionality described was what was presented by me and the sales team, but apparently, the committee members had been confused about which vendor provided what specific features and functionality due to the lengthy time period between vendor presentations. Resulting in confusion of the vendor information, and therefore, thought another vendor provided the functionally we presented and went on to select that vendor.

I quickly reached out to the committee members to clarify the apparent confusion, but the announcement had already been made public, and the prospect's decision was not open to reconsideration.

AUDIENCE'S MIND-SET AND PERSPECTIVE

The salesperson needs to be aware and understand when creating or designing a presentation that this information is going to be delivered to an audience who may be unfamiliar with the information being presented. This situation is similar to a student looking through a high school or college classroom textbook containing *lots* of words and trying to absorb it all in one sitting. This may be similar to the presentation audience, where the audience is trying to absorb all the information during a presentation and may feel overwhelmed if the solution appears to have *lots* of features and functionality.

Therefore, the salesperson should reflect back to when they needed to read a book containing a substantial number of words for a class, work, etc., and needed to be able to reference important areas of the book. What do most people do to indicate the most important areas of the book's information? Many people utilize some indicator (highlighter, mark pages, etc.), allowing them to quickly refer back to review important areas and information.

This highlighting technique is similar to how a salesperson should think about preparing and presenting the company's solution offering(s). Although there are probably *lots* of features and functionality in the solution offering(s), it is the salesperson's responsibility to figure out what is the most important to the prospect (criteria, SAT questions, etc.). Then, the salesperson must make sure they are able to communicate these points so the audience understands the value and benefits of each of the highlighted points and spend time on the most important ones, rather than on all the other features and functionality the solution offering(s) can provide.

It is said that audience members will remember, on average, approximately 20–30 percent of the information provided in a presentation. If this is the case, salespeople should be spending time focusing on the value proposition (values and benefits) and the most important and major elements of the purchasing criteria and less time on nonessential decision-making factors/elements.

264

Prospects have a tendency to evaluate a solution's capabilities to address their needs from five major areas:

1. Solution offering(s) fit and match to purchasing criteria (needs and goals).
2. Ability to be integrated into their environment and situation (can the solution offering be integrated into current or existing technology, can it be single sourced, one-stop shop, etc.).
3. The reputation of the vendor and solution offering(s); industry knowledge and longevity, industry focus, market-leading position and market share, Research and Development (R&D), references, etc.
4. Vendor's people (reputation for implementation, training, customer service and support, company notoriety and prominence for participating in their industry, company values, etc.).
5. Economic and financial parameters. Is the solution offering(s) a solid financial decision?

BE PREPARED FOR SURPRISES

The salesperson should be aware of and prepared for individual(s) who haven't been communicated with prior (utilizing the SAT and W-6 indicator questions) to the presentation. Therefore, the salesperson may not have a clear understanding of what these individual audience member(s) may be expecting, as well as, their motivations and individual position is in regard to the solution offering(s). This situation certainly provides circumstances where audience members may come to the presentation with a different understanding or take a different position during the meeting.

Should this situation happen, it is important for the salesperson to acknowledge any concern(s) and try to quickly explore the reason for any misinterpretation or misunderstanding. Then, if the salesperson feels there is time to pursue the concern further without taking too much time away from the group, there should be an attempt to extract additional information around the person's concerns without alienating that person or putting them in a defensive position.

If it appears the concern(s) is going to take longer than a few minutes to address and/or take the presentation off schedule or distract the audience, then it may be best to ask the individual if it would be okay to continue with the presentation, and you will be glad to talk with them during a meeting break.

UNIQUE PREPARATION METHOD

One unique and strategic method for preparing and practicing for a presentation is to consider and give the presentation your competition may be providing and delivering to the same prospect.

I had a coworker who had researched our number one competitor so thoroughly, he was able to perform a presentation on the competitor's company and solution offerings as they matched up against our own company and solution offering(s). During company sales meetings, he would deliver a presentation as if he was the competition's salesperson, highlighting what was considered to be the competition's value proposition, strengths, and benefits. He would also provide thoughts and feedback on their considered weaknesses at the conclusion of the performance. This provided valuable insight to how the competition may be positioning themselves against our company in sales opportunities, as well as making us aware of some possible "traps" or "hurdles" the competition may be trying to set for our salespeople and company to address.

This situation of a salesperson knowing the competition so well put him in a unique position and provided a new perspective and advantage when matched in selling opportunities. Being familiar with the competition's offerings, value(s), and benefit(s) and how they compared to our company's allowed him and our sales team to diffuse possible "traps and hurdles"...or perhaps set up a few for the competition to address.

PERFORMING AND PRESENTATION ANXIETY

Shortly after beginning my sales career, I was encouraged by a coworker to become a member of a local group that focused on public speaking. This allowed focusing on improving speaking and performing skills, which was badly needed!

After joining the group and only attending a couple meetings, there was an existing member who delivered an outstanding speech to the group. After the meeting, I approached him to introduce myself and to ask if he would be willing to share any of his secrets as he was one of the most polished and accomplished speakers I had witnessed.

During our conversion, he stated that when he first joined the speech group, he was so terrified of public speaking; he could not even stand up and say his own name in front of the group. He was fearful to speak because he did not know if he would lose control of what words may come out of his mouth, so he found it easier to just not begin speaking in the first place.

However, he stayed committed to working on improving his ability to speak among friends and coworkers, and within a few months with the group, he was able to deliver 1-2 minute speeches, which he felt was a monumental victory.

He continued on with the group, and within a couple years, he found himself becoming a professional speaker, delivering 45-60 minute presentations to large audiences around the world.

He was so thankful to the people within the speech group for all their encouragement and support they offered, he continued to be a member of the group and would come back periodically (when his speaking schedule allowed) to *practice* delivering speeches along with offering encouragement to fellow members.

Yes, you read that correctly. He is a professional paid speaker, and yet he still *practices* preparing and delivering speeches (performances).

During our conversation, he offered some of the best presentation advice I have ever heard.

He stated his performances and speeches began being valuable and fun for his audiences when he "stopped focusing on himself" and began focusing and thinking about the audience...about their needs, their expectations, and why they were attending his performance.

Thanking him for his time and advice, I began focusing on the audiences, their needs, and their expectations and delivering information that would benefit them and their businesses.

Simply changing the thought process about my performance and the presentation provided benefits to the audience:

1. Making the presentation more enjoyable and engaging.
2. Focusing on the audience's needs (important purchasing criteria and elements).
3. Focusing on the audience's expectations and building in flexibility and versatility into the presentation.
4. Being able to involve and be involved with the audience. This provides interaction, engagement, and exchanges with the audience.
5. Making preparing and delivering the performance and presentation more enjoyable.

Another benefit of focusing on delivering a good performance and experience for the audience is it takes the mind-set and emphasis off of the presenter. This will allow the focus to be shifted toward delivering the message and information to the audience.

Early in my career, I put more focus on presenting and focusing on what and how things were said, rather than the audience's expectations and informational needs.

However, after my conversation with the individual from the speaking group, I changed my perspective and found it more advantageous to focus on the audience needs rather than my own.

I have a friend who has competed in the Professional Rodeo Cowboy Association (PRCA) for well over 25 years, competing in almost every rodeo across the United States. He has qualified multiple times to compete at the National Finals Rodeo, where the top 15 qualifiers in the world compete every year for the World Championship. He has performed and competed in front of thousands of people in thousands of venues and has stated he still gets anxious before performing.

If someone who competes at the highest professional level for over 25 years still has anxiety, it is okay if an individual still experiences some level of anxiety when performing or presenting...no matter in what arena they are competing! He claims the key is to utilize and channel any anxiety into positive energy, excitement, and anticipation rather than allowing it to take away or diminish from the performance and the audience's experience.

So take the rodeo champion's advice and channel any anxiety before a performance toward being upbeat. Focus on the moment, the opportunity, and the situation at hand. Realize it is okay to feel some anxiety before a performance and presentation. Just make sure it does not affect the overall audience experience or the valuable message and information being delivered.

IMPORTANCE OF NOT SELLING NEGATIVE

When it comes to sales opportunities, my philosophy has been to provide focus and attention on the needs and goals of the purchaser(s) and to illuminate the strengths of my company and its reputation, people, quality and strength of the solution offering(s). Then utilize and leverage this information to present why my company and its solutions are the best choice for the prospect, rather than communicating information about the competitor(s).

If a salesperson encounters a situation where a prospect(s) makes a comment regarding something they may have heard or read regarding a competitor, and would like the information confirmed and/or explained, I recommend responding with, "I do not have any specific information regarding the situation and therefore would not want to provide any inaccurate information."

Then, if the salesperson wants, they could offer suggestions, such as websites, articles, publications, or customer references where the information may be able to be vetted.

In most cases, by setting this professional ethical precedent, the prospect(s) appreciate and understand the salesperson's level of professionalism and will not continue to ask the salesperson to state/claim anything about the competitor(s).

This goes back to the saying, "Treat people like you would like to have them treat you."

―――――――

SUMMARY

During the presentation, it is important to establish and build credibility quickly.

One of the ways to make the salesperson's presentation more enjoyable and memorable is to build the presentation around a theme that resonates with the prospect.

Incorporating current technology elements will allow variation in the presentation format and assist in keeping the audience's attention by engaging and stimulating their thought patterns with interesting and various elements while making it engaging, interesting, and memorable.

Share stories that the audience can relate to, resulting in emotional, intellectual, and visual connections and/or attachment to the situation and story.

The goal should be to design and create mental scaffolding, constructing a walkway where the prospect(s) can mentally and conceptually walk along with the salesperson during the presentation.

Individuals who are not familiar with a certain concept, idea, or element need to hear it at least *three* times in order to remember it.

Utilize the PEEERC technique, allowing the audience multiple opportunities and chances to absorb the information communicated and hear the message in different and various ways.

Provide a *value statement(s)* after each significant point in a presentation, such as, "S-M Enterprises is the leading provider in distribution solutions, *and the reason that is important is* we spend 100 percent of our time focused on the distribution industry's issues, concerns, and goals."

It is unlikely that a salesperson will get a second chance to deliver a presentation to the same audience. This indicates the importance of the salesperson providing their best effort and performance: practice, practice, and more practice.

The salesperson needs to be aware and understand when building or designing a presentation that this information is going to be delivered to an audience who may be unfamiliar with the information being presented.

Purchaser(s) have a tendency to evaluate a solution from 5 major areas: solution offering(s) fit and match to criteria, ability to be integrated into their environment and situation, vendors and solution offering(s) reputation, vendor's employee peformance, and economic and financial parameters.

Keep in mind, salespeople may never know when they will see audience members again. Therefore, they should do everything possible to leave a positive impression.

LESSON 17
NEGOTIATIONS

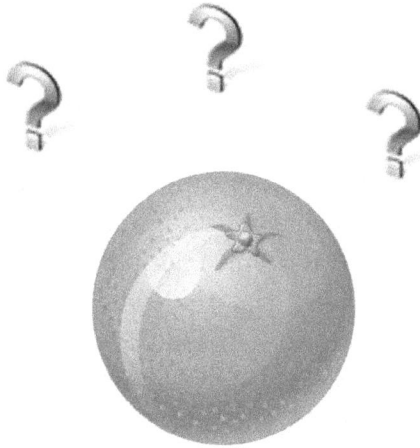

Many individuals feel negotiations and negotiating are more difficult than finding something that rhymes with the word...*orange!*

Depending on the company's solution offering(s), target market(s), industry(s), prospects, and customers, negotiations may affect multiple areas of the contract agreement, such as the initial purchase elements (price, delivery, implementation, training, returns, etc.), as well as ongoing business transactions (annual fees/support/maintenance, quantities, etc.).

Contract negotiations should *not* be something that is unexpected or eluded but rather viewed as another step in the sales cycle. Negotiations and negotiating are simply another element and part of the selling process. The salesperson should expect it...and be prepared for it when it happens. Again, consider how people make decisions.

Think about how you, your friends, and your family make purchasing decisions. Other individuals more than likely utilize the same or similar process(es), method(s), knowledge, and technique(s) when making a significant/substantial purchase. As a result, most people are motivated in pursuing and receiving the best value and deal possible, involving the best solution offering(s) to fit their need(s)/criteria, including such things as quality, service, reliability, and within their financial parameter(s).

Most individuals' purchasing patterns, mechanisms, and mannerisms are formed and established in their youth and/or early adulthood. These patterns usually continue through their personal, business, and professional lives. Individuals' purchasing decisions, much like their personalities, are different and unique to them. Some individuals naturally make decisions quickly, and others may take days, weeks, and even months to make decisions. It is simply their purchasing pattern.

As a salesperson, it is beneficial to understand the individual's and committee's decision-making style(s) and pattern(s). One indicator may be how an individual (or committee/group) reaches decisions on smaller items during the sales cycle. It would be beneficial to a salesperson to determine the decision-making process and procedures for those individual(s) involved by presenting smaller decisions early in the process.

If decisions early on in the sales cycle seem to take an extended period of time, it may be an indicator that decisions about vendor selection and/or final decision on any proposal(s) may also take longer. Having the salesperson be aware of the decision-making pattern is helpful in determining and forecasting the opportunity's close date.

PRACTICE NEGOTIATING

The more one practices something, the more proficient and more comfortable they become at performing the task/activity. Therefore, it makes sense, like the other elements of the sales cycle, to practice negotiating to become proficient.

One way of improving this skill is to practice in one's everyday activities. One might consider making negotiating a standard part of their daily personal lives by attempting to request a little better deal when conducting commerce with individuals and companies during their own personal business transactions.

ASK FOR HELP

One technique to practice negotiating is to simply ask for a *favor* or *help* with improving the deal/transaction, such as:

1. Ask for the "nice person" discount from the sales associate.
2. Ask if you are the "lucky" customer of the day, week, etc., qualifying for a discount.
3. Ask individuals in the service industry if they can help out with the pricing "this time" by offering a better rate, such as hotels, motels, rental cars, rental equipment, etc.
4. Ask the sales associate and salesperson if they can "throw in" (add) something else of value/benefit to the deal.
5. Ask if they have a coupon available that can be utilized for this purchase.
6. Ask for the future "employee" discount, etc.

You may be pleasantly surprised by how many times individuals are willing to assist in making the deal/transaction a little more attractive and enhanced for the purchaser, but it usually needs to be requested.

This negotiating practice activity is not necessarily directed at saving a few dollars, but rather keeping in the practice and mind-set of constantly negotiating and learning to read people's reactions in the negotiation process.

It also allows practice recognizing people's characteristics, personalities, body language, facial expressions, and posture, and how their characteristics might provide a correlation to their reaction to the request along with predicting the outcome.

It has been my experience that if the person requesting the favor or help has a friendly approach with their request(s), individuals are okay with being asked. Besides, what is the worst result that can happen? The transaction or deal cannot be improved. However, it has been my experience that people are oftentimes willing and able to provide some type of concession to make the deal better.

These personal transactions allow a salesperson to get in the mindset of negotiating on a daily basis. Then, when a prospect begins negotiating, it will seem familiar, and the salesperson will feel comfortable with the process, as this is something the salesperson does *every day!*

WHY PRACTICE NEGOTIATING

There are many individuals who compete in professional sports (other than sales) and depend on their personal performance during competitions for their livelihood.

Each of these individuals continues to work daily on improving all aspects of their skill set (methods, techniques, etc.). What you might find surprising is that these individuals continue to work on the "basic" skills, which in the sales world would include such items as performing, presenting, and negotiating.

Examples:
1. Professional rodeo contestants continually work on perfecting the basics of their individual sporting event.
2. Professional football teams continue to work on their basic skill set and techniques daily.
3. Professional bodybuilders continue to work and perform basic strength, speed, and coordination movements daily.

If other professionals focus and practice on the basics on a daily basis, why not sales professionals?

A LITTLE EXTRA

The term *lagniappe* (LAN-yap) is defined as a small gift given to a customer by a merchant at the time of a purchase (such as an extra doughnut when purchasing a dozen) or, more broadly, "something given or obtained gratuitously or by way of good measure." The word entered English from Louisiana French, derived from the American Spanish phrase *la ñapa* (something that is added). The term has been traced back to the Quechua word *yapay* (to increase; to add). In Andean markets, it is still customary to ask for a *yapa* when making a purchase. The seller usually responds by throwing in a *"little extra."*

One might witness an example of this when making a purchase at a candy store where the candy is selected from a bulk container. When someone makes a request for purchasing a certain amount/weight of a particular candy, the merchant then takes a candy scoop and estimates the amount that has been requested.

Then, both the purchaser and the merchant stand on each side of a scale (located atop a counter), observing as the candy from the scoop is slowly poured into a paper bag while both individuals witness the scale reflecting the candies weight. As the weight (amount) of candy approaches the requested amount, the merchant begins slowing down the pouring speed of the candy into the bag, watching the weight reflected on the scale. As both the purchaser and merchant watch the scale reach the requested weight (amount), and with the purchaser continuing to watch, the merchant adds a few more candies, letting the purchaser know they are getting more than requested at "no additional charge." How does this make the purchaser feel about the merchant?

Purchasers of a company's solution offering are many times looking for the same thing..."*something extra.*"

This approach is something to keep in mind when working with prospects as they are looking to work with a salesperson and vendor who is willing to provide *something extra or a special deal* or potentially add something without making it a chargeable item on an invoice. Consider what could be provided in the way of lagniappe to prospect(s)/customer(s). Areas to be considered could be special pricing, additional services, extended support/maintenance, extended subscription(s), etc.

GIVE-TO-GET (G-T-G) NEGOTIATIONS

When negotiating, it is good practice to "gain" something for "giving" something. Getting in this practice will provide and sets the stage for:

1. Building goodwill within the relationship and allowing the salesperson to appear to be flexible, as well as willing to work with the prospect(s) in an attempt to accommodate requests.
2. Setting a precedent early. Although the salesperson is willing to attempt to accommodate prospect(s) requests, the purchaser(s) should also be willing to provide (give) something in return. This sets the stage, allowing the salesperson to provide purchasers' requests back to their management, with the prospect(s) knowing they in return will also need to be willing to provide something that moves the sales opportunity forward. This mind-set allows the salesperson to set negotiation parameters early in the process, avoiding looking inflexible in the mind of the prospect(s) as the opportunity gets closer to the decision and contract signing.

When prospects/customers request concession items such as discounting, etc., the salesperson is willing to make the request to their sales management with the prospect(s) aware they should be willing to offer something in return, such as moving the contract signing and/or implementation to an earlier date, etc.

Example:

Prospect states, "We are fairly close to making a final decision to move forward with your company's proposal. However, if we could get another five percent discount, it would really help us finalize the decision with the committee."

Salesperson's response: "<u>Mr./Ms. (Prospect)</u>, my company and I are very excited about having you and your company join our family of customers, and the ongoing synergy and relationship of our two companies working together will be beneficial for both companies. I am certainly willing to do everything possible to make sure this can happen. However, here is the situation. The company tracks sales, revenue, and implementations on a quarterly basis to ensure it has appropriate personnel and resources available to meet your organization's and other customers' implementation and services timeline(s) and expectation(s). Your current purchasing criteria reflects a project timeline of signing a contract with a vendor by end of the second quarter and implementing it by the end of the third quarter."

"I will certainly be glad to pass your request for the additional discount along to my company's management team, and along with the request, can I also share with my management team if they are willing to provide the additional five percent discount, your organization is willing to finalize the decision earlier, allowing moving up the contract signing date to be completed by the end of the first quarter and implemented by end of the second quarter? If this is something your company is willing to consider, I will approach my management team and let you know their response in regard to the additional discount concession."

This approach of "Give-to-Get" (G-T-G) helps set the stage early with the prospect, letting them know you are willing to try to accommodate their request(s) with your management team; however, the prospect should also expect to be willing to give something in return for receiving the concession(s).

This approach of G-T-G also helps alleviate the prospect(s) continuing to ask for additional concessions (discounting, additional items, etc.). It also assists in setting the stage for prospects' internal conversations as they discuss potential options. The interior adviser(s) can let the prospect's decision committee know they can ask for concession(s), but the salesperson may be expecting something in return, so what are they willing to give as a concession?

This G-T-G strategy will also let the salesperson know where they stand in the opportunity. If the prospect(s) are willing to give-something-to-get-something, then the salesperson has a good chance of moving forward toward closing the sales opportunity. If, however, the prospect(s) continues to ask for concessions and is not willing to consider giving something in return, the salesperson needs to quickly determine and confirm their position within the account. They need to determine if this is a valid opportunity or if the salesperson is being positioned to drive down the pricing for a competitor, which the prospect is more interested in selecting.

NEGOTIATION CONSIDERATIONS

1. What is the purchaser's motivation and purchasing criteria?
2. How well does the solution offering(s) meet their decision criteria (RFP, etc.)?
3. How well does the solution offering(s) "fit" or acclimate into the purchaser's environment and situation?
4. Does the solution offering(s) meet/exceed their current/future needs?
5. What is the budget for this project (what is the funding timing, and what internal procurement process/procedures are required for the purchase to be completed)?
6. What is the time frame for funding (budget approval, new budget year, etc.)?
7. What and whose approval is needed to move forward with the proposal, and are different approval(s) needed based on the project investment amount(s)?
8. Discounting/Concessions. Find out early in the sales process if/ what concessions are going to be requested and/or needed to close the opportunity.

9. Should the project be divided up into smaller deals or phases based on budget and/or timing (allowing moving forward with current funding/approval available and continuing into a new budget and/or multiple budget areas)?

10. Explain to the potential purchaser(s) how to compare competitive proposals (apples to apples).

11. Point out any savings the purchaser(s) will receive by the proposed solution offering eliminating/reducing other areas of current expense(s).

12. Make sure the purchaser(s) clearly understands the value proposition (values and benefits), therefore avoiding commoditizing the proposed solution offering(s).

13. Put concessions provided in real dollar amounts/figures rather than reflecting a percentage amount.

14. G-T-G: Attempt to *get* something for every concession *given*. What would the prospect be willing to give to gain something in return?

15. Illuminate potential exposure(s)/risk(s) for not purchasing the company's solution offering(s).

CONTRACT NEGOTIATION ITEMS

1. The salesperson should confirm they are conducting negotiations with the appropriate individual(s) and/or organizational committee member(s).

    • Does this individual(s) have the authority to negotiate and sign a contract?

    • Are the individual(s) who are "required" to make and sign the contract decision involved in the negotiation(s) process? The salesperson should confirm they are negotiating with the appropriate level of decision-making personnel.

2. Address the prospect's/customer's concerns early, avoiding any unknown or last-minute items that may jeopardize or put the opportunity at risk.

a. If more than one decision maker is involved, make sure to get them together for negotiation discussions (avoiding good guy, bad guy negotiating). If this does not happen, the salesperson should triangulate (confirming understanding from each individual involved) the information, ensuring all decision makers understand where the negotiations currently stand and the actions for completing the deal.

b. The salesperson should make sure to understand the purchasing philosophy that may be utilized for this particular opportunity. Remember, most individuals do not purchase strictly on price for items requiring significant investment (e.g., people do not usually purchase the cheapest house, car, etc.). They select the solution that provides and meets the purchasing criteria and then set out to negotiate the best deal possible.

c. Avoid letting purchaser(s) "commoditize" the solution offering(s). This can be accomplished by putting a value (dollar amount) to each function/process/task the solution offering(s) provides, or a cost savings (dollar amount) for each function/process/task the solution offering(s) eliminate and communicate these figures to the prospect(s). Make sure if prospects are attempting to compare competitive proposals, they understand the *value* of your solution offering(s) and that they are completing an apples-to-apples comparison and providing dollar amounts for any additional value and benefits your solution offering(s) provides.

d. Communicate your company's contract agreement process(es), including structure, procedures, and timing, including such items as contract finalizing and signing, down payment, implementation/installation processes, training, shipping of items, invoicing and payment terms, etc.

e. Validate that the customer feels comfortable with their decision. Remember how it feels to make a major purchase and the excitement shared with others. Avoid the customer questioning or regretting their decision by surprising them with some previously unannounced contract item at the last minute or shortly after signing the contract agreement.

f. Consider mentioning any opportunity cost(s) of not purchasing your solution offering(s).

NEGOTIATION TIMING

Prospects may begin negotiating at different stages and timing within a sales cycle. Some may start right from the beginning, and others may wait until getting closer to the end or just before signing the contract. Therefore, negotiation items should be identified and discussed well in advance to avoid closing delay(s).

A friend of mine was in the market for purchasing a new vehicle. Since he might be picking up the vehicle from the dealership, he asked for a ride, enabling him to drive the new vehicle from the dealership's lot. I observed him negotiating with the dealership's salesperson and sales manager in an attempt to get the best possible deal on the vehicle he had selected.

Once he was satisfied he had negotiated the best deal possible, he had the salesperson produce the required purchasing paperwork. As the salesperson handed him a pen to sign the paperwork to acquire the vehicle, my friend accepted the pen and then politely stated, "Oh, and of course the vehicle will be coming with a full tank of gas, right?"

The salesperson, not wanting to lose a sales opportunity over a tank of gas, responded, "Of course!"

COMPETING AND NEGOTIATING ON PRICE

One way for a salesperson to avoid competing solely, or mainly, on price alone is to make sure steps are taken to *NOT* commoditize the solution offering(s). Therefore, separating the solution offering(s), value(s), and benefit(s), from competition.

However, if a salesperson competes solely or mainly on price, then one strategy is to commoditize the solution offering(s), therefore coercing the competition to compete on the salesperson's and company offering(s): pricing, level(s), and term(s).

In most cases, prospects are predominantly interested in purchasing value(s) and benefit(s), and how the solution offering(s) is going to improve their lives/business, making sure it is going to meet their purchasing criteria. Then, they are interested in completing the purchase at the best possible price.

It is imperative the salesperson understand and be able to communicate their company's solution offering(s) and associated value(s) to prospects, as well as educating them on how to compare (apples to apples) and contrast competitive proposals. Many times, a prospect(s) will overlook what may be *included* in a solution offering(s). These *included* features and functionality will allow them to discontinue utilizing another application(s) or service(s), therefore reducing the "overall total cost of ownership."

SALESPERSON SUGGESTION(S)

One negotiation technique that has been utilized is for the salesperson to actually suggest what the prospect might want to request in the form of a negotiation concession. Salespeople should prepare a list of concession items that might be requested as a result of negotiations and what concession(s) the company may be willing to consider. A good place to start is researching what other prospects/customers have requested and what items the company has agreed to in the past, as well as what new ideas (recent events, etc.) may be considered.

Any concession that would be offered as a suggestion from the salesperson would be preapproved, or something that is common for the company to provide during negotiations that improves the deal for a customer, along with the opportunity to win the deal for the salesperson.

During the selling cycle, the salesperson utilizes the W-6 indicator questioning technique to learn more about the prospects budget parameters for the proposed project and acquiring the company's solution offering(s).

As an example, during the analysis process, it is discovered the funding for the project will be coming from multiple departmental budgets, and each of these departmental budgets is limited to how much each will be contributing. The initial purchase price of the solution offering will be coming from one single, larger departmental budget, and then recurring fees (e.g., annual maintenance/support fees, upgrades, etc.) will be provided by other, smaller departmental budgets.

In this situation, the salesperson might suggest having the prospect(s) request to have multiple years (3-5) of annual fees included along with the initial purchase price, allowing it to be included and purchased with the larger departmental budget.

Another example is to have additional solution(s) and/or service(s) included with the initial pricing proposal at reduced or no charge, such as additional training hours, additional implementation/installation services, additional application(s) or module(s), etc. When a salesperson suggests negotiation item(s) it:

1. Lets the prospect know the salesperson understand negotiations and is willing to work with and even assist them with this process.
2. Sets the stage. The salesperson has already provided something early in the sales cycle, and this may help avoid or lessen any additional concessions requested toward the end of the sales cycle.
3. Provides the ability for the salesperson to have improved flexibility and control of what is being negotiated. By suggesting item(s) the prospect(s) should ask for in the way of negotiating, the salesperson is in a better position to provide those concession(s), along with letting the prospect know the associated value (dollar figure) of the concession.

NEGOTIATION OBJECTIONS

There can be a myriad of objections or reasons for the opportunity to not close and the prospect(s) to not move forward with the solution offering(s) proposal, such as "It is just too expensive for us."

When hearing objections, it may possibly mean the prospect(s) feels:

- The solution offering(s) does not meet their purchasing criteria (needs and goals) or does not meet enough of the purchasing criteria to move forward.
- The solution offering(s) requires a larger investment than competitive options being evaluated.
- They have not yet achieved a comfortable confidence level in regard to the company and its solution offering(s), and therefore are not sure it is a prudent decision.

Should a salesperson begin to hear or receive these types of responses, they should confirm that the prospect(s) are considering elements such as:

1. How does your company's reputation, customer base, industry focus, and references compare to the competition?
2. How seamless and efficient of a transition is it going to be to move to your solution offering(s) versus other options, considering such items as personnel involvement, data conversion, etc.?
3. Is the total value and total cost of ownership (initial and recurring) being considered against other options (competition)?

Being able to address questions and challenges to your company's proposal is something a salesperson should be prepared and able to discuss. While discussing questions and/or rejections on the proposal, the salesperson should make sure to effectively address and provide answers, and to do this they should:

1. Confirm and acknowledge they have heard and *understand* the question and/or issue.
2. Articulate their understanding back to the individual, ensuring clear understanding of the question.
3. Provide answer(s) or potential resolution options. If the salesperson is unsure of the answer, they should take notes, providing

assurance they understand the question(s) and will get back to the individual(s) with a response.

- They should also let individual(s) know the time frame to expect an answer back.

4. Establish agreement with the purchaser(s) that the resolution option(s) presented is agreeable and acceptable.

It is important that the salesperson not appear unsettled by any of the question(s)/challenge(s) to the proposal offering(s). The salesperson should remember...there is not only a sale on the line, but also a future reference.

CONTINUE TO MONITOR

The salesperson should be aware that there may be times when challenges to their proposal may be either expressed openly and shared directly with the salesperson, or may be more subtly expressed within the decision committee/group. Either way, it is the responsibility of the salesperson to make sure questions and challenges are addressed to the decision maker's satisfaction, which is why it is imperative to constantly monitor and verify/confirm with decision maker(s) how they feel about the company's solution offering(s) and any proposal(s).

The salesperson should be aware that any challenges to the proposal offering may be presented in various ways and priorities. Some may seem relatively easy to address, such as a simple misunderstanding of information stated or presented, or more difficult and complex, such as company's reputation, past experience(s) with the company, etc.

It is imperative to identify any of the issues and address them quickly in order to allow the proposal to be evaluated correctly and appropriately as it pertains to the purchasing criteria. It is not advisable to ignore questions/challenges to the proposal, thinking they may simply not matter, or be weighed heavily, toward the final decision.

Also, avoid any urges to shift the focus from your company's solution offering(s) to the competitor(s). It can be tempting to begin reacting to challenges with responses like, "We cannot provide the feature/functionality being requested, but neither can any of the competitors."

The salesperson should continue to focus on what they and their organization can provide and address how the question(s), challenge(s), and issue(s) will be addressed and resolved with the proposed solution offering(s).

COOLER HEADS PREVAIL

Keeping emotions in check during negotiations may seem like an elementary concept, but it is important to remain professional and communicate to the prospect(s) that you are continuing to support them and their request(s) and trying to assist them by communicating their question(s) and concession request(s), while also representing your company's business objectives.

The prospect(s) probably realize it is not good business nor realistic for your company to lose money on opportunities, and whether they realize it or not, the reality is, the prospect(s) wants the company to make a "reasonable" profit on each deal, allowing the company to remain in business and continue to provide support and future solution offering(s) enhancements.

The salesperson should keep in mind the prospect(s) is exercising their attempt to get the best deal possible given their business environment, decision criteria, and financial parameters.

I have been involved in situations where prospects have initially made a decision to go with a competitor but remained professional and positive, letting them know me and my company would be around if things did not work out with the vendor selected. I then kept in touch with the prospect during their implementation process, leaving the door open in the event everything didn't go as planned. Within a brief time, I received communication back from prospects stating their selected vendor was not working out. Therefore, they would like me come back and see them to discuss how we could re-evaluate moving forward with my company's solution offering.

HONEY OR VINEGAR

It has been said one can catch more bees with honey than with vinegar! This is certainly true, and I find it interesting more people have not realized this, especially when approaching strategic opportunities, such as sales opportunities.

In most markets and industries in which individuals work, it is customary to have some level of working knowledge of the competitor's solution offering(s) participating in the same industry.

An account in California provided an RFP containing the standard information (environment, situation, purchasing criteria, time frame, etc.). Upon responding to the RFP, the prospect selected the top three vendors and invited them in to provide a two-hour presentation. My company was fortunate enough to be selected as one of the top three.

After all the vendors had provided the presentations, the prospect called the vendors that were not selected to notify them of the news. My company was included in the group of two not selected.

I thanked them for their time and for the opportunity to respond to the RFP and for taking time to allow me to present the solution offering(s) and to let me know if there was anything me or my company could provide or if they encountered any unexpected issues with the selected vendor or the implementation.

I also asked if it would be okay to continue to follow up with them periodically to see how things were going with the implementation/installation and to provide any updated information from my company, such as upcoming industry events and our solution offering(s) new features/functionality, etc.

Within a few months, this particular prospect contacted me stating that the implementation with the selected vendor was not going well. The vendor was experiencing difficulty delivering what was provided in their RFP response and presentation. The prospect requested that I come back and meet with them, which subsequently resulted in them ceasing moving forward with the originally selected vendor and moving forward with my company's solution offering(s) without going back through the RFP process again.

During the ongoing conversations and implementation of my company's solution offering(s), I asked the customer why they contacted me from the remaining two companies from the original RFP process.

Their response was, "You didn't act like you lost the opportunity, and you continued to provide value and invest time in how we were doing and if our needs were being met. So, we figured if you and your company continued to be interested after not being originally selected for the project, then we could count on you and the company taking even more of an interest in us being successful if we became an actual customer."

The lesson...a salesperson can gain more business by being professional and continually interested in people (prospects/customers) than they can expressing defeat and becoming disengaged after not being initially selected.

FREE TRIALS AND/OR SAMPLES

Whether free trials and/or samples are provided depends on the solution offering(s) and the company philosophy. In certain industries and markets, this may be appropriate and make sense to offer and provide to potential prospects.

There are advantages and disadvantages for offering and providing "free" and/or "limited" trials.

The advantage is that it provides the prospect(s) an opportunity to actually utilize (test-drive) the solution offering(s), providing an opportunity to gain a better understanding of how the solution offering(s) works, as well as having hands-on experience to explore features/functionality of the solution offering(s) that may assist in finalizing the purchasing decision.

The disadvantage is that the "free" and/or "trial" requires little to no financial investment or commitment for the prospect(s), so there is very little incentive for the user(s) to actually access, explore, and utilize the solution offering(s). Another potential issue is that individuals at the prospect's organization are busy performing their daily job tasks, so the trial period time frame may expire before any individual(s) get an opportunity to evaluate the solution offering(s).

If trials and/or samples are available and offered, they should be provided with an associated *investment* and/or time frame. Even if the investment is a trivial amount, it provides an incentive for the user/organization to begin the evaluation process. The investment made for the trial could also be provided with a money-back guarantee or refund should the decision be made to not move forward, or it can be applied to the purchase price should the user/organization decide to move forward and purchase the solution offering(s).

ONCE NEGOTIATIONS ARE COMPLETED, BE QUIET!

Salespeople should recognize a chance to "be quiet" and stop selling *after the prospect(s) agrees to the contract agreement items and to complete the sales opportunity!*

Salespeople feel compelled to continue to sell even after the prospect(s) agrees to move forward with the proposed solution. This can happen when the salesperson begins to feel confident about the deal being almost completed, and may inadvertently say something that is contrary to the prospect's understanding or expectation. Causing the prospect to state, "Hold on, that is not what we want or intended to do!"

Introducing new information now has the deal and potential successful "win" quickly at risk of being withdrawn, potentially extending the sales cycle and putting the deal is jeopardy.

This is commonly referred to as grabbing defeat from jaws of success!

Here is an example of a situation where I continued to sell after the prospect(s) agreed to the proposal negotiations and just needed to get the contract agreement signed to complete the deal. Then, I almost lost the opportunity because I did not realize I was risking anything and did not realize it was time to stop selling.

I had been working with a prospect on a computer software and hardware deal during the months of October and November, and the prospect was waiting for December (year-end) to conclude the purchase. As the end of the year began to draw closer, I continued to work with the prospect, ensuring everyone involved understood what items and elements would be needed to ensure the project completion timeline.

With only a few weeks left in the year, I began to get concerned about the possibility of meeting the requirements needed to complete and implement the proposed project, so a conference call was scheduled with the prospect's team to get everyone up to speed and on the same page as individuals were beginning to take holiday vacations, days off, etc., and this could impact completion times of required steps and elements (signing contract, training, implementation/installation, etc.).

Wanting to make sure we would be able to address any questions and/or topics, a request was made to several individuals from my company to participate on the call as these individuals were considered experts in their specific areas of the hardware and software applications.

The conference call began customarily with greetings, introductions, and making sure everyone on the call was up to date on recent and activities since the presentation meeting a few weeks ago. Then, I asked for any new or follow-up questions anyone may have. The president of the prospect's company asked a question in regard to the hardware requirements and shipping timing for the new system, which had also been discussed during the presentation meeting. However, the hardware shipping time frame had changed due to a large end-of-year demand on the hardware vendor, and therefore, the time frame stated during the presentation had changed, putting the project at risk of not being completing by the end of the year.

The president of the prospect's company quickly became concerned, stating that if this project was not completed within the next two weeks, they would need to wait until next year during the same time frame (delaying the project and deal twelve months), which now became a big concern since I had forecasted this opportunity to my company's sales management for a year-end close.

The crux of the issue was whether the hardware system was going to be shipped from the manufacturer to my company to be staged and have the software application(s) loaded, prepared, and set up and then shipped to the prospect's office to complete installation, or if the hardware would be shipped from the manufacturer to the prospect's office and then the set up and installation completed remotely, utilizing both company's people. The difference between the two approaches would be time, as well as monetary investment.

On-site implementation at the prospect's office would be faster but would require more monetary investment for the prospect. Having the hardware shipped to my company for the software installation and configuration (hot staging) would require less monetary investment but would require more time to complete, involving two shipping destinations, two receiving destinations, etc.

After discussing the available options that could meet the time constraints, the prospect's team made a decision. The hardware would be shipped from the manufacturer to the prospect's location, allowing it to meet the prospect's year-end timeline. However, this would require an increase in the down payment required to complete the deal.

After discussing and finalizing the new strategy to meet the prospect's year-end deadline, I was summarizing what had been discussed and what would be required from each party.

Then, rather than taking the opportunity to stop selling and thanking them for their time and business, I continued to sell to the prospect. I was sharing with individuals on the call additional items, requirements, and potential investment outcomes associated with the new purchasing and implementation strategy when something was shared that made the president cut me off immediately, stating, "Hold on, that's not what we want to do. If the changes are going to cause that to happen, then we will wait until next year."

The president's comment got everyone participating on the call concerned about the completion of this project.

So, rather than taking the opportunity to be quiet and quit selling after everyone agreed to the plan, I spent the next forty-seven minutes trying to explain that what had been stated was not going to affect how their purchase was going to take place. I had just been sharing some additional information regarding options that other purchasers had selected and not how we were going to handle and address their situation and needs.

Salespeople should not miss an opportunity to quit selling and be quiet after the prospect(s) have agreed to negotiations and are willing to move forward with completing the opportunity and signing the contract agreement. Once the salesperson has received agreement to move forward, resist introducing risk by continuing to sell the solution offering(s) unless you are confident that what is being said matches the prospect's understanding and goal(s).

NEGOTIATION LESSON

Each year, the National Western Stock Show and Rodeo is held in January in Denver, Colorado. The entire event runs for three weeks and includes a national animal (stock) show along with one of the largest professional rodeos held in the United States. Some of the events are held a few days prior to the official start of the Stock Show and are called the "Pre" Stock Show.

Upon approaching the parking lot to attend the "Pre" Stock Show, the attendant politely stated it would be $15.00 for parking, which was gladly paid as the parking is close to the proximity of the events being held in the Denver Coliseum venue.

Returning the next day, which was the official first day of the Stock Show, the parking attendant said it was $20.00 to park. I inquired as to the increase in price, and the attendant politely stated it was due to the increase in demand for parking spots.

Not being excited about the opportunity to pay the additional $5.00 investment for the same parking location, I seized the opportunity to utilize well-honed sales and negotiation skills on this particular parking lot attendant by briefly presenting the situation and reasons for letting me go ahead and pay the same price as the day before.

The parking lot attendant listened politely and then responded, "Sir, I completely understand what you are saying and appreciate your valid points. However, I have approximately 4 parking spaces left in this lot, and there are approximately 20 cars lined up behind your vehicle that would like to park in this lot because it is so close to the events and venue."

The attendant went on to say, "There are several other parking areas that are much further away from the events, which require walking about half a mile to a bus, which will then take you around to pick up additional passengers from other outlying parking lots. It will take approximately 30-40 minutes to arrive at the venue once getting on the bus. However, the parking lots only cost $15.00 to park. Be sure to wear your coat because it is cold today, and the forecast is predicting snow showers this afternoon. However, this particular parking lot will allow you to simply walk a short distance to the venue, therefore not needing to carry around a coat all day. Now, if you do not feel you would like to invest $20.00 for this parking lot, please turn around and let one of the next cars in line have your parking spot."

I quickly reached into my pocket and produced the requested $20.00 for parking and paid the attendant. I politely said, "Thank you for the parking space, as well as the negotiation lesson!"

The $20.00 was not only worth the parking spot but also worth the negotiation lesson provided!

SUMMARY

Contract negotiations should not be something that is unexpected but rather viewed as another step in the sales cycle. Negotiations and negotiating are simply another element and part of the selling process that the salesperson should be prepared to address. Like the other areas of the sales cycle, practice negotiating to become familiar and comfortable with the process. Then, when prospects begin negotiating, it will seem as if this is something you do every day.

One way to avoid competing mainly on price is to make sure the solution offering(s) are not being commoditized. Purchaser(s) are interested in purchasing value(s) and benefit(s), and how the solution offering(s) is going to address their need(s) and *then* completing the purchase at the best possible price point.

During negotiations, it is good practice to "gain" something for "giving" something. Salespeople should prepare a list of concession items that might be requested as a result of negotiations and what concession(s) the company may be willing to consider.

The salesperson needs to be aware that although there is not a scoreboard involved in each sales opportunity, the purchaser(s) are keeping score between you and the competition.

If during the negotiations process, the salesperson feels like individuals (committee) are trying to play the "good person, bad person," it may be beneficial to associate what one person is saying to what all the decision group is saying and triangulate what the salesperson is being told in an attempt to confirm the information before acting upon it.

Another method of negotiating and investment justification is breaking down the overall investment to reflect "total cost of ownership" divided by the expected utilization time frame, units, etc., allowing the purchaser(s) to view and understand the incremental investment in perspective to the overall value(s)/benefit(s) received toward the individual's and organizational needs and goals.

Depending on the salesperson's authority granted by their company to finalize negotiation pricing, terms, etc., it may be acceptable for the salesperson to defer final negotiation requests made by the prospect(s) to their company's management (known as deferring to a higher power). This allows the salesperson the opportunity to go back to their management team (if needed) and get approval or alternative option(s) without potentially damaging the relationship with the prospect(s).

If trials and/or samples are offered, provide these with an associated "investment" and/or "time frame." Even if the investment is a trivial amount, it provides an incentive for the user/organization to begin and complete the evaluation process.

Resist continuing to sell after the prospect(s) agrees to the contract agreement items and to complete the sales opportunity.

It is important that the salesperson not appear distracted by challenge(s) to the proposal offering(s). The salesperson should remember there is not only a sale on the line, but also a future reference.

LESSON 18

CLOSING CONTRACT OPPORTUNITIES

Many people view the closing of a sales opportunity as the grand finale and therefore put lots of emphasis on a salesperson's ability to close deals.

As proof of this, just take a look at a sales role/position job advertisement. In the description or requirements, it will state something to the effect of "Must be able to close deals," "looking for closers," "only closers need apply," etc. What they are referring to is whether the person applying for the sales role/position can successfully manage a sales cycle to fruition.

The definition of a sales representative sort of implies the person should have the abilities that would be beneficial to completing the elements needed to successfully complete a sales process and therefore close a deal. If a person is spending time in a designated territory/region, informing individuals and companies of what their organization provides to companies and to industries but is not generating sales revenue and closing deals, then that person could be considered in a marketing role as opposed to a sales role.

From my experience, if a salesperson has completed their responsibilities appropriately and assisted the prospect(s) through the proper sales steps and elements, then the completion of the opportunity is the next logical step and element in the sales cycle.

Referring back to an earlier statement within this book, regardless of what title a salesperson introduces themselves (sales representative, sales executive, account manager, etc.), if an individual is spending time, effort, energy, and resources with prospect(s) and providing information such as communication, presentation, proposal, etc., then the prospect(s) probably is aware and understands that the individual is a salesperson, thus realizing that at some point in the process, the salesperson may provide them with an opportunity to make an investment in their solution offering(s).

One technique to assist in closing the sales process is to "trial close" after reaching certain points during the sales cycle while identifying and addressing challenges/issues at each step and then confirming the prospect(s) is willing to continue to the next step in the sales process/cycle.

It has been my experience that the closing of a sale should be a win-win-win combination...win for the customer as it provides improvement(s) to individuals and/or an organization...win for the salesperson's company as it generates revenue, market share, etc...and win for the salesperson, providing them a new customer and reference.

CLOSING ITEMS

Providing "trial close(s)" during the sales process assists in confirming and determining where the salesperson stands in the opportunity and where additional time, energy, and effort may need to be spent and applied in addressing any outstanding issues, challenges, goals, etc.

Trial close(s) assist in identifying and addressing objections during the sales cycle, making it more effective for the salesperson to complete the sales process while attempting to avoid surprises along the way, especially at the end of the cycle when asking for signing the contract agreement.

It is advisable to not skip over or leave out any of the sales steps without receiving confirmation from the prospect(s) and gaining agreement that it is okay to continue to precede. If steps are skipped/left out without confirmation, the salesperson risks having the prospect(s) bring up an item(s) that might have been overlooked or that they thought did not need to be addressed, only to find out these element(s) are issues and brought up during the closing step.

When this happens, the salesperson may need to go back and address some earlier step(s) and elements in the sales cycle, potentially delaying the sales process and completion. This situation can also provide the salesperson with the opportunity to explain to their sales management why the opportunity may be delayed and/or potentially at risk.

Salespeople should view the closing step and element as another step in the sales process, which happens to involve the customer signing formal paperwork to complete the contract agreement. Just like the other steps and elements in the selling cycle, the salesperson gets approval and agreement to move forward as the contract agreement signing is simply the purchaser putting it in writing. If a closing and contract signing is handled and addressed appropriately, this step can take place as inherently as any of the other steps in the sales cycle.

CONTRACT SIGNING ITEMS

The following are items that should be performed and provided after receiving a signed contract agreement.

1. Make sure to send a 'Thank-You" for their business. Send to all personnel involved in the selection decision. Something personal (handwritten note, etc.) is preferred, but making sure to provide a "Thank-You" is essential.

2. Communicate receipt of each of the contract document(s) and items. Let the customer know what document(s) have been

received, such as signed contract, purchase order, down payment, etc., therefore avoiding delays as each of the parties are assuming there are potential delays due to the actions of the other, and potentially affecting the project timeline.

3. Stay involved in the continuing stages of the contract fulfillment, providing any additional information or requested sales items.

4. Maintain ongoing communication with the customer, setting expectations as to the timing of the next steps (shipping, training, implementation/installation, etc.).

5. Ask if they are aware of other companies that might be looking for solution offerings and if they are willing to be a reference.

SUMMARY

Closing of a sales opportunity should be a win-win-win combination...win for the customer as it provides improvement(s) to individual(s) and/or an organization...win for the salesperson's company as it generates revenue, market share, etc...and win for the salesperson, providing them a new customer and reference.

Provide "trial closes," confirming and determining where the salesperson stands in the opportunity, and where additional time, energy, and effort needs to be spent and applied in addressing any outstanding issues, challenges, goals, etc.

Skipping over or leaving out sales steps without receiving confirmation from the purchaser(s) may cause delays and risk with closing the opportunity.

Salespeople should view the closing step and element as another step in the sales process, which happens to involve the customer signing formal paperwork to complete the contract agreement.

LESSON 19

IMPLEMENTATION/ INSTALLATION

Certain companies' solution offering(s) have some type of implementation and/or installation process associated with them. If a salesperson's company provides a solution offering(s) that currently does not require implementation and/or installation, then this provides information for potential future reference.

Implementation and/or installation are traditionally executed after the contract is completed and signed by the customer. Depending on the implementation and/or installation factors, the level of direct involvement from the salesperson may vary. However, it is imperative to the ongoing relationship for the salesperson to continue to:

1. Stay involved and up to date with the customer's and their company's implementation/installation teams.
2. Communicate with the customer as to the status and progress of implementation/installation steps and timing.
3. Monitor project plans (stages, dates, etc.) with both the customer's team and your company's team.
4. Inform the customer that you are continuing to monitor the progress along with any issues that may be encountered.

5. Participate and assist with the implementation/installation meetings and ongoing steps and processes to stay involved and apprised of the project's progress.

6. Communicate with the customer after the sale and during implementation/installation. This will serve the salesperson well in regard to future references, allowing the customer to speak well of the company's services, personnel...and the salesperson.

LESSON 20

FOLLOW-UP AND REFERENCES

In the sales world, there are few things more beneficial and valuable than a customer referral. This is when an existing customer shares with a prospect the value(s), benefit(s), and success(s) they have experienced while doing business with your company and utilizing its solution offering(s).

It is encouraging to receive a phone call from a prospect who has heard good things about your company's solution offering(s) and would like to schedule a time to learn more about what the company is providing to customers and explore what might be able to be provided to them.

One of the reasons this type of opportunity is so valuable for a salesperson is that an existing customer is able to speak and communicate more directly about their specific experience(s), benefit(s), and result(s)/achievement(s) they have received and how it has impacted their business more directly than a salesperson. In essence, the reference can speak more directly from experience(s) and utilization than a salesperson may be able to provide. The reference usually has instant credibility and can utilize their industry's language, terms, etc., which allows the prospect to quickly and easily understand the results and outcomes.

REFERENCE SELLING

During my career, I have been fortunate to have reference accounts that would communicate to others in their industry looking for the type of solution I was selling, "If you don't speak to Steve before making a purchasing decision, then you are making a mistake." This recommendation resulted in prospects contacting me to learn more about what my company and its solution offering(s) could provide for them.

How valuable was their recommendation? Think about the probability of a salesperson's success if they were to approach a prospect announcing if they did not speak to them before making a particular purchasing decision. They were making a mistake with their business!

It is also beneficial if the reference accounts participate in industry associates and events, and are well-known in their (and your) industry and amongst their peers.

This is another good reason for continually meeting and reinforcing the relationship with existing customers who are willing to speak with prospects who may be able to utilize the company's solution offering(s).

REFERENCES AND CUSTOMER VISITS

It is important to the salesperson's ongoing success to stay in touch with reference customers, such as:

1. Schedule periodic calls to the individual(s) who are providing references to see how the company's solution offering(s) continues to meet their current and future expectations, needs, and goals.
2. Schedule time to meet with individual(s) within reference accounts when in their area, and schedule time to meet with them at events (industry events, trade shows, seminars, etc.).
3. If the salesperson's company allows, it is also beneficial to:
    - Plan off-site meetings, where the salesperson gets an opportunity to interact with individuals on an informal and personal level.

- Bring a cup of their favorite coffee, tea, etc., to a meeting at their office(s); provide lunch for meetings, meet for dinner when in town, etc. These can be simple and inexpensive ways to show appreciation for them providing information and references.

SUMMARY

In the sales world, there are few things more beneficial and valuable to success than a customer referral, so make sure to communicate with reference customers on a regular basis.

One of the reasons a reference is so valuable for a salesperson is that an existing customer can speak and communicate more directly about their specific experience(s), benefit(s), and result(s)/achievement(s) they have received and how the offering has positively impacted their business.

Most references have instant credibility and can utilize their industry's language, terms, etc., which allows the prospect to quickly understand the information and results.

Consider ways to show appreciation for references assisting with sales opportunities.

LESSON 21

CONCLUSION AND CLOSING THOUGHTS

In each sales opportunity, the salesperson should assume the potential purchaser(s) are saying, *"So what?"* as it relates to information being provided and presented regarding the company and its solution offering(s), along with value(s), benefit(s), feature(s), function(s), action(s), process(es), procedure(s), and statistics/facts.

Prepare for the performance and presentation, set the stage for the presentation, begin with a powerful and attention-grabbing opening, and connect with and engage the audience quickly and often. Utilize the SAT and W-6 indicator questions to address purchasing criteria, such as need(s), challenge(s), issue(s), and goal(s). Make sure to provide and present information in an easy-to-understand and memorable manner.

Design, plan, and practice the performance and presentation to engage the audience emotionally and intellectually.

Provide information that connects the dots, along with utilizing proof sources to reflect results that can be expected, showing the logical conclusion of how purchasing the company's solution offering(s) would allow the prospect to reach and achieve their goal(s).

SUMMARY

Salespeople should sell to each potential purchaser(s) as they would a friend because the goal is to have the prospect join the company's family of users, resulting in a W-3...*Win* for the customer, *Win* for the company, and *Win* for the salesperson's career.

LESSON 22

EPILOGUE

Sales and selling is one of the most optimistic professions in the world, touching everyone's lives and all of our futures.

Two very popular and wealthy people were interviewed regarding their past successes and to provide their prediction for the future. They both were extremely positive on the future for individuals, especially those who "want and try" to succeed.

I would also like to echo these words of encouragement. I feel everyone can achieve whatever level of success they strive to reach. This reading is a small example of what can be accomplished if someone puts their mind to a goal.

Sales is a profession that provides people countless opportunities to meet and encounter numerous individuals they may have not otherwise had the opportunity or experience to meet; assist individuals and organizations in a way they might not have otherwise; communicate with people they may have not otherwise; work with and beside dedicated and outstanding professionals; and gain unique knowledge of markets and industries, many acquaintances, and, most of all...*many friends.*

It provides an opportunity to enjoy many aspects of what the world has to offer while helping individuals and organizations improve what they do every day.

I hope this book has provided inspiration and encouragement for you to continue to grow both as an individual and as a professional salesperson. Embrace the challenges and opportunities a sales career can provide. Enjoy the experiences and the journey a sales career offers, realizing it is just not the destination but also the journey that provides lifelong experiences. Enjoy and embrace the opportunities you win and learn from the opportunities you may not win (initially).

Do not be afraid to take chances and forgive yourself for mistakes. It is human to make mistakes. Just make them quickly, and try not to repeat them!

Remember it is possible that any given performance and presentation may not go perfectly as planned, but understand it is okay and continue moving forward and learning from the experience for future opportunities.

I encourage you to embrace each sales opportunity and role (much like life itself) as a moment in time. Enjoy and embrace life as it is today, knowing it may only be this way for a period of time, so enjoy the journey as things will most likely change moving forward.

There's an old saying I learned from my grandparents: "We should all strive to find a career and occupation we enjoy, ensuring we do not have to get up and go to 'work!'" It is my recommendation to select an occupation and career you view as a labor of affection and not only a job.

Strive to take life to the "**NEXT LEVEL**":
N...New opportunities every day.
E...Extra effort to win deals—and enjoy life.
X...eXtraordinary...You be eXtraordinary—You be great!
T...Technology...embrace and utilize it to make your life better.
L...Learn something new each day.
E...Excitement...about your life and opportunities.
V...Value people and relationships (career and personal).
E...Enthusiasm about your life...be one *in* a million, not one *of* a million!
L...Live and Love *everyday*!

The world of sales will continue to evolve over the coming years, and salespeople will continue to play an important role in society and in commerce as people will continue to conduct business with people.

It is with unbridled excitement and optimism that I share my thoughts regarding selling and the sales process in this writing. I believe if you incorporate the ideas shared in this book you will improve your effectiveness and elevate your sales resulting in an enjoyable and successful sales career.

Following the steps, techniques, and methodologies provided and incorporating them into your repertoire will allow *"Uncloaking The Mysteries"* and achieving success...with and in...**The Business Of Sales**.

Good Luck in Selling...and Good Luck in Life!

CONTACT INFORMATION

For more information about The Business Of Sales training programs and consulting, please contact:
Phenom Inc.
4164 Austin Bluffs Parkway, #343
Colorado Springs, CO 80918
Info@TheBusinessOfSales.net
TheBusinessOfSales@gmail.com

GLOSSARY AND ACRONYMS

Advertising: The activity of attracting public attention to a product or business. The business of designing, writing, and producing advertisements for publication and/or forms of broadcast.

Analysis/Analytics: The separation of a whole into its constituent parts for individual study; the stated findings of such a procedure.

Blog: A type of website usually arranged in chronological order from the most recent post (or entry) at the top to the older entries toward the bottom. Written on a particular topic communicating ways to learn, share ideas, and do business around the world.

Commission(s): A fee or percentage allowed to a sales representative or an agent for services rendered.

Consumer(s): One that utilizes economic goods.

Customer(s): One that purchases a commodity or service.

Goods: Having the qualities that are desirable or distinguishing in a particular thing. Serving the desired purpose or end.

Internet: An electronic communications network that connects computer networks and organizational computer facilities around the world.

Informal Organization Chart: Influencer(s) on decision maker(s) that do not necessarily represent the formal hierarchal organization chart.

Inner Circle: A small and often influential group of people on decision maker(s).

Marketing: The commercial functions involved in a company's global message about the company and image. The commercial functions involved in transferring goods from producer to consumer.

Merchandise: Goods bought and sold in business.

Methodology: A body of practices, procedures, and rules used in a discipline or an inquiry; a set of working methods.

Offer/Offering: To put forward for consideration, such as a proposal. To present in order to meet a need or satisfy a requirement.

Performance: The act or style of performing a work or role before an audience.

Product/Products: Something produced by human or mechanical effort or by a natural process.

Prospect(s): A potential buyer or customer.

Prospecting: Looking at likely candidates as a potential purchaser or consumer.

Proposition: A plan suggested for acceptance; a proposal. A subject for discussion or analysis.

Purchase/Purchasing: To acquire by effort. Acquisition through the payment of money or its equivalent.

Sale(s)/Sell(s): The exchange of goods and/or services for an amount of money or its equivalent.

Salesperson: A person who is responsible for selling solution(s) and/or services.

Service(s): Work performed as an occupation or a business. Installation, maintenance, or repairs provided or guaranteed by a dealer, manufacturer (vendor).

Solution/Solutions: The method or process for solving a problem. The answer or disposition of a problem.

Technology: The application of scientific method and material used to achieve a commercial or industrial objective. Body of knowledge available to a civilization that is of use in fashioning implements, practicing manual arts and skills, and extracting or collecting materials.

Telemarketing: Use of the telephone in marketing.

Value: Worth in usefulness or importance to the possessor; utility or merit. A principle, standard, or quality considered worthwhile or desirable. To rate according to relative estimate or worth or desirability.

Value Proposition: A representation of value provided and delivered, summarizing the benefits a vendor proposes a consumer will receive in return for the customer's associated payment or other value transfer.

World Wide Web: A part of the Internet accessed through a graphical user interface and containing documents often connected by hyperlinks; also called the *Web*.

ACRONYMS

- **CARE:**
  C = Current environment.
  A = Analysis.
  R = Reason(s) for adding and/or converting.
  E = Expectations.
- **CIIR:** Circumstance(s), Issue(s), Impact(s), Resolution(s)/Option(s).
- **CRM:** Customer Relationship Management.
- **ERP:** Enterprise Resource Planning.
- **G-T-G:** Give-To-Get.
- **NEXT LEVEL:**
  N = New opportunities every day.
  E = Extra effort to win deals...and enjoy life.
  X = eXtraordinary...You be eXtraordinary...You be great!
  T = Technology...utilize to make your life better.
  L = Learn something new each day.
  E = Excitement...about your life and opportunities.
  V = Value people and relationships (career and personal).
  E = Enthusiasm about your life (be one *in* a million, not one *of* a million!
  L = Live and Love!

- **PEEERC:**
  P = Presentation.
  E = Explain.
  E = Expand.
  E = Explore.
  R = Review.
  C = Confirm.
- **PDA:** Personal Data Assistant.
- **RFP:** Request for Proposal.
- **RFQ:** Request for Quote.
- **ROI:** Return on Investment.
- **SALES:**
  S = Systems.
  A = Analysis.
  L = Learning.
  E = Excellence.
  S = Success.
- **SAT:** Sales Analysis Tool.
- **SIC:** Standard Industrial Classification.
- **SYSTEM:**
  S = Solutions...what does your solution(s) offering provide to address prospect's needs and goals?
  Y = whY...should they select your company over other options available?
  S = Successes..."proof sources" and references acknowledging successes.
  T = Technology...utilize and leverage today's technology to engage prospects.
  E = Effort...work smarter and provide extra effort to win each sales opportunity.
  M = Memorable...make a positive impression with individuals within an opportunity.

- **W-6's:**
  1. **W**ho.
  2. **W**hat.
  3. **W**here.
  4. **W**hen.
  5. **W**hy.
  6. ho**W**